SAP® NetWeaver BI Integrated Planning for Finance

 **PRESS**

SAP PRESS is a joint initiative of SAP and Galileo Press. The know-how offered by SAP specialists combined with the expertise of the publishing house Galileo Press offers the reader expert books in the field. SAP PRESS features first-hand information and expert advice, and provides useful skills for professional decision-making.

SAP PRESS offers a variety of books on technical and business related topics for the SAP user. For further information, please visit our website: *www.sap-press.com*.

Norbert Egger, Jean-Marie Fiechter, Sebastian Kramer, Ralf-Patrick Sawicki, and Stephan Weber
SAP Business Intelligence
2007, 653 pp.
ISBN 978-1-59229-082-6

Marco Sisfontes-Monge
CPM and Balanced Scorecard with SAP
2006, 387 pp.
ISBN 978-1-59229-085-7

John Jordan
Production Variance Analysis in SAP Controlling
2006, 120 pp.
ISBN 978-1-59229-109-0

Manish Patel
SAP Account Detemination
2006, 96 pp.
ISBN 978-1-59229-110-6

Kumar Srinivasan, Sridhar Srinivasan

SAP® NetWeaver BI Integrated Planning for Finance

Galileo Press

Bonn • Boston

ISBN 978-1-59229-129-8

1st edition 2007

Aquisitions Editor Jawahara Saidullah
Development Editor Jutta VanStean
Copy Editor John Parker, UCG, Inc., Boston, MA
Cover Design Nadine Kohl
Layout Design Vera Brauner
Production Iris Warkus
Typesetting SatzPro, Krefeld
Printed and bound in Germany

Contents at a Glance

Contents

4   SAP NetWeaver BI Integrated Planning — User Interface ... 201

PART III: DEVELOPING PLANNING APPLICATIONS

5   Essential Tools for Developing SAP NetWeaver BI Planning Applications 245

Foreword by Kellie Gypin

As recently as 20 years ago, success in business was built around having a good idea and working hard. That is a far cry from today, where simply working hard has been replaced by working flexibly and nimbly, and "working smart." In the world of business, competition is the name of the game. It is becoming increasingly important to create a competitive edge through market awareness and knowledge.

Highly successful enterprises are those that have established a clear pattern of rapidly generating market insight. They efficiently and effectively respond to the changing conditions. These companies distinguish themselves in a number of ways, but there is a central theme that allows them to remain a market leader: They understand the power of business intelligence and the advantage of a strong business-planning discipline.

Adoption of Business Intelligence (BI) analytics is not always easy or successful. Many enterprises fail to properly implement BI solutions and thereby put themselves at a competitive disadvantage. Why do these companies fail to fulfill their vision? A few patterns of behavior show up repeatedly. Many organizations treat BI implementations as technical exercises for Information Technology (IT). Their solutions lack significant business value which then result in poor adoption.

Other organizations suffer from a low level of "BI activism." There is a lack of commitment and enthusiasm to drive adoption of BI analytics. Users do not embrace a data integrity rigor or the concepts of information analysis. In other places, IT organizations do not understand the potential or complexity around specialized solutions to deliver BI analytics. In these companies, IT organizations attempt a "one-size-fits-all" approach when actually a suite of different tools and specialized solutions are needed to be successful. Alignment of business solutions and technology enablers is crucial to ensure a "best-in-class" advantage in business intelligence analytics and financial business planning.

With financial business planning, we see a similar premise concerning value and complexity. One of the most common sets of activities in financial management is planning. Very simply put, planning is setting direction and ensuring follow- through. Planning involves inputs, processes, outputs, and outcomes. Inputs go through a process where they are examined, predicted, and integrated to achieve a set of goals. Outputs and outcomes are the results or benefits. A strong planning discipline is essential for applying BI analytics to an organization's execution plan. It is important to understand that planning cannot guarantee a desired outcome. It will, however, allow an organization to be prepared for challenges and obstacles that stand in the way of success.

Developing sound and executable business plans is critical to being competitive in today's business world. There are many companies who do not succeed. These enterprises operate at a disadvantage with respect to the "best in class" and, without improvements, fall further behind. So why do these companies fail to fulfill their goals? Some companies build their plans on inaccurate or invalid information. Not knowing how others have addressed key problems in the past, they rely on untested assumptions or hunches instead of reality.

Many times new ideas put forward have already been tested by others and were not successful. Other companies forget that a plan is an outline of a future goal and should not be written in stone. Adaptable planning is essential to success. Companies must plan for flexibility and allow for adjustments. Plans that can't change should not be written. Other organizations do not understand that planning must be allowed to be more free-form than other traditional financial activities. Hard structures and absolute models need to be minimized in planning or companies risk losing flexibility and creativity.

It is easy to see why successful planning requires a special mindset and a flexible set of solutions. SAP has long recognized the crucial role planning plays in a successful business. The company has continued to invest in technology capabilities that advance their solutions. Today, SAP is becoming recognized as a true market leader with the recent delivery of SAP NetWeaver BI Integrated Planning. More and more people are striving to learn how to develop a robust and flexible planning solution supported by solid business process. There is a great desire to understand how to leverage SAP's toolkit.

This book is a tutorial and reference for those interested in desiring a deeper understanding of SAP's solution for integrated financial planning. I am pleased to introduce this book and the authors. The authors have a deep knowledge base built on many years of working with SAP's business intelligence (BW) and planning solutions. They have demonstrated a drive to always learn and excel. I have been very impressed by their collective ability to grasp key business issues and apply excellent judgment in delivering solid and flexible solutions. I am confident that anyone who is seeking a broad understanding of SAP's BI Integrated Planning will benefit from this book.

Kellie H. Gypin
Director, BI/Planning and Performance Management
Mead Westvaco
Charleston, SC

Foreword by Kevin Harrington

In recent years, business intelligence (BI) has emerged within companies as a very strategic endeavor utilized to advance corporate objectives. Corporations have recognized the ability to leverage business data into a greater understanding of the market conditions in which they compete. At the same time, advances in technology have enabled the collection, interpretation, and subsequent analysis of the transaction base to advance the objectives of each business enterprise.

This publication outlines the manner in which companies can align business intelligence activities with corporate planning objectives. The authors focus on the setting of planning objectives within the integrated BI tool suite provided by SAP NetWeaver 7.0. Readers of this publication will find a practical guide on how to evolve traditional business intelligence functions into a corporate planning initiative through the implementation of SAP NetWeaver 7.0.

It is a necessity for any corporation, large or small, to establish a business-planning direction that outlines the financial objectives of the company. In conjunction with business planning objectives is the necessity to monitor performance to plan. SAP has provided a capability within its SAP NetWeaver Business Intelligence suite for companies to monitor and measure performance against predefined criteria. The material in this book is a comprehensive guide for SAP users who are looking to implement functions within SAP's business planning products.

The authors have been personally involved with implementing the products described in this book. The knowledge shared here comes from actual field experience working with corporations. Their practical and real-world approach to solving BI solutions will be invaluable to readers attempting to implement SAP's NetWeaver BI planning products.

Kevin Harrington
Director, Business Intelligence, Global Information Solutions
Avnet, Inc.
Phoenix, Arizona

Acknowledgments

This book has been produced with the help of several people who have reviewed the materials and offered invaluable suggestions. Their contributions and advice have helped us to realize the objectives of this book.

We would like to offer our thanks and special appreciation to the following people for their contributions.

- ▶ The editors of this book, Jawahara Saidullah and Jutta VanStean, for guiding us through the book development process.
- ▶ The production manager of this book, Iris Warkus, for managing the production and successful release of the book.
- ▶ Sue Mevers at MeadWestvaco, who reviewed the initial chapters of the book and provided us with several suggestions for the presentation of the chapters.
- ▶ Mukul Agrawal at Halliburton, who reviewed the initial chapters of the book and provided the business perspective to planning that has been incorporated in the book.
- ▶ Peter Tomany at Avnet, who reviewed the initial chapters of the book and offered several ideas to consider in the functional areas of planning.
- ▶ Our late father, A.R. Srinivasan, who throughout his life instilled in our minds the importance of excelling in what we do.
- ▶ Our mother, Saroja Srinivasan, for her advice to be ambitious and to constantly pursue opportunities that would make a difference.
- ▶ Our older brother, Raghunath Srinivasan, for his encouragement to write this book and for his advice all the way through to completion.
- ▶ Kumar Srinivasan's family — thanks to my wife Vidya, and my children, Sandhya and Sanjay, for their support and patience as I spent long hours writing the book.
- ▶ Sridhar Srinivasan's family — thanks to my wife Jayashree, and my children, Harini and Ashwin, for providing the motivation and enthusiasm during the writing of this book.

Kumar Srinivasan
Sridhar Srinivasan

The importance of planning is growing in this era of rapid technology development, global competition, modernization, and ever-changing customer needs. Understanding the market in its entirety, developing a clear vision, and executing and scheduling various activities are all integral parts of planning. These issues pose challenges for businesses in planning effectively and competing successfully in the marketplace.

Introduction and Overview

In simple terms, planning in business involves thinking ahead and coming up with a set of activities a company will execute in the future. It is a complex process because many factors have to be taken into consideration when undertaking it. For example, any business has to plan for multiple resources relating to a skilled workforce, investment decisions, or production capacity, depending on the nature of the business. To ensure that these activities are performed optimally, a good planning system must be in place.

A good idea or a good product does not necessarily guarantee the success of a company. A company should make decisions to sell the right product, at the right time, and through the right channel. The plan to achieve the organization's goals needs to be clearly defined as well as refined throughout the entire planning process.

While strategic planning objectives are usually set by upper management, a company may create multiple plans at lower organizational levels to help achieve these strategic planning objectives. It is therefore imperative to ensure total coordination and oneness of objectives among the different plans. This should be taken into account when planning decisions are made. Let's take a look at what planning tools you have at your disposal.

Software Planning Tools

In the past, a majority of organizations have used Excel spreadsheets for financial planning. This approach has many limitations, including accessibility issues, lack of security, insufficient control mechanisms on who can modify data, and the inability to clearly understand how the planning data was derived.

SAP NetWeaver 7.0, which includes the SAP NetWeaver Business Intelligence (BI) Integrated Planning tool, is new-generation software that addresses these issues effectively. It also significantly reduces the time and resource requirements of organizational planning. The Integrated Planning tool is a part of SAP NetWeaver BI, an enterprise data warehouse that aids and integrates planning. It is a sophisticated software tool aimed at giving customers an edge in the market place by helping them reduce total cost of ownership (TCO). The tool provides the flexibility to plan, budget, and forecast for any area of business. It also provides an environment that allows the integration of data from various application areas such as finance, marketing, production, and human resources for the purpose of planning. Further, the availability of enterprisewide data in SAP NetWeaver BI, which is used as the basis for planning, makes it a compelling choice for businesses to take advantage of this environment and use the planning software.

SAP NetWeaver BI Integrated Planning and the Finance Department

To realize the objectives of an organization, the different components of financial planning, such as cash-flow management, asset management, cost and overhead management, investment management, balance-sheet management, and profit and loss management need to be planned and closely monitored. The SAP NetWeaver BI Integrated Planning tool provides a comprehensive set of tools to integrate data from different sources to enable planning, set up a process for planning, analyze the progress of the plan with respect to the actual outcome, and effectively monitor the outcome of the plan.

Let's now see how reading the book in front of you will help you make the most of the SAP NetWeaver BI Integrated Planning tool.

How this Book Can Help

The objective of this book is to help technical developers, functional analysts, consultants, and managers who work primarily in the areas of SAP Financials and SAP NetWeaver BI understand and make the best use of the capabilities of the the SAP NetWeaver BI Integrated Planning tool. This book is unique in that it explains the features of the software through extensive examples in a simple and easy-to-understand manner. Let's now look at the structure of the book to better understand its contents.

Structure of the Book

This book is divided into three parts, as follows.

Part I: Planning and Evolution of SAP Planning Software

The first section of the book includes this Introduction and Overview and Chapter 1. It presents an introduction to planning in general and the evolution of the planning software in SAP specifically. The different planning options available to an organization as well as the importance of Strategic Enterprise Management (SEM) are described in this section. Further, the reader is introduced to SAP NetWeaver BI, the enterprise data warehousing solution from SAP, and the SAP NetWeaver BI Integrated Planning tool, both of which are available with SAP NetWeaver 7.0. Let's get a quick glimpse of what Chapter 1 will cover.

▶ **Chapter 1: An Overview of Business Planning**
  This chapter starts with highlighting the importance of planning in an organization. It explains the concept of planning and presents the suitability and usability of different options available for planning in an organization. The need for financial planning is also discussed.

Next, we present the evolution of planning software in SAP to help readers understand the developments in this area. The planning applications suitable for development in different SAP systems—R/3, SEM Business Planning and Simulation (BPS), and SAP NetWeaver BI—are discussed to explain how SAP has used an incremental approach to make available an efficient and stable software platform for different planning scenarios. We describe the capabilities of NetWeaver 7.0 to introduce the reader to the way a comprehensive planning application can be developed from within SAP NetWeaver BI using the Integrated Planning tool.

Part II: Developing Planning Applications Using SAP NetWeaver BI Integrated Planning

The second part includes Chapters 2, 3 and 4. This section is critical to understanding how to develop planning applications using the SAP NetWeaver BI Integrated Planning tool. To make the concepts more accessible, we use a case study that helps explain how to develop a comprehensive planning application for the finance area using SAP NetWeaver BI Integrated Planning. We also use extensive examples to demonstrate the various features available for this purpose. Here's a brief introduction to each of the chapters in this section.

▶ **Chapter 2: Introduction to SAP NetWeaver BI Integrated Planning**
This chapter identifies the two options available for developing planning applications: SAP NetWeaver BI Integrated Planning and SAP BPS. It explains the advantages of SAP NetWeaver BI Integrated Planning over SAP BPS and discusses the considerations for designing a data model to suit the planning application. A case study for the area of financial planning showcases the capabilities of BI in NetWeaver 7.0. This case study is then used as the basis for the examples in all of the following chapters.

▶ **Chapter 3: SAP NetWeaver BI Integrated Planning — Configuring a Financial Application**
This chapter discusses in detail the BI Integrated Planning tool in NetWeaver 7.0. Using the case study introduced in Chapter 2, along with several examples, we discuss the various features available in BI Integrated Planning. We also elaborate on how you can leverage the tool to develop high-value financial planning applications.

▶ **Chapter 4: SAP NetWeaver BI Integrated Planning — User Interface**
This chapter demonstrates how to integrate the planning objects you developed in SAP NetWeaver BI Integrated Planning into an intuitive planning application for users. It shows you how you can use the Business Explorer (BEx) Query Designer to develop a query for entering planning data. This chapter also explains how the query and planning objects can be included into user interfaces for Excel, and the Web using the BEx Analyzer and Web Application Designer tools respectively.

Part III: Developing Planning Applications

The third part includes Chapter 5 and Chapter 6 and is an essential complement to the information presented in the second section. The topics covered in these sections are required reading when developing planning applications. Section III covers a wide array of topics that include managing locking mechanisms, using the Status and Tracking System (STS) application for facilitating and monitoring the planning process, transporting planning objects, administering authorization, retracting plan data from SAP NetWeaver BI back to the R/3 system, and examining performance considerations when developing planning applications. Here's a short introduction of each of the chapters in Section III.

► **Chapter 5: Essential Tools for Developing SAP NetWeaver BI Applications**
This chapter covers a range of topics you must understand and know how to use when developing a planning application. It includes the following areas.

  ► **Locking**
  This topic involves locking in the context of plan data and the steps to reduce locking contention when multiple users run planning applications at the same time.

  ► **Status and Tracking (STS)**
  The STS application is an out-of-the-box application to monitor the planning process. The steps to customize the application for a planning process are explained with the help of an example.

  ► **Authorization**
  Who can access a planning application or planning objects depends on users roles in the organization. This topic lists the different authorization objects you can use to configure users'access to planning applications.

  ► **Transport**
  The planning application and planning objects must be transported across the system landscape; i.e., from the development system to the quality and production systems. The process of transporting objects is discussed here.

  ► **Retraction**
  The data from some planning applications can be created in SAP NetWeaver BI and sent back to the SAP R/3 system. This chapter lists the applications for which data can be retracted and provides a basic overview of the steps involved in the process.

  ► **Performance**
  Performance determines usability and contributes to users' confidence in working with the application. The best planning application may

not be viable if there are performance issues. This chapter highlights the importance of performance and explains the steps to understand and troubleshoot issues.

▶ **Chapter 6: SAP NetWeaver BI Integrated Planning Implementation and Best Practices**
This chapter presents useful tips that will contribute to the successful development and implementation of a planning application.

Now that we have reviewed the contents of the book, we will explain how to use it effectively.

Using this Book

This book is primarily aimed at technical developers, functional analysts, consultants, and managers working in the areas of SAP Financials and SAP NetWeaver BI who might be required to develop a planning application using the SAP NetWeaver BI Integrated Planning tool.

The chapters and examples have been selected to make it easier for readers to understand the importance of planning and how SAP NetWeaver BI Integrated Planning can be used to build a complete financial planning application. The examples used to explain the features of the SAP NetWeaver BI Integrated Planning tool have been selected so that readers can reproduce them in their own environments to gain hands-on experience with the tool.

The book employs an easy-to-follow step-by-step format and can be used by all members of the team who are interested in understanding how to develop a planning application with the SAP NetWeaver BI Integrated Planning tool. For members of the team who are involved in the management of the project, reading this book will help in understanding the product and improving project management. Other team members will learn about the features in the SAP NetWeaver BI Integrated Planning tool that can help them develop a high quality planning application.

Finally, it is important to read the chapters in the order they are presented to get a step-by-step understanding of the concepts discussed.

Summary

The introduction and overview provided in this chapter explain the key components and use of this book. In Chapter 1, we will discuss the concepts of financial planning, the evolution of the planning software provided by SAP and the role of the information technology department in the process of planning.

Summary

PART I
Planning and the Evolution of SAP Planning Software

This chapter introduces general business planning concepts, explains how the planning software in SAP has evolved over time to meet the planning requirements of business users, and outlines the role of the information technology (IT) department in development of a planning application.

1 An Overview of Business Planning

We start this chapter by discussing the definition and importance of planning along with the duration, types, and applicability of planning for different business areas. We further explain the difference between planning, forecasting, and budgeting. We conclude with the considerations you should take into account during planning.

We then discuss the evolution of planning software in SAP. We explain how the ability to create planning applications was limited to a few areas in the SAP R/3 system before SAP introduced a specific tool for the purpose of financial planning in the SAP Strategic Enterprise Management (SEM) system's Business Planning and Simulation (SEM-BPS) module. The SEM-BPS module was later integrated into SAP Business Warehouse (BW) as a part of the SAP NetWeaver release. In the subsequent release of SAP NetWeaver, SAP NetWeaver 7.0, SAP then made the SAP NetWeaver BI Integrated Planning tool available. Chapters 2 through 5 of this book focus on the development of a financial planning application using this tool.

In the next section of this chapter, we discuss the role of an organization's IT department in developing and delivering planning applications to business users. We list the skills the SAP NetWeaver BI Integrated Planning team should possess to successfully develop and implement a planning application.

Finally, we provide a summary of what we have learned in this chapter along with a preview of the topics we will discuss in Chapter 2.

Let's now take a look at the key concepts of planning in general, the evolution of the planning software in SAP and the role of the IT department in planning.

1.1 Concepts in Business Planning

Planning in business has become increasingly important for a number of reasons. These can include the following:

- Rapid changes in technology
- Need for organizations to optimize resources to stay competitive in the global market
- Changing geopolitical situations
- Changing customer needs
- Need for organizations to strategically position themselves for future growth

Planning, in simple terms, involves thinking ahead and coming up with a set of activities an organization will perform in the future. From another perspective, it is the process of modeling or projecting future business activities. Planning is a key component of the management cycle that allows companies to position themselves in complex environments. The process of planning identifies the individual tasks involved in reaching a goal, provides the time frame for executing the tasks, and determines the resources needed for their successful completion. Planning is an iterative activity in which the actual performance is measured against set targets and refined accordingly.

1.1.1 Planning as Compared to Budgeting and Forecasting

It's important that you understand that planning differs from budgeting and forecasting, and why. Budgeting is the process of allocating resources once the planning process is completed and a plan has been approved and accepted by management. Budgeting is the start of the action phase following the planning process. In the budgeting process, the requisite details are worked out for the implementation of the plan. This is also the period where financial allocations are made to the various departments, such as finance, sales, IT, or human resources.

Forecasting deals with the actual realization of the plan and is used as a monitoring mechanism to facilitate the success of planning. Business environments do not remain the same; the situation that was planned for yesterday may be different today. Forecasting provides this information in a timely manner so that corrective action can be taken when there is a significant difference between the current state and what was planned for during the planning process.

1.1.2   Planning Timelines

Planning timelines fall into three categories: short term, medium term, and long term. Let's look at each of these categories in more detail.

Short-Term Planning

Short-term planning usually covers a period of one year or less. It's used when a business has clear-cut, short-term goals. Examples of short-term planning include cutting costs and increasing labor productivity; for example, by putting a freeze on new hires and effectively training the existing workforce. Short-term planning is also suitable for businesses in industries that are constantly changing and where it is difficult to make reliable long-term projections.

Medium-Term Planning

Medium-term planning usually covers a period of one to three years. Medium-term planning is applicable if a business can reasonably plan the outlook for the next three years. For example, a company could develop a medium-term plan to increase market share in a particular segment of its business.

Long-Term Planning

Planning is considered long term when the duration of the plan exceeds three years. This type of planning usually involves investment of a large amount of capital to achieve stated objectives. Long-term planning is also applicable for businesses where there is a lengthy time gap between initial project investments and the final realization of sales and profits. For example, this is the case with companies in the utility, steel, or bio-technology industries.

Planning Timeline Considerations

The level of detail in short-term planning is high because it addresses the immediate future. With medium-term planning, the level of detail is reduced. With long-term planning, planning occurs at a very high level.

There is no one solution regarding which planning timeline to choose; the choice depends on business requirements. Typically, companies will use different timelines in planning for different areas of their business.

In general, routine business operation plans that address the immediate future are good candidates for short-term planning. Programs and plans that involve large capital investment and that take longer periods of time to mature and yield results usually involve long-term planning.

For example, if a business wants to reduce costs in the immediate future, it may come up with a short-term plan to do so. The same company also may have a long-term plan to gain the biggest market share in its industry.

1.1.3 Planning Types

Several planning types are available to provide clarity to the process of planning by clearly differentiating the objective of the plan. The planning type is based on the planning timeline and the granularity of the planning process. Let's take a look at the different planning types, including operational, tactical, and strategic planning.

Operational Planning

Operational planning typically means planning for the short term and is generally conducted at the operational level of a company. This type of planning usually has an immediate objective in mind. For example, a plan might have as its objective improvement in productivity by control of variable cost. This type of plan might involve employees who execute the action items of the plan in the planning process. This participation increases the likelihood of the successful execution of the plan.

Tactical Planning

Tactical planning is associated with planning for the medium term and is generally conducted at the middle-management level of a company. It is suitable for projects that can be completed in less than three years. For example, a company might start an initiative to improve the quality of its product, an objective which might take a couple of years to realize. Note that, although this plan might also be in agreement with an existing long-term plan, it would still be developed at the middle-management level.

Strategic Planning

Strategic planning is associated with planning for the long term. It is generally conducted at the organizational level of a company, and upper management typically plays a significant role in the planning process. For example, an organization might decide to allocate significant funds to research and development (R&D) to develop a new line of products. It will likely take more than three years to develop these products, and the company might need to develop a plan to finance the development process.

Strategic planning usually begins at the top level of management and moves down the company hierarchy. The planning objectives and processes are agreed upon by upper management, and might be split into further sub-plans during implementation.

In Figure 1.1, you can see how the different types of planning are categorized based on the granularity of the plan (high level vs. detailed level) and the required time (less time vs. more time) to achieve the objectives of the plan. Operational planning requires the shortest time and has the highest level of granularity. Strategic planning, on the other hand, requires the most time and has the lowest level of granularity.

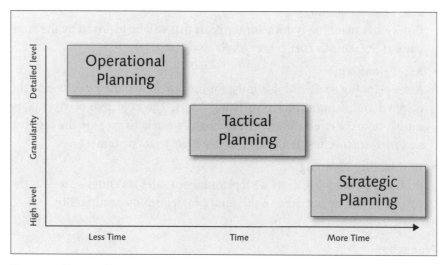

Figure 1.1 Planning Types

1.1.4 Planning Area

The planning area is the business area for which you develop a plan. For the purposes of this book, you need to understand the relevance of financial planning with respect to the business areas of finance, production, human resources, and marketing. We'll look at each of these areas in detail.

Finance

The finance department is the control room of any business. It is responsible for planning, implementing, and directing the financial aspects of the business. Examples of financial planning include investing in a new venture, maintaining an optimal cash position (liquidity), reducing cost, and increasing profits. The focus of this book is to illustrate the development of a financial planning application for a company that has an objective to increase its gross profit margin.

In this context, it is helpful to discuss different areas of financial planning.

▶ **Liquidity Planning**
  Liquidity planning focuses on maintaining optimal cash flow for running the business. This involves taking into account the current cash position of a company, estimating the inflow of cash from customers and the outflow of cash to vendors and employees, and planning a company's liquidity over the next few months.

▶ **Cost Center Planning**
  Cost center planning is done for the costs that will be incurred by the company at the various cost-center levels.

▶ **Asset Planning**
  Asset planning deals with planning for the purchase of new assets, and the disposal and maintenance of existing assets. The objective of asset planning is to make effective use of a company's assets to provide the capacity and performance needed to deliver products to its customers.

▶ **Profitability Planning**
  Profitability planning deals with planning for sales revenues as well as the costs that will be incurred in the future to determine profitability.

Production

Companies need to plan how much they should produce, at what time, and at what location. This is important to satisfy customer needs. Companies also need to plan to produce their products in the most optimal manner to fulfill customer requirements and demand. Different variables such as seasonal trends, geographical demand, and user behavior should be taken into account when planning for production. The financial implication of the production plan should be consistent with the overall financial plan of the company. Inventory and overhead costs incurred as a result of the production plan should be kept at minimal levels.

Human Resources

Any business must have the workforce required to run the business. Workforce requirements need to be planned based on a company's overall growth objectives. When there is a shortage of employees in the industry, you'll have to decide how to proceed. You have several options:

- Hire new employees
- Train existing employees
- Bring in people from the outside as consultants

This area of planning is especially important in industries that require many employees and where specialized skills are necessary to realize business objectives. The costs associated with meeting labor requirements have a direct impact on the financial plan.

Marketing

The marketing department provides the necessary information to plan the products a company can sell and the price at which they can be sold. The distribution of products and services to customers should also be taken into account. The sales plan can be arrived at using actual sales in past years, revaluation based on future trends in the industry, the geo-political environment in which the company has sales operations, and the strategic vision of the company.

The above areas are critical for the survival of the business and have a direct or indirect effect on the financial plan of the company. Planning for these areas is important to ensure the smooth functioning of business.

1.1.5 Common Scenarios for Planning in Business

Companies need to plan for different scenarios, depending on their individual requirements at different points in time. In this section, we discuss some of the more common planning scenarios, including gross profit margin planning, profit and loss and balance sheet planning, investment planning, labor planning, sales planning, and demand planning.

Gross Profit Margin Planning

In this scenario, you plan the revenue from sale of a company's products along with the costs that will be incurred to produce or buy the product from suppliers. This usually starts with gathering external information on product demand. Market research can provide this information. Often, prior-year revenue results can indicate a trend for future sales planning. This information, along with the strategic vision of the management and the estimate of demand provided by the sales force, help the company to plan the quantity and prices of its products.

The expected manufacturing cost can be arrived at by using standard costing method. This process should take into account any expected increase in material, labor, and overhead costs in the future. The expected revenue and expected manufacturing costs are used to determine the expected gross profit margin.

Profit and Loss and Balance Sheet Planning

This type of planning is related to the financial area of a business. The projected profit and loss is prepared along with the balance sheet to see if it meets the returns expected by the business. This might also provide clues as to which areas might need corrective action. For example, the projections might show that overhead costs are increasing every year. Based on this information, management might need to take corrective action.

Investment Planning

Investment planning is also associated with the financial aspect of business. It focuses on new investments the company plans to make. The expected rate of return for the investment is a key metric in investment planning.

Labor Planning

Labor planning means planning workforce requirements for a company. This plan should take both new projects and expected expansion into account, and might require additions to the workforce. The labor plan should also take into account expected attrition from the workforce, both through retirement and labor turnover. Human capital is crucial to any business, and labor planning is vital to ensure that a company employs the right people with the right skills to operate the business successfully.

Sales Planning

Sales planning involves creating a plan to sell a company's products. The focus should be on developing a marketing plan that would be most beneficial to the company while keeping prices competitive. The sales plan should reflect the overall strategic vision of the company. For example, if a company decides to place a lot of emphasis on just a few products, then the sales plan needs to reflect this objective.

Demand Planning

Demand planning starts when the process of sales planning is complete. Provided that production capacity exists, demand planning uses the existing sales forecast to plan for material, labor, and machinery to produce the products.

1.1.6 Planning Considerations

You should plan in a manner that ensures that company goals are accomplished. Plans should be aligned with the strategic objectives of the company. The following key points should be considered when planning:

▶ **Importance**
Planning is an important component of every business because it contributes to the success of a company. There are many cases where good planning and execution have paved a company's road to success, and also where inadequate planning or no planning resulted in the failure of a company. Management needs to understand the importance of planning in helping the company to be successful in its business operations. Planning ensures that upcoming tasks happen in a way that you foresee them to happen and improves your chances of success.

▶ **Skills**
Planning requires the ability to take many different factors, both internal and external to the company, into account. It takes a lot of experience, maturity, and knowledge to develop a successful plan. People entrusted with the responsibility for planning should possess the following skills.

▶ **Internal company knowledge**
Those involved in developing a new plan need to understand how the new plan relates to other projects that are currently under way and those that are likely to be undertaken by the company in future. Also, cross-functional aspects always need to be taken into account. For example, if a plan is being developed to improve production capacity, the question of financing needs to be addressed before arriving at a decision.

▶ **Reliable Data**

The data that is used in planning should be reliable. For example, if you use market research and intelligence information as the basis for planning, the data you use for this purpose should come from a trustworthy source. You must also take the possibility of error in the data into account.

▶ **Governance**

A good governance process should be established for planning. The levels of responsibility should be clearly defined so that there is no ambiguity. The people involved in planning should clearly understand their roles in the process.

▶ **Communication**

Good communication among all people involved is of vital importance during all aspects of planning. This ensures that the various participants stay well-informed about planning progress and take the appropriate actions at the various stages of the plan's implementation.

▶ **Monitoring**

A sound review process should be in place to monitor the execution of the planning process. The availability of such a process helps to identify any deviations from the plan and aids in taking corrective action.

▶ **Planning Method**

There are two types of planning methods:

  ▶ Top-down

  ▶ Bottom-up

With top-down planning, upper management decides what will be done and employees at lower levels of the company hierarchy implement the process. This planning method is typically used for strategic decision-making; for example, when upper management decides which areas of the business the company should focus on long term.

With bottom-up planning, planning starts at the lower levels of a company's hierarchy and is sent to upper management for approval. This planning method is typically used used for operational planning. Bottom-up planning is helpful in getting employees to be committed to the plan, and, because they are involved in the planning process, it increases the likelihood that the plan will be successful.

▶ **Participation**
The planning process is more likely to succeed if the people responsible for executing it are consulted when the planning goals are initially set. This encourages participative decision-making and promotes cooperation from everyone involved in implementing the plan. It also provides an opportunity for management to solicit employee feedback regarding the identified planning objectives.

▶ **Issue List**
If issues come up during the planning process, they should be recorded so that the organization can track progress towards issue resolution. There should also be a system in place for employees to raise such issues.

▶ **IT Department**
While we will look at the role of the IT department in more detail in Section 1.3 of this chapter, it is appropriate to include a brief overview of this topic here. The planning process involves collecting and integrating information from different sources, such as finance, production, marketing, or human resources, and sometimes also from external sources. The integration of this information needs to be facilitated by the IT department, which ensures that a planning process is created that can meet the demands of the business in a reliable and timely manner. The IT department must be able to handle this responsibility effectively.

▶ **Flexibility**
The planning process should be flexible so it can be adjusted to changes as needed. This makes the process less rigid and more open.

The topics introduced in this section have helped you understand the basic concepts in planning. In the next section, we will discuss in detail the evolution of planning software in SAP.

1.2   Evolution of Planning Software in SAP systems

Planning applications have been available in SAP systems for some time. However, over the years, the applications have been improved to provide comprehensive functionality that aids the process of planning and analysis of the planning data. SAP has used this incremental approach to make available an efficient and robust planning software platform for different planning scenarios. Our discussion of the following topics will help you understand the evolution of planning software in SAP systems:

- ▶ Origin of planning in the SAP R/3 system
- ▶ Introduction to SAP Strategic Enterprise Management (SEM)
- ▶ Introduction to SAP NetWeaver and the integration of planning software into the SAP Business Warehouse (BW)
- ▶ Introduction to SAP NetWeaver 7.0 and the SAP NetWeaver BI Integrated Planning tool

Now, let's go on to look at each of these topics in more detail.

1.2.1 The Origin of Planning in the SAP R/3 System

The planning software currently used in SAP has its roots in the R/3 system, where the following planning applications were provided:

- ▶ Sales & Operations Planning (SOP)
- ▶ Cost Center Planning
- ▶ Controlling-Profitability Analysis
- ▶ Investment Planning

While you can use the operational systems in SAP R/3 to plan for a majority of the functional areas of a business, these systems do not provide flexibility for planning at different levels or detailed analysis of the various planning scenarios.

1.2.2 Introduction to SAP Strategic Enterprise Management (SAP SEM)

The main objective of SAP Strategic Enterprise Management (SAP SEM) is to help an organization best position itself with respect to its competition and surrounding factors relevant to its business.

SAP SEM is the process through which an organization makes high-level decisions, using various management techniques and analysis tools. The strategic decisions that are made as a result of this process identify the areas on which the organization wants to focus and guide the long-term plans of the company. It is important to ensure that these decisions agree with the overall vision of the company.

SAP SEM helps an organization recognize business opportunities and threats ahead of time and decide on appropriate actions. The decisions made and the actions taken are monitored to ensure that the end result does not deviate from the original aim.

SAP SEM covers a wide range of areas and includes business consolidation, planning, performance measurement, stakeholder management, risk management and information collection. We set up business processes in SAP SEM with respect to these areas to bring optimal benefit to the organization and to interested parties involved in its business. While SAP SEM has a financial focus, its principles and practices can be applied to any area of business to improve the overall efficiency and growth in an organization.

SAP has provided various components in SEM that can be classified as follows:

▶ Business Consolidation

▶ Business Planning and Simulation

▶ Corporate Performance Monitor

▶ Stakeholder Relationship Management

▶ Business Information Collection

All of the components used in SAP SEM use the SAP Business Warehouse (BW). The individual components run on top of the SAP BW architecture. The data processed in SAP SEM applications are stored in SAP BW InfoCubes.

Business Consolidation (SAP SEM-BCS)

Business consolidation provides for internal and external reporting functions. Consolidation of data is especially helpful when a company has operations spread across the globe and needs to report the operations of the business using standard accounting practices.

The process of business consolidation plays an important role in calculating the monetary value of a business during acquisitions and amalgamations. Business consolidation incorporates the following features:

▶ Inter-company profit is eliminated when a company is doing business among its subsidiaries. This means that internal business profits among the company's subsidiaries are eliminated when reporting profits at the company level.

▶ Currency translation is used to report all data in one currency. This applies when a company does business in multiple countries using different currencies and finds it necessary to understand and report the operations of its business in one currency.

▶ Accounting data consolidation, to include the subsidiaries of a company and to report on the financials for the company as a whole. This may apply when using standard accounting principles like US GAAP.

▶ Elimination of equity ownership of investment in subsidiaries when reporting financial statements.

Business Planning and Simulation (SAP SEM-BPS)

The SAP Business Planning and Simulation (SAP SEM-BPS) component is used to plan, forecast and budget for the operations of a company. Planning is a generic task and is applicable to all areas of a business.

SAP developed standard applications in SAP R/3 to support planning. Some examples of standard planning applications are cost center planning, profitability analysis, investment planning and so on. These planning applications can be customized to fill the need of the business using the SAP SEM-BPS tool.

To configure a planning application, you use a planning workbench. You can use manual planning layouts to enter and modify plan data. You can also define planning functions to automate the generation and modification of plan data.

Corporate Performance Monitor (SAP SEM-CPM)

The SAP Corporate Performance Monitor (SAP SEM-CPM) is one of the key components of the SEM module and includes several capabilities. It is used as a tool to identify strategies and to measure performance against the strategies and objectives set by management.

The SAP SEM-CPM component includes two parts: strategy setting and performance measurements. These are used as follows:

▶ **Strategy Setting**
In setting strategy, the emphasis is on identifying strategies a business wishes to pursue. One of the important areas of strategy definition is the Balanced Scorecard. The Balanced Scorecard recognizes the importance of both quantitative and qualitative aspects of the business when identifying the strategies. Besides the quantitative information like quantity, sales, and profit, other factors such as morale of employees and customer satisfaction are taken into account in this process.

▶ **Performance Measurements**

In the performance measurement area, a Measure Builder is used. The Measure Builder helps to compare performance with respect to a particular measure. A company might, for example, include employee training as a measure with several values. Over time, the actual performance for the measure is recorded. The actual values can be compared with the standard values to evaluate performance.

Stakeholder Relationship Management (SAP SEM-SRM)

The SAP Stakeholder Relationship Management (SAP SEM-SRM) is related to disseminating information about the company to interested parties and partners. The objective of this component is to determine the various groups that are interested in the company's business and provide timely information to them. The groups interested in a company's business include investors (stock holders), employees, suppliers, customers, government, and the public.

Business Information Collection (SAP SEM-BIC)

The SAP Business Information Collection (SAP SEM-BIC) provides external market information relevant to a company's business. The business intelligence is collected from sources such as the Web, market research (surveys of demand and competition in the industry), assessment of political and economic factors, and trends in the industry that affect the business. The information compiled through these sources is available for organizations during decision-making processes.

The data collected in this process is stored as documents and constitutes the knowledge base of the company. It is based on events and factual data affecting the business.

It is important for the company to provide required information to the public and regulators. For example, if a company is involved in a business that affects the environment, it is essential to disclose the operations of the company and their impact on the environment to the groups affected.

As you can see, SEM covers a wide area of financial applications and plays an important role in managing an organization's growth and long-term survival.

From SAP SEM-BPS to SAP NetWeaver

The SAP SEM-BPS component is an important part of SAP SEM and is used for planning, budgeting, and forecasting. The introduction of SAP SEM-BPS helped customers develop planning applications in the area of SEM. The range of applications that could be developed using SAP SEM-BPS was primarily limited to the area of financial applications. This prompted SAP to make the planning software available on a common platform that can be used for any area of business. This resulted in SAP integrating the SAP SEM-BPS software with SAP BW to provide SAP BW-BPS in SAP NetWeaver.

1.2.3 Introduction to SAP NetWeaver

SAP NetWeaver contains multiple components to enable the integration of people, processes and information using a common interface, the SAP Enterprise Portal. Figure 1.2 illustrates SAP's vision for SAP NetWeaver.

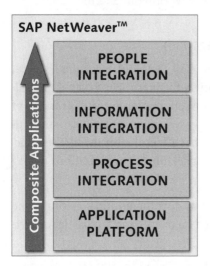

Figure 1.2 SAP NetWeaver Vision (Source: SAP AG)

People integration is achieved through the SAP Enterprise Portal. Process integration is facilitated through the SAP Exchange Infrastructure (XI). SAP XI manages process integration by serving as the single point for exchanging data among the various systems in the enterprise. The transfer of data from the source to a destination is managed entirely from SAP XI.

SAP NetWeaver also supports pre-packaged applications to extract data from multiple back-end systems through xApps (cross-application solutions). An example of an xAPP in SAP is XRPM (Resource and Program management).

This application gets information from the SAP Financial System, HR System, Project Systems, and Product Lifecycle Management.

Information consolidation is made possible through SAP BW, SAP Knowledge Management (KM), and SAP Master Data Management (MDM). SAP MDM provides the tools to harmonize master data from various source systems into SAP BW. SAP BW 3.5 was delivered as the data warehousing component solution with SAP NetWeaver. One of the significant features of this release includes the integration of the SAP SEM-BPS planning software into SAP BW, delivered as SAP BW-BPS.

SAP BW is the foundation on which the SAP BW-BPS tool runs. As a result, you need basic understanding of SAP BW in order to develop planning applications in this environment.

Introduction to SAP BW

In SAP BW, transaction data is stored in InfoCubes and Operational Data Store (ODS) objects. Examples of transaction data are sales and manufacturing data. The InfoCube and ODS objects are defined to contain characteristics and key figures. Characteristics represent entities of data; for example, customer, material, plant, and so on. Key-figure InfoObjects represent the quantitative data associated with the characteristics; for example, amounts and quantity.

Master data is stored in InfoObjects. Examples of master data are *customer* and *material*. An InfoObject might have other dependent InfoObjects that are referred to as attributes and that provide more information about the data. For example, a customer InfoObject has other InfoObjects such as region, country, and address listed as attributes.

An InfoCube is based on the extended star-schema architecture and is made up of a fact table and a number of dimension tables. Related characteristics in an InfoCube are grouped together and referred to as *dimensions*. A dimension ID is created in the dimension *table* for each unique combination of data for the characteristics values in a dimension. A record in a fact table is made up of the individual key-figures and the dimension IDs associated to a transaction. The individual characteristic in a dimension and the corresponding attributes of a characteristic are related using surrogate IDs (also called SIDS).

An ODS is also made up of characteristics and key figures. This architecture is based on a relational database model for storing and accessing data. In the case of an ODS, the data is stored in a transparent table.

Data Extraction

SAP BW is a tool you can use to extract and analyze the following types of data:

▶ Data from SAP R/3 systems and other new dimension products such as SAP Customer Relationship Management (CRM) and SAP Advanced Planning and Optimization (APO)

▶ Non-SAP data from flat files and other databases such as Oracle and Informix

▶ Data from Web applications using Web services

Business Content

The power of SAP BW lies in its ability to pull data from SAP systems (R/3, CRM, etc.) and non-SAP systems using preconfigured business content extractors. Some business-content data sources also provide the flexibility to handle delta and can be set to extract only changes in the source system since the last time the data was extracted into BW.

The SAP BW system also comes with a number of pre-configured objects such as InfoCubes, ODS objects, InfoSources, queries, Web templates, and security roles. This helps in expediting the process of development of data warehousing projects.

Reporting

A Business Explorer (BEx) Query can be designed using the Query Designer front-end tool provided by SAP to report and analyze data stored in SAP BW. Other reporting tools are available, including the BEx Analyzer, which is an Excel add-on tool used to create and execute queries, and the Web Application Designer tool, which is used to design Web templates and to deploy queries and management dashboards on the Web.

1.2.4 Introduction to SAP NetWeaver 7.0 and SAP NetWeaver Business Intelligence (BI)

SAP NetWeaver 7.0 was released by SAP as a solution for different IT scenarios. SAP 7.0 is built on what was offered before as SAP NetWeaver. It contains a number of services and includes the SAP NetWeaver BI software. Figure 1.3 that depicts the technical architecture of the SAP Business Intelligence system. The system contains an ODS to contain detailed level data that supports operational reporting, the Data Warehouse Layer with subject-oriented data that supports strategic decision-making, and the data mart with customized and summarized data to support a specific analytical requirement.

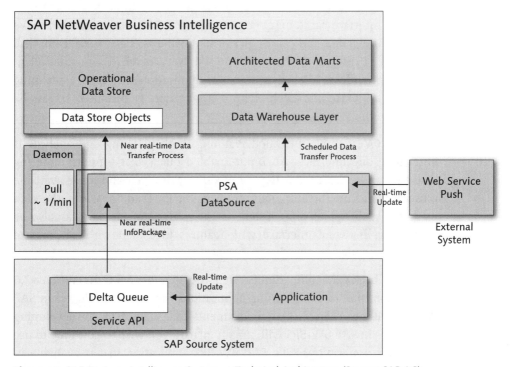

Figure 1.3 SAP Business Intelligence System — Technical Architecture (Source: SAP AG)

SAP NetWeaver BI replaces the term SAP BW used in earlier releases. SAP NetWeaver BI is enterprise-wide data warehouse software used to store and analyze data. The tool also lets you configure planning applications for any area of business. Other significant enhancements have been made in SAP NetWeaver BI with the objective of improving the user experience and lowering the total cost of ownership (TCO).

Note that with the introduction of NetWeaver 7.0, the release numbers in business-intelligence and other individual components no longer have relevance. Any major changes to the product will be released as part of the SAP NetWeaver stack of products.

BI Integrated Planning Tool

The new SAP NetWeaver BI Integrated Planning tool in version 7.0 greatly improves the planning functionality that was introduced earlier in SAP BW-BPS with SAP NetWeaver. In SAP BW-BPS, planning was done with manual layouts using the SAP GUI or a Web interface. The analysis was done in yet a different interface based on queries designed in BEx. These functions have now been integrated and can be performed using a single interface in SAP NetWeaver BI Integrated Planning. The SAP NetWeaver BI Integrated Planning tool provides a Web dynpro-based application to model a planning environment. Once the Web dynpro application is installed, it can be accessed on the Web using a URL.

In SAP NetWeaver BI Integrated Planning, both planning and analysis is done using one interface. An Input-Enabled query that supports entering plan data can be designed using the BEx query designer and made available to users either from the BEx Analyzer (using the Excel add-on) or on the Web (using the Web Application Designer). The analysis of the data can also be done using the same interface with features to drill down and perform detailed reporting.

In terms of backward compatibility, after you upgrade to SAP NetWeaver 7.0 you can continue to use planning applications that were developed in SAP BW-BPS without changes. Any investments that were made in developing applications in SAP BW-BPS will remain intact if you wish to continue to use the existing applications. The SAP BW-BPS application that is available in version 7.0 can also be used to develop the planning model for planning applications. However, SAP does not intend to develop any new planning functionality for the SAP BW-BPS application going forward. Improvements and enhancements in the planning software will be made only in the SAP NetWeaver BI Integrated Planning software. To take advantage of the new features and to reduce TCO, we recommend developing planning applications using the SAP NetWeaver BI Integrated Planning tool.

Next, we will discuss the role of the IT department to support the development of a financial planning application.

1.3   The Role of IT in Developing a Planning Application

Leadership for a project that involves the development of a planning application should originate from the business side because the sponsorship, direction, and guidance for the project are driven by the business. The IT department, however, plays an important role in development and execution of such a planning project. IT is responsible for developing a planning application that is simple and easy to use and that at the same time meets the requirements of the business. In addition, users expect a system that is stable and that will help them complete the planning process in a timely manner.

For an SAP NetWeaver BI Integrated Planning project, many skills are required to develop a planning application. Let's look at each of the skilled positions in detail:

▶ **Planning Analyst**
Someone from the business side who is skilled in the functional areas of planning would be ideal for this position. This person must be able to design a planning application that meets the needs of the business user community. He must be also be able to communicate the requirements to the technical members of the team, for the purpose of implementation. The person must also be able to clearly identify any design limitations and must be able to communicate these limitations during the blueprint phase of the project. If there are limitations that are not identified in the blueprint phase of the project, the project might run into delays.

▶ **SAP NetWeaver BI Architect/Developer**
Because planning is done in the SAP NetWeaver BI system using the SAP NetWeaver BI Integrated Planning tool, an experienced SAP NetWeaver BI architect or developer should work on the project. A poorly designed SAP NetWeaver BI system will be a detriment to developing a successful planning application. The principles associated with a good SAP NetWeaver BI system should be practiced when designing planning applications. This becomes even more important when the planning data involves a number of business areas and needs to be integrated. The SAP NetWeaver BI architect or developer should have a thorough understanding of the steps involved in configuring a planning application using the SAP NetWeaver BI Integrated Planning tool. The architect or developer also needs to have a good understanding of the user interfaces available in the SAP NetWeaver BI Integrated Planning tool. These interfaces will be developed and deployed as the planning application to business users.

47

▶ **SAP ABAP Developer**

It is advantageous to have someone on an SAP NetWeaver BI Integrated Planning project who knows how to code using the object-oriented language ABAP. This person can help when custom coding is required. He should also be familiar with the SAP NetWeaver BI architecture and the SAP NetWeaver BI Integrated Planning tool to better understand the project requirements.

▶ **Infrastructure Team**

The infrastructure team will be responsible for securing the data and enabling the smooth functioning of the systems on which the planning applications run. The team does this by ensuring system availability and good performance. This team will likely include members from the Basis team responsible for the technical configuration of the systems, the database team responsible for the efficient functioning of the database, and the security team responsible for secure access to systems.

▶ **Project Manager**

An experienced project leader should direct the IT team that is involved in the implementation and support of SAP NetWeaver BI Integrated Planning applications.

The team responsible for the planning application development should start prototyping the application early on. Ideally, this would start during the blueprint phase of the project when discussions are taking place and the design of the system is still evolving. The advantage of developing a prototype at this point is that key parts of the system can be developed and shown to users to elicit early feedback, while making sure that the application will meet the requirements.

The design of the planning application should be flexible so that it can be enhanced if there are additional requirements after the system goes live. However, redundancy and flexibility should be weighed against each other and which will outweigh the other will depend on individual requirements.

Finally, the IT team needs to test the application before releasing it to users. The testing procedures should ensure that the key processes work as expected. In addition, response time needs to be acceptable and heavier use by multiple users should be simulated during testing.

1.4   Summary

This chapter has provided you with a basic understanding of the concepts involved in planning in general, has traced for you the evolution of planning software in SAP, and has discussed the role of the IT department in the planning process.

In Chapter 2, we will take a detailed look at the concepts and terminologies used with the SAP NetWeaver BI Integrated Planning tool. In addition, we will introduce you to a case study we will use throughout the book to help you learn how to develop a planning application using the SAP NetWeaver BI Integrated Planning tool.

PART II
Developing Planning Applications Using SAP NetWeaver BI Integrated Planning

This chapter introduces you to the concepts and terminologies used with the SAP NetWeaver Business Intelligence (SAP NetWeaver BI) Integrated Planning tool. The chapter discusses the planning framework in SAP NetWeaver BI and the data model suitable for a planning application. It further presents a case study in the area of financial planning to illustrate the capabilities of the SAP NetWeaver BI Integrated Planning tool in SAP NetWeaver BI 7.0.

2 Introduction to SAP NetWeaver BI Integrated Planning

We start the chapter by introducing the SAP NetWeaver BI system, describing the different objects used in the system and explaining the process of extracting, transforming, and loading data from a source system. We also compare the processes used to load data in the SAP NetWeaver BI 7.0 system and the SAP BW 3.x. system. The chapter further describes the process of reporting on data that has been loaded. In addition, it highlights the use of SAP Business Content and how you can use it to expedite the development of BI applications.

Next, we discuss the two options available for planning in SAP NetWeaver BI Integrated Planning and SAP BW BPS and explain why the SAP NetWeaver BI Integrated Planning option is the preferred method for developing new planning applications. We also present the factors to take into consideration when designing the data model for a planning application.

Later in the chapter, we introduce a case study that presents a scenario for creating a planning application. This case study is used with all of the examples in the book.

Finally, we explain the creation of the data model for storing plan data. The basic building blocks for storing and analyzing data in SAP NetWeaver BI are explained using the case study requirements. Let's start by looking at some of the basic concepts used in the SAP NetWeaver BI system.

2.1 Objects Used in SAP NetWeaver BI

Before you develop a planning application, you'll need to understand the objects used to store data in the SAP NetWeaver BI system. These include InfoObjects and InfoProviders and are used to store master, text, hierarchy, or transaction types of data.

2.1.1 InfoObjects

An *InfoObject* is the basic object for building a data model in SAP NetWeaver BI. There are four different types of InfoObjects, which we will describe here:

▸ **Characteristic**
A Characteristic InfoObject represents a business entity or an attribute related to an entity. Examples of business entities include customer, material, and employee.

Characteristic InfoObjects that provide further information about an entity are called *attributes*. Attributes are used together with a parent Characteristic InfoObject. For example, attributes in the customer Info-Object include customer address and phone number.

A Characteristic InfoObject can be configured to store master, text. and hierarchy data, as follows:

  ▸ If an InfoObject is configured to store master data, it will contain the master data table with the InfoObject and its associated attributes. For example, the InfoObject might contain a customer number along with city, state, zip code, and country information.

  ▸ If an InfoObject is configured to store text data, it will contain the InfoObject's text values. For example, a customer's name can be stored as a text value.

  ▸ If there is an inherent parent child relationship in the data, the Info-Object can be defined as a hierarchy. The hierarchy is useful for analysis when the data contains a relationship. For example, the reporting relationships between manager and employees can be defined as a hierarchy.

▸ **Time Characteristic**
You use the Time Characteristic InfoObject to set the value for the time-related data of a transaction. Some examples of Time Characteristics are the calendar month, calendar year, or fiscal year associated with a sales transaction.

▶ **Unit Characteristic**

The Unit Characteristic InfoObject provides meaning to quantitative data. Currency and Unit of Measure are examples of Unit Characteristics. For example, the sales amount for a transaction can be recorded as a currency (such as US dollars or Japanese Yen) and the quantity sold can be recorded as a unit (such as kg or lb).

▶ **Key Figure**

The Key Figure InfoObject represents the quantitative measure associated with a transaction. Examples of Key Figure InfoObjects are quantity and amount associated to a sales transaction (e.g., a sales quantity of 5 kg or a sales amount of $500.00). Key Figures are typically associated to a Unit Characteristic. The Key Figure contains the value of the quantitative measure (value of sales quantity = 5) and the Unit Characteristic contains either a Unit of Measure (the unit associated to the sales quantity = kg) or Currency (unit associated to the sales amount = USD). The value of the Unit Characteristic can also be hard-coded in the definition of a Key Figure.

2.1.2   InfoProviders

An *InfoProvider* is the object used to report data in the SAP NetWeaver BI system. It is built using InfoObjects of all of the four previously discussed types (Characteristic, Time Characteristic, Unit Characteristic, and Key Figure). There are two types of InfoProviders:

▶ Physical

▶ Logical

Physical InfoProviders

Physical InfoProviders are used to store data. They include Characteristic InfoObjects, InfoCubes, and DataStores, and are also referred to as *data targets* because they physically contain data. Let's look at them in more detail:

▶ **Characteristic InfoObjects**

As mentioned earlier, Characteristic InfoObjects can be loaded with master, text, and hierarchy data.

▶ **InfoCube**

An *InfoCube* is a collection of InfoObjects and represents the extended star-schema architecture used in SAP NetWeaver BI.

An InfoCube is made up of a Fact Table and a number of Dimension Tables. Related Characteristics in an InfoCube are grouped together under Dimensions. When you load data into an InfoCube, a Dimension ID is created by the system for each unique combination of Characteristics in a Dimension. A record in a Fact Table is created using the individual Key Figures and the Dimension IDs associated with a transaction. The individual Characteristics in a Dimension and the corresponding attributes of a Characteristic are related using Surrogate IDs (SIDS). The InfoCube is the recommended approach for reporting in SAP NetWeaver BI because it takes full advantage of the extended star-schema architecture.

▶ **DataStore**

DataStore is the new name for Operational DataStore (ODS) used in SAP BW 3.x. It is a transparent relational database table and usually serves as the first layer for extracting data from a source system. The data loaded in a DataStore is often used for detailed analysis because it contains the raw data extracted from the source system. The data extracted into the DataStore can be further loaded into another InfoProvider, depending on the particular reporting requirements.

Logical InfoProviders

Logical InfoProviders do not physically contain data but are instead used for reporting. They include InfoSets, MultiProviders, and Virtual InfoProviders:

▶ **InfoSets**

InfoSets let you join objects that store data. For example, you can join two DataStore objects together to create an InfoSet for reporting. You can then use the InfoSet to report the data on the combined objects. The joins created in an InfoSet are database joins. Defining an InfoSet using inner and outer joins provides considerable flexibility. Using an outer join, all of the data defined in the left object of the InfoSet can be reported. For example, you can report on the sales of all customers, including those that did not have any sales reported in a particular period. One of the new features of the InfoSet in SAP NetWeaver BI 7.0 is that you can use an InfoSet to combine data from an InfoCube and another InfoProvider. In prior releases, it was not possible to include an InfoCube in the definition of an InfoSet.

▶ **MultiProviders**

MultiProviders let you report on data contained in more than one physical InfoProvider. For example, you can use a MultiProvider to report data from an InfoCube and a DataStore. The MultiProvider provides a union of data in the underlying InfoProviders. This helps combine the data available in more than one InfoProvider. The queries designed on a MultiProvider can be set to run in parallel on the InfoProviders included in the definition. While the queries run separately, the resulting data is combined and reported in an unified manner.

▶ **Virtual InfoProviders**

Virtual InfoProviders enable remote access of data from a source system connected to the SAP NetWeaver BI system.

2.2 Extracting, Transforming, and Loading Data in SAP NetWeaver BI

Now that you're familiar with SAP NetWeaver BI objects, you'll also need to learn the steps involved in creating and loading data into these objects and how to report on the data. However, let's first look at the concept of a DataSource and its role in SAP NetWeaver BI.

2.2.1 DataSource

A DataSource, as its name implies, specifies the source from where data is extracted into SAP NetWeaver BI. DataSources can be configured to extract data from a variety of source systems, including the following:

▶ **SAP Systems**

SAP systems from which data can be extracted into SAP NetWeaver BI using the Service Application Programming Interface (API) include SAP R/3, SAP CRM and other New Dimension products offered by SAP.

▶ **Flat Files**

You can extract data from standard files, such as Microsoft Excel files, by defining a DataSource in the SAP NetWeaver BI system that corresponds to the file layout for extracting data.

► **Web Applications**
You can use an XML interface to extract data from a Web application using the Simple Object Access Protocol (SOAP).

► **DB Connect**
You can use DB Connect to establish a direct connection to a variety of external databases systems such as Oracle and Informix.

► **Universal Data Connect**
This connection type provides access to external relational databases and multidimensional databases via a J2EE server.

► **Third Party Systems**
You can use a Business Application Programming Interface (BAPI) in conjunction with third-party tools to extract data into the SAP NetWeaver BI system. Examples of third-party systems include Informatica and Ascential.

2.2.2 Flow of Data in SAP NetWeaver BI (Extraction, Transformation, and Loading)

You can configure the flow of data in SAP NetWeaver BI in two ways. They include the new Data Transfer Process (DTP) that has been introduced in SAP NetWeaver BI 7.0 and the DTP that originally existed in the BW 3.x system.

The New Data Transfer Process in SAP NetWeaver BI 7.0

Starting with SAP NetWeaver BI 7.0, a new data flow, shown in Figure 2.1, is available for extracting and loading data. The new Data Transfer Process provides a flexible and improved process for extracting data from a source system, transforming the extracted data and subsequently loading the transformed data into a data target.

> **Note**
>
> You can continue to use the data flow and structures that were developed in BW 3.x as the extraction, transformation, and load (ETL) process in the new release. You can also use ETL as the process for new development. However, SAP recommends that you use the new process introduced in SAP NetWeaver BI 7.0 when developing new applications.

The following are the phases and components of the new Data Transfer Process in SAP NetWeaver BI:

▸ **Persistent Staging Area (PSA)**

A PSA table is generated when a DataSource is activated in SAP NetWeaver BI. The PSA table is a transparent table and will be the first layer for storing data. When data is requested for a DataSource from a source system, the data will initially be loaded into the corresponding PSA table of the DataSource.

▸ **Transformations**

A transformation process must be defined between a source and target object in SAP NetWeaver BI. The objective of the transformation is to map data coming from a source to a target using specific rules. The transformation process also lets you apply changes to data coming from a DataSource.

The DataSource (PSA), InfoSource, DataStore, InfoCube, InfoObject, and InfoSet can be used as source objects for the transformation. The InfoSource, DataStore, InfoCube, and InfoObject can be used as target objects in the transformation.

Transformation rules enable mapping of a field or InfoObject to a target InfoObject, setting a constant value to a target InfoObject, developing a routine in ABAP to perform the mapping, creating a formula, looking up master-data attributes to determine the value of a target InfoObject, and performing time determinations.

The InfoSource concept in the new process is different from the InfoSource concept that was used in BW 3.x. In the new process, the InfoSource acts as an optional, additional layer of transformation when two or more transformations are required before data is transferred from a DataSource to a data target. In BW 3.x, it was mandatory to use the InfoSource as an intermediary layer to transfer transaction data.

▸ **Data Transfer Process**

The DTP facilitates the flow of data in SAP NetWeaver BI from one persistent object to another, moving the data from the source to the target using the rules specified in the transformation. For example, after data is transferred from a source system into the PSA, the DTP is used to load data from the PSA to a data target. The PSA, InfoObject, InfoCube, and DataStore objects are examples of persistent objects in the SAP NetWeaver BI system. Note that the DTP can encompass one or multiple transformations.

▶ **InfoPackage**

The InfoPackage is the object used to request data for a DataSource from the source system. Once data is requested by the InfoPackage, the data for a DataSource is transferred from the source system to the PSA table.

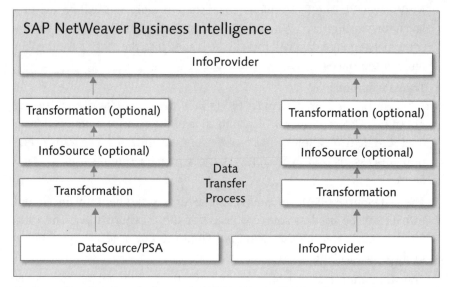

Figure 2.1 New Data Transfer Process in SAP NetWeaver BI 7.0 — Source: SAP AG

The Data Transfer Process in BW 3.x

The flow of data in the BW 3.X DTP, as shown in Figure 2.2, consists of the following components:

▶ **Transfer structure**

The transfer structure mirrors the structure of the DataSource in the source system.

▶ **Communication structure**

The communication structure represents the data structure of the data target.

▶ **Transfer rules**

Transfer rules map the transfer structure to the communication structure to set a value for the InfoObject in the communication structure.

Transfer rules allow mapping of a field or InfoObject to a target Info-Object, setting a constant value to a target InfoObject, developing a routine in ABAP to perform the mapping, and creating a formula to determine the value of a target InfoObject.

▶ **Update rules**

Update rules are the next level of transformation for InfoObjects, InfoCubes, and DataStores and provide flexibility for further transformation of data before data is loaded into a data target. For example, an Info-Source can provide data to multiple data targets, but additional transformations may be required before loading data to a specific data target. This process is facilitated by the use of update rules. InfoObjects that are defined for flexible updating can use update rules for further transformation before data is loaded into the data target. It is possible to load Info-Objects with master, text, and hierarchy data directly without the use of update rules.

▶ **InfoPackage**

The InfoPackage is the object that is used to load data from a DataSource in a source system into a data target. A setting in the InfoPackage determines where the data is loaded. The data target could be an InfoObject, InfoCube, or DataStore.Another setting in the definition of an InfoPakkage specifies the process of loading data to a data target, as follows:

▷ **Load data in the PSA only**

With this setting, the data is loaded only to the PSA table. A subsequent process will manually need to be executed for the data in the PSA to be loaded to the data target.

▷ **Load data in the PSA and data target**

With this setting, the data is loaded to the PSA and the data target. The PSA and the data target can be set to load one after the other or in parallel.

▷ **Load data in the data target only**

With this setting, the data is loaded to the data target only. This setting is used when it is not necessary to store the data extracted into a PSA table. This setting requires less storage because data is not loaded into the PSA table.

Note
Please note the difference in use of the InfoPackage in the new DTP in SAP NetWeaver BI 7.0 and the Data Transfer Process in BW 3.x. In the new data flow, the InfoPackage is used to load data only to the PSA; in the BW 3.x system, the InfoPackage is used to directly load data into data targets.

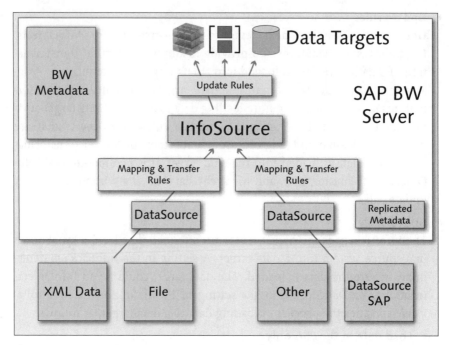

Figure 2.2 Data Transfer Process Used Primarily in BW 3.x — Source: SAP AG

2.2.3 Process Chains

Process Chains are used to automate the process of extracting, transforming and loading data in the SAP NetWeaver BI system. In addition, they can be used to administer the data in the SAP NetWeaver BI system effectively. A Process Chain provides different types of processes for managing data within the SAP NetWeaver BI system.

For example, the InfoPackage that is executed to request data from the source system, and the DTP process that is used for moving data within the SAP NetWeaver BI can be automatically scheduled in a process chain.

2.3 Reporting in SAP NetWeaver BI

The SAP BEx Query Designer is the tool that is available for reporting data in SAP NetWeaver BI. It is an add-on tool offered as part of SAP NetWeaver BI and enables drill-down and analysis of data.

Based on reporting requirements, the Characteristic and Key Figure Info-Objects can be included in the query definition. Filters can be set to restrict the report to specific selections. Once a query is designed, two options are available for deployment of the query to the user. They are as follows:

▶ **BEx Analyzer**
The BEx Analyzer is an add-on tool that lets you execute SAP NetWeaver BI queries in Microsoft Excel and provides spreadsheet capabilities for reporting. In addition, you can execute a query as a workbook.

▶ **Web Application Designer**
The Web Application Designer is a tool for reporting on the Web. A Web template can include Web items to display data in various formats, such as tabular and chart formats. A query designed in the BEx Query Designer can be defined as the provider of data to a Web item in a Web template. One of the common Web items used for displaying data is the analysis Web item, which lets you display data in a tabular format. The Web template also provides an option to develop a complete reporting application.

In SAP NetWeaver BI 7.0, the BEx Analyzer and the Web Application Designer provide the same features for reporting. However, the Web Application Designer allows users to execute reports and planning applications on the Web and provides certain advantages over using the BEx Analyzer. The Web executes reports faster and users don't need the BEx add-on to be installed on the computer to execute reports on the Web. The reports can be executed if a user can connect to the SAP NetWeaver BI system from the Web. With the integration of the SAP Enterprise Portal (EP) with SAP NetWeaver BI, the advantages of EP can be fully realized using the Web as the reporting tool.

2.4 SAP Business Content

SAP Business Content consists of pre-configured objects provided by SAP that help accelerate the process of development of a SAP NetWeaver BI application. Business Content is available in the following areas:

▶ **DataSources**
There are DataSources supplied by SAP to bring data from R/3 to the SAP NetWeaver BI systems. The logic for extracting the data is supplied with the data source. This greatly reduces the time and effort in extracting the data. Some of the DataSources have delta capabilities for extracting data. A DataSource that is delta-enabled brings over only the data that was created or modified since the last extraction from the source system.

▶ **InfoObjects**
SAP supplies standard InfoObjects used in business applications, for example, Customer, Plant, Material, Material Group InfoObjects, etc.

▶ **InfoProviders**
There are standard business content InfoProviders available for a wide area of applications. These include InfoCube, DataStores and MultiProviders.

▶ **Queries and Web Templates**
The queries and Web templates used for reporting are also available as business content for a wide range of applications.

In addition to the above, Business Content is available for objects that are used to load data; for example, InfoSources, Transfer Rules, Update Rules, Transformations, and DTPs. The processes for controlling data loading in SAP using InfoPackages and Process Chains are also delivered by SAP.

You can see from our discussion so far that the process of setting up the SAP NetWeaver BI system is greatly facilitated through Business Content supplied by SAP. While the Business Content may not be able to provide a solution for all of the reporting and analysis requirements of a business, it can be used as the starting point to prototype a solution. Business Content can subsequently be enhanced to meet the reporting requirements of specific users.

In the next section, we will review the framework for developing a planning application in the SAP NetWeaver BI system.

2.5 Planning Framework in SAP NetWeaver BI

SAP NetWeaver BI provides a flexible and stable framework for planning data. The data in SAP NetWeaver BI can be used as a source of data for the purpose of planning. A planning application can be developed for any area of business using the tools available in SAP NetWeaver BI.

Beginning with SAP NetWeaver BI 7.0, two options are available in SAP NetWeaver BI to develop planning applications. They are as follows:

▶ **SAP Business Planning and Simulation (BW BPS)**
Business Planning and Simulation (SAP BW BPS) was integrated into SAP BW with the release of SAP NetWeaver. It is also supported in the SAP NetWeaver BI 7.0 release. The SAP GUI must be installed on the developer's computer for configuring planning applications. When using SAP

BW BPS for planning, you create the objects required for the planning application using the Planning Workbench. The planning objects are then integrated into a complete planning application and made available to end users either on the SAP GUI or on the Web. Users employ the layouts included in the planning application to make any necessary changes to plan data. Automatic changes to data are supported through the use of Planning Functions. Subsequently, users can perform reporting and analysis of plan data using a query that is created using the BEx Query Designer. The query is deployed to the user on the BEx Analyzer or on the Web using the Web Application Designer tool.

▸ **SAP NetWeaver BI Integrated Planning**
SAP NetWeaver BI Integrated Planning was introduced with the release of SAP NetWeaver BI 7.0. The Web-based planning modeler in SAP NetWeaver BI Integrated Planning provides the necessary tools to develop planning objects and planning applications on the Web. With the SAP NetWeaver BI Integrated Planning option, the process of creating planning objects is done through a Web-based modeler. This modeler supports the entire configuration of the planning objects required for the planning application. After planning objects are created, a query is created in the BEx Query Designer for the user to create, modify and analyze plan data. Users can create or modify plan data using input-enabled queries. These queries are then integrated into a planning application using the BEx Analyzer or the Web Application Designer tool and presented to end users as a complete planning application. The BEx query is also used for reporting and analyzing the plan data.

2.5.1 Comparing SAP BW BPS and SAP NetWeaver BI Integrated Planning

The main advantage of using SAP NetWeaver BI Integrated Planning over SAP BW BPS for developing a planning application is that it provides a common interface for data entry, reporting, and analysis of plan data. The ability to leverage the elements created in the SAP NetWeaver BI reporting environment by using the BEx Query Designer tool is an added benefit when using the SAP NetWeaver BI Integrated planning option. This brings down the total cost of ownership (TCO) and provides the flexibility of enabling a Web-based configuration.

SAP NetWeaver BI Integrated Planning is the SAP recommended option to develop new planning applications. You still can use SAP BW BPS to modify and run applications that were developed in the older releases.

2.6 High-level Overview for Creating a Planning Application

The initial process of identifying the planning requirements is the same when using either SAP BW BPS or SAP NetWeaver BI Integrated Planning. The planning process starts with determining the requirements of a planning application. The requirements are collected and analyzed, and the necessary relationships are identified.

We will now review the high-level steps needed to create a planning application using the SAP BW BPS and the SAP NetWeaver BI Integrated Planning tools.

> **Note**
>
> The prerequisite for developing a planning application in SAP BW BPS or SAP NetWeaver BI Integrated Planning is the existence of a Real-Time InfoCube, which is used to maintain plan data using either tool.

2.6.1 SAP BW BPS: Steps to Develop a Planning Application

You'll need to perform the following steps when using the SAP BW BPS option for planning. The planning objects are configured using the Planning Workbench (Transaction BPS0).

1. Create a Planning Area by identifying the appropriate Business Area. For example, you can create a Planning Area for a sales planning application. In the definition of the Planning Area, you specify a Real-Time InfoCube. This InfoCube will contain the plan data that is associated to the sales planning application.

   A multiple Planning Area can be used if more than one InfoCube is required for planning. For example, one InfoCube can serve as reference data and another InfoCube can store the plan data.

2. Create a Planning Level based on a Planning Area. Planning Levels provide flexibility when creating a planning application. Let us take the example of sales planning for a company that is divided into different units, each producing a different set of products. A Planning Level can be created for each unit, depending on the planning requirements for each individual unit. The Characteristics and Key Figures required for the respective Planning Level are selected during this step.

3. Create Planning Packages based on a Planning Level. Planning packages help to configure planning at a more granular level. For a sales unit in a

company, for example, a salesperson may be responsible for planning only a few products. A planning package can be created so the salesperson can enter or modify plan data only for the products for which he is responsible.

4. Create Planning Functions to automatically generate and modify the plan data. There is great flexibility when using Planning Functions. SAP provides a number of standard functions for the purpose of planning. Formula extension (FOX) and user-exit Planning Functions can be developed to support complex requirements of planning.

5. Create a Planning Sequence to execute more than one Planning Function as a single unit by combining the functions into a Local Planning Sequence. The Planning Functions included in a Local Planning Sequence should belong to the same Planning Level.

   Global Planning Sequences work much like Local Planning Sequences but provide additional flexibility. Planning Functions from any Planning Level can be included into a Global Planning Sequence. Global Planning Sequences can also be executed in the background.

   The configuration of Planning Functions and Planning Sequences are also performed in the planning workbench from the SAP GUI.

6. Create Manual Planning Layouts to enable users to enter plan data. Manual Planning Layouts are created based on Planning Packages. They provide the option to create or modify existing plan data. There are three different options that are available for manual planning: ABAP List Viewer (ALV in R/3), Microsoft Excel, and Web:

   ▶ When using the ABAP List Viewer interface for creating or maintaining plan data, users will need the SAP GUI installed on the computer for executing the planning layout.

   ▶ The Microsoft Excel option can be used take advantage of the extensive features offered in Excel. There are some limitations when using the Microsoft Excel interface on the Web because all of the features are not available when using this medium.

   ▶ The advantage for users when using the Web for planning is that it does not require the SAP GUI to be installed on the computer. The application can be accessed from any computer using an Internet connection that can access the company's network.

Figure 2.3 shows the planning cycle in SAP BW BPS.

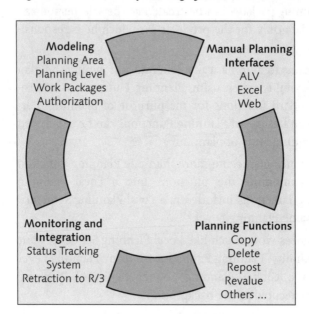

Figure 2.3 Planning Cycle in SAP BW BPS

Next, we will discuss the steps to develop a planning application using the SAP NetWeaver BI Integrated Planning tool.

2.6.2 SAP NetWeaver BI Integrated Planning — Steps to Develop a Planning Application

The following is the list of steps you'll need to perform when using the SAP NetWeaver BI Integrated Planning tool for planning. The planning objects are configured using the Web-based Planning Modeler.

1. Assign an InfoProvider as the basis of planning. The InfoProvider selected should be a Real-Time InfoCube. If a MultiProvider is selected, at least one InfoProvider in the definition of the MultiProvider should be a Real-Time InfoCube. The Real-Time InfoProvider would contain the plan data. If a MultiProvider is used, the other InfoProviders in its definition that are not Real-Time InfoCubes would contain the reference data that will be used for planning purposes.

2. Assign an Aggregation Level for the selected InfoProvider. Aggregation helps to support flexible planning for different levels. In the example of sales planning for a company, a company plan at a material group level, and an Aggregation Level can be created for that level. The Characteristics and Key Figures required for the Aggregation Level are selected in this step.

3. Assign Filters based on an Aggregation Level. Filters help to restrict planning to specific Characteristic values. For example, in a sales unit a salesperson might be responsible for planning only a few products. A Filter can be created for the salesperson to enter plan data only for the products that fall under his responsibility.

4. Create Planning Functions to automate the process of creating or modifying plan data. There is considerable flexibility when using Planning Functions. A number of standard functions are available for this purpose. The configuration of Planning Functions is performed using the Web Modeler.

   Different types of Planning Functions can be used depending on the requirements of the planning application. We will discuss this in detail in Chapter 3 when we configure a planning application.

5. Create Planning Sequences to execute Planning Functions in sequential order. Planning Sequences are configured in the Web modeler to include an Aggregation Level, Filter, and Function. Planning Sequences can also be integrated into a process chain.

6. Create an interface where users can manually enter or modify plan data. To do so, you design an Input-Enabled query using the BEx Query Designer tool. There are two options when deploying this query to users, either using the BEx Analyzer or the Web. The BEx Analyzer tool uses an Excel add-on interface and the BEx Web Application Designer tool uses the Web interface. As described earlier, the advantage of deploying the planning application over the Web is that the users do not require the SAP GUI to be installed on their computer to access the planning application.

The Planning Function and the Planning Sequence created in the earlier steps can be configured to be triggered from the user interface; i.e., the BEx Analyzer workbook or the Web template.

Figure 2.4 represents the process for planning when using the SAP NetWeaver BI Integrated Planning tool.

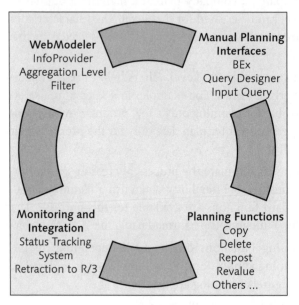

Figure 2.4 Planning Cycle in SAP NetWeaver BI Integrated Planning

Status and Tracking System (STS)

The Status and Tracking System (STS) is an out-of-the box application from SAP that lets you define, track the status of, and monitor an active planning process. This application is available for both the SAP BW BPS and the SAP NetWeaver BI Integrated Planning tools. The STS application has to be customized before it can be used in a planning process An SAP NetWeaver BI hierarchy can be created that identifies the relationship of individuals involved in the planning process. After the hierarchy is defined, it is associated to a planning process. The roles and responsibilities of individuals identified in the planning process are defined in the configuration of the STS application. This information is used in the STS application to monitor the progress of an active planning process.

For example, let's say sales planning is initiated at a company where sales analysts enter the planning data for their respective areas and submit the data to their managers for approval. The managers review the data, approve or reject it, and send it back to the sales analysts for further changes. If there are many layers of approval in the planning process, the importance of communication and the availability of current status information are critical for the success of the planning process. STS helps with this need by providing real-time status information.

The initial configuration for the STS application is done from within the SAP GUI. Once the configuration is complete, the final application is made available to users on the Web.

Retraction

Plan data generated in SAP BW BPS and SAP NetWeaver BI Integrated Planning can in some cases also be retracted to SAP R/3 systems. This functionality is available for a few standard applications such as cost center planning, profitability analysis planning, and investment management planning.

From the above discussion, you can see that the entire process of planning is supported by SAP NetWeaver BI. The availability of enterprise data makes the process of generating plan data easier. It also enables the integration of data from various sources. This is the case, for example, with balance-sheet planning, which requires profitability analysis, profit and loss, and investment management data.

We will now discuss the points you need to consider when modeling a planning application in SAP NetWeaver BI.

2.7 Modeling Considerations in Planning

Before modeling a planning application in SAP NetWeaver BI, several considerations will have to be taken into account. This section discusses the relevant issues concerning the different approaches and the data model and type of InfoProvider required for planning.

2.7.1 Standard InfoCube versus Real-Time InfoCube

The most common form of storing data in SAP NetWeaver BI is the InfoCube. There are two types of InfoCubes, the Standard InfoCube and the Real-Time InfoCube. The InfoCube designed to store plan data in SAP NetWeaver BI must be defined as a Real-Time InfoCube. Table 2.1 compares the features and functionalities of Standard InfoCubes and Real-Time InfoCubes.

Standard InfoCube	Real-Time InfoCube
Primarily used for loading data through the standard extraction process via an Info-Package Transformation or Data Transfer Process. Used for loading transaction data.	Primarily used for entering and modifying data through a planning application using Planning Objects and Planning Functions.
Optimized to be read-efficient.	Optimized to be write-efficient.
Data can be reported using the BEx Analyzer.	Data can be reported using the BEx Analyzer.
Aggregation and compression of data are possible.	Aggregation and compression of data are possible.
Can be used for loading data only through the standard extraction, transformation and loading process.	Can be set to load mode using a switch. When this mode is set, data can be loaded using the standard extraction, transformation, and loading process. After the data is extracted, the switch can be reset to planning. In this mode, data can be entered or modified using Planning Functions.

Table 2.1 Differences between Standard InfoCubes and Real-Time InfoCubes

Please note the following key points about requests to load data into a Standard or Real-Time InfoCubes:

▶ When data is loaded into a Standard InfoCube, a unique request is opened. It is closed after the data is successfully loaded into the InfoCube. The traffic light associated with a closed request is green.

▶ When plan data is loaded into a Real-Time InfoCube, a request is created and stays open until the data exceeds 50,000 records. The traffic-light icon associated with an open request is yellow. You might find that the threshold of 50,000 records is not always the level at which a request is actually closed. Calculation of this number occurs in the system after a user saves data. If the number of records in the open requests plus the number of new records when saving the changes exceeds 50,000, the request will be closed. When the request is closed, the traffic light associated with the request turns green.

▶ A request that is open will not be available for reporting if the query is not enabled as a query used for planning. Such a request can be reported in a BEx query using a special variable for the requested InfoObject. This variable is 0S_RQTRA. It's available as standard Business Content and can be used in a query after activation.

- A request that is open with respect to a Real-Time InfoCube can be closed by executing the function module RSAPO_CLOSE_TRANS_REQUEST. If you do so, you will be prompted for an InfoCube name. Enter the name of the InfoCube that contains the open request. Once the request is closed, aggregates defined for the InfoCube will be rolled up to reflect all closed requests.

- The Process Chain now includes a new process type that can be used to close an open request in a Real-Time InfoCube. This process type is titled *Close Request of Real-Time InfoPackage* and is available under the **Load Process and Post-Processing** area for process types in the process chain.

2.7.2 Key Figure Model vs. Account Model

An InfoCube InfoProvider is used as the basis for planning in the SAP NetWeaver BI environment. It therefore helps to understand the design considerations that are relevant to planning when setting up the InfoCube Info-Provider. Recall that an InfoCube is made up of Characteristics and Key Figures. The Characteristics represent entities such as product, customer, or plant. Key figures represent an amount or quantity value. For example, in the case of a sales InfoCube, Key Figures could be sales quantity, sales amount, etc.

To illustrate this concept further, let's use the example of a sales InfoCube that is used for storing three different types of sales data: actual, plan, and forecast data. In this context, the quantity Key Figure can represent actual sales, plan, or forecast data. There are two approaches when configuring the data model for this purpose:

- Key Figure model
- Account model

Key Figure Model

With the Key Figure model, the three different types of Key Figures can be included into the InfoCube to store the quantity values. In this case, the values will be stored in the respective Key Figures depending on the type of transaction data; for example, sales or plan.

Account Model

In the case of the Account model, only one generic quantity Key Figure is created. An additional Characteristic, for example Type, is included in the InfoCube and identifies the type of transaction. The value for this Characteristic will determine whether the quantity value is associated with sales, plan, or forecast. The necessary restrictions will have to be applied using this Characteristic when analyzing or reporting the data on the Key Figure when using the Account model.

Examples of the Key Figure Model and the Account Model

Table 2.2 shows data based on the Key Figure model. Here you can see that a single sales record has three different amounts in the same record. These represent three different amounts: sales price, rebates, and freight. Table 2.3 shows data based on the Account model, where three records are generated using an additional Characteristic type with only one Key Figure. The value in the type Characteristic represents the type of data contained in the amount Key Figure.

Customer	Product	Sales Price	Rebates	Freight
C1	P1	$100	$5	$2

Table 2.2 Example of the Key Figure Model

Customer	Product	Type	Amount
C1	P1	Sales Price	$100
C1	P1	Rebates	$5
C1	P1	Freight	$2

Table 2.3 Example of the Account Model

The Key Figure model enables increases in the width of individual records in an InfoCube as additional Key Figures are added to the structure, thus helping to distinctly represent the data. The Account model increases the number of records in the InfoCube where there is a record for each value represented in the Key Figure.

Pros and Cons of Account and Key Figure Models

From a performance point of view, the Account model typically generates more records and takes longer to retrieve data. In addition, restrictions have to be applied when designing queries created against an InfoCube that uses this model. But this model also provides greater flexibility when additional Key Figures have to be included after initial design.

The Key Figure model works well when the number of Key Figures in an InfoCube remains stable over a period of time. It's also easier to use, and you don't have to worry about additional restrictions in reporting and planning. However, if a Key Figure has to be added after the initial design, the InfoCube has to be modified. The addition of a new Key Figure for planning purposes also requires a change to the planning configuration.

One of the things to look for when evaluating the Key Figure model is to determine the percentage of Key Figures that will contain values. If, for example, an average of only two of the 10 Key Figures included in the InfoCube have values filled in for a record when loading transaction data, it may be advantageous to use the Account model, despite the fact that it generates more records than the Key Figure model.

The source of the data also dictates the model. For example, when sales data is extracted from Controlling-Profitability Analysis (CO-PA) in R/3, the structure of the data in the source makes it easier to use the Key Figure model. However, with the help of FOX Planning Functions (available in SAP NetWeaver BI Integrated Planning and SAP BW BPS), it is possible to convert data from one model to the other as required.

Which model you choose when designing an InfoCube is up to you. However, it's best to make your decision based on business requirements.

We are now finished with our review of some of the important considerations for modeling a planning application. In the next section, we will present a case study that will help you understand the requirements for a particular planning scenario and guide you through the process of developing a planning application.

2.8   Case Study for Financial Planning

The case study we introduce in this section will be used as the basis for later developing a planning application using the BI Integrated Planning tool. This section will give you an overview of a fictitious sample company, along with detailed information about its operations. It will also explain the objectives the company wants to realize from planning.

The objective of the case study is to project the *gross profit margin* of the company's operations. The gross profit margin is a measurement of the efficiency of the company's operations. It is the company's total sales revenue minus its cost of goods sold. It can also be expressed as a percentage.

2.8.1 Rich Bloom, Inc. — Sample Company for the Case Study

The sample company for our case study is Rich Bloom, Inc., a popular clothing retailer. The company has a large presence in the USA and also has operations in Europe, with companies set up in the UK and Germany.

Rich Bloom, Inc.'s products and business model have been well received in the market, and it has been expanding since it was founded in 2000.

The company is incorporated as follows:

▶ Rich Bloom, Inc., incorporated in San Diego, California (parent company)
▶ Rich Bloom Ltd., incorporated in London, England (subsidiary)
▶ Rich Bloom AG, incorporated in Frankfurt, Germany (subsidiary)

The details of the company's product line are as follows:

▶ The company sells clothing for teenagers. It has the following product lines:
  ▶ RB T-Shirt
  ▶ RB Shirt
  ▶ RB Jackets
  ▶ RB Designer Jeans

The details of the company's sales are as follows:

▶ The company sells most of its products to large department stores, which in turn sell them to retail customers. Rich Bloom, Inc. also has a few retail stores of its own that sell directly to retail customers.
▶ The RB T-Shirt and RB Designer Jeans product lines are especially popular among teenagers and have contributed to large profits for the company in recent years.
▶ The company introduced RB Jackets in 2006 and has been selling them at a promotional price. The promotional price is 20% less than the original

price. The company plans to continue using the promotional price for sell-ing this item for all of 2007.

From a financial and monetary transaction standpoint, the company is organized in the following manner.

- Each location uses a unique code, as follows:
    - 20 — Rich Bloom, Inc., San Diego, CA, USA
    - 25 — Rich Bloom Ltd., UK
    - 30 — Rich Bloom AG, Frankfurt, Germany
- The subsidiaries operate as independent entities but report their opera-tions to the parent company. Each of the companies has its own produc-tion centers to cater to market demand.
- The currencies for transactions are the respective currencies of the coun-tries in which the companies operate. They are as follows:
    - US Dollar — Rich Bloom, Inc., San Diego, CA, USA
    - British Pound — Rich Bloom Ltd., UK
    - Euro — Rich Bloom AG, Frankfurt, Germany

For the purpose of analysis and reporting the operations of the company as a whole, the operations of the subsidiaries are converted into the currency of the parent company, which is US Dollars (USD). The calendar year is used as the fiscal year for reporting.

2.8.2 Requirements of the Case Study

Rich Bloom, Inc. has a fully functional SAP R/3 system. It also implemented SAP BW four years ago and has fully realized the benefits of using this tool for analysis. It recently upgraded the SAP BW system to SAP NetWeaver 7.0 and wants to do financial planning in SAP NetWeaver BI. The actual and his-toric sales and cost data for the last four years are maintained in SAP NetWeaver BI. A decision has been made by upper management to use the SAP NetWeaver BI Integrated Planning tool for financial planning.

The company's management is convinced that it can increase sales and reduce costs by implementing a robust process for planning. A good plan-ning system will help the company anticipate demand for its products and position itself to meet customer requirements. The company also believes that it can reduce production-related labor and material costs by having a good planning system for procurement in place. Moreover, labor costs and other overhead costs can be planned effectively to increase productivity. The objective of the planning in this case study is to project the gross profit margin of the company's operation.

Rich Bloom, Inc. also wants to compare the plan data with actual and historical data to see how well it is expected to perform over time. The planning application will use the current and historical sales revenue and cost of sales data as the source for planning for the future. This, in addition to marketing research, will form the basis for projecting the gross profit margin.

The company has decided to use the bottom-up approach for planning. Using this method, the initial planning of sales revenue and cost of sales for the individual sales areas will be done by the sales representatives. The sales representatives will complete the sales-revenue and cost-of-sales plan for their respective areas and send it to the sales manager for approval. The sales manager will then combine the data from all of the sales reps, make any necessary changes, and send it on to the regional manager. This process will continue up the hierarchy to upper management until all of the plan data is consolidated and approved.

Proposed Planning Application

To meet the outlined requirements, a planning application needs to be developed and made available to the users involved in the planning process. The planning application should satisfy the following aspects of planning:

▶ The functional aspects of planning should be incorporated into the planning application.

▶ It should meet the planning requirements of the business.

▶ It should be flexible to efficiently accommodate planning process changes.

▶ It should be comprehensive with respect to the integration of various sources of data.

▶ It should be reliable and easy to use.

Determining the Required Information

The company has determined that it needs the following pieces of information to plan effectively:

- ▶ Company Organization
  - ▸ Company Code
  - ▸ Controlling Area
  - ▸ Cost Center
  - ▸ Business Area
- ▶ Product
  - ▸ Material
  - ▸ Material Group
- ▶ Customer
  - ▸ Customer
  - ▸ Sales Organization
  - ▸ Sales Office
  - ▸ Distribution Channel
  - ▸ Division
- ▶ Country
  - ▸ Country
- ▶ Period
  - ▸ Calendar Year
  - ▸ Calendar Period
- ▶ Quantity
  - ▸ Plan Quantity (including units)
- ▶ Value
  - ▸ Group Currency (the currency of the parent company — US Dollars)
  - ▸ Local Currency (the currency of the country where the transaction occurs — based on the company code)

The above elements correspond to the different entities and planning Key Figures of the business and will be used to develop a data model for the purpose of planning.

In the next section, we will delve into the details of building a data model to suit the planning requirements of our sample company. In the subsequent chapters, we will explain the process of configuring the planning objects and the integration of the planning objects into a comprehensive application. The planning application will be used for creating, modifying, reporting, and analyzing the plan data.

2.9   Building the Data Model in SAP NetWeaver BI

In the previous section, we looked at the details of a company that has decided to use the SAP NetWeaver BI Integrated Planning tool to plan the gross profit margin of its business. In this section, we will start building the objects required for supporting this case study. Note that we will build the objects sequentially. This will give you a clear understanding of the steps involved to create the necessary objects before building a planning application.

An InfoCube called Sales will store the actual sales and cost data for the last four years. It will also be used as one of the sources of data for the purpose of planning for the future. Market research will also be used to determine the current trends in clothing in the teenage market. The data in the Sales InfoCube will be loaded with data from the SAP R/3 system on a daily basis.

An InfoCube called Plan that will store the plan data will also need to be created. The structure of the Plan InfoCube will mirror the structure of the Sales InfoCube. The Plan InfoCube will be configured as a Real-Time InfoCube.

The InfoObjects to be included in the Sales and Plan InfoCubes are listed in the following tables and are SAP-delivered unless indicated by the words *Custom InfoObject*:

▶ **Characteristics**
The Characteristics and their values are listed in Table 2.4.

▶ **Time Characteristics**
The Time Characteristics and their values are listed in Table 2.5.

▶ **Unit Characteristics**
The Unit Characteristics required are listed in Table 2.6.

▶ **Key Figures**
The Key Figures (quantitative measures) required for reporting are listed in Table 2.7.

Characteristic	Values
0COMP_CODE	20, 25 and 30 20 — Rich Bloom Inc., San Diego, CA, USA 25 — Rich Bloom Ltd., London, UK 30 — Rich Bloom AG, Frankfurt, Germany
0CO_AREA	1000

Table 2.4 Characteristics and Values

Characteristic	Values
0COSTCENTER	CC1 and CC2 CC1 — Cost center for T-Shirts, Shirts, and Jackets CC2 — Cost center for Designer Jeans
0BUS_AREA	B1 and B2
0SALESORG	20, 25 and 30 20 — Rich Bloom Inc., San Diego, CA, USA 25 — Rich Bloom Ltd., London, UK 30 — Rich Bloom AG, Frankfurt, Germany
0SALES_OFF	SO1, SO2 AND SO3 SO1 — US sales office SO2 — UK sales office SO3 — Germany sales office
0DISTR_CHAN	70 (Direct Distribution)
0DIVISION	D1 and D2 D1 — Shirt division D2 — Jeans division
0VTYPE	10, 20 and 60 10 — Actual 20 — Plan 60 — Forecast
0VERSION	00, 01 Actual data is always stored with version 00 Plan data is stored with version 01
0MATERIAL	CK2000, CK2001, CK2002 CY7000 CK2000 — T-Shirts CK2001 — Shirts CK2002 — Jackets CY7000 — Jeans
0MATL_GROUP	Material group is also an attribute of material CK — Shirts CY — Jeans
0CUSTOMER	C1-C4, C20-C21, C30-C31 C1 — C4 — Customers in the USA C20 — C21 — Customers in the UK C30 — C31 — Customers in Germany

Table 2.4 Characteristics and Values (cont.)

Characteristic	Values
0COUNTRY	US, GB and DE US (United States of America) GB (United Kingdom) DE (Germany)
ZRES_PERS (Custom InfoObject)	Dummy Characteristic that is included only in the Plan InfoCube; used for STS Data type: CHAR Length:13

Table 2.4 Characteristics and Values (cont.)

Time Characteristic	Values
0CALMONTH	Calendar period for sales/plan data
0CALYEAR	Calendar year for sales/plan data

Table 2.5 Time Characteristics

Unit Characteristic	Values
0D_UQTY	Used in Key Figure 0D_QTY
0CURRENCY	Used in Key Figures ZCTAMT_GC and ZSLAMT_GC.

Table 2.6 Unit Characteristics

Key Figures	Values
0D_QTY	Quantity in units (Key Figure of type unit; associated with 0D_UQTY unit measure)
ZCTAMT_GC (Custom InfoObject)	Cost amount in group currency (Key Figure of type currency; associated with 0CURRENCY currency measure)
ZSLAMT_GC (Custom InfoObject)	Sales amount in group currency (Key Figure of type currency; associated with 0CURRENCY currency measure)

Table 2.7 Key Figures

2.9.1   Create and Activate InfoObjects

Based on the requirements listed in the case study, we will now start building the necessary objects. The InfoObjects listed in the above tables are required for building the data model. You will notice that most of the Info-Objects have a technical name that starts with *0*. These are SAP-supplied Info-

Objects. Before an InfoObject that is delivered by SAP can be used, however, it must be activated. Let's start by checking the status of InfoObjects and learn how to activate them if they're not yet active.

Steps to Check the Status of an SAP-Supplied InfoObject

As illustrated in Figure 2.5, the following are the steps to check the status of an SAP-supplied InfoObject:

1. Open the **Edit InfoObjects: Start** window using Transaction **RSD1**.

2. Under **Type**, select **Characteristic** and next to **Version**, select **Active/Revised** (see Figure 2.5, callouts 1 and 2).

3. In the text field next to **InfoObject**, enter the name of the InfoObject to check (see Figure 2.5, callout 3).

4. Click the **Display** button (see Figure 2.5, callout 4).

If the InfoObject is not yet active, the following message displays in the status bar of the window:

Enter valid Characteristic...

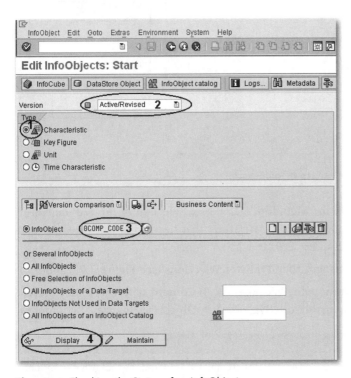

Figure 2.5 Checking the Status of an InfoObject

Steps to Activate an SAP-Supplied InfoObject

By default, none of the SAP-supplied InfoObjects are active so let's start by activating them. The process, illustrated in Figures 2.6, 2.7, and 2.8, is as follows.

1. Open the **Data Warehousing Workbench: BI Content** window using Transaction **RSA1**.

2. In the left pane, select **Object Types** (see Figure 2.6, callout 1).

3. In the right pane, under **Grouping**, select the option **Only Necessary Objects,** and for **Collection Mode** select the option **Collect Automatically** (see Figure 2.6, callouts 2 and 3).

4. Under **InfoObject**, double-click **Select Objects** (see Figure 2.6, callout 4). This opens the **Input help for Metadata** dialog box.

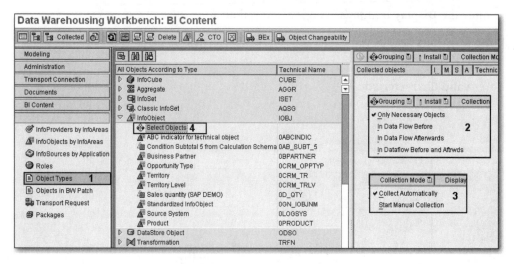

Figure 2.6 Settings to Activate an InfoObject

5. In the **Input help for Metadata** dialog box, select all of the SAP-delivered InfoObjects required for the case study that need to be activated, as outlined in Tables 2.4, 2.5, 2.6, and 2.7.

6. When you're finished, click **Transfer Selections** (see Figure 2.7, callout 5).

7. In the **Data Warehousing Workbench: BI Content** window, under **Install**, select the option **Install** to activate the InfoObject (see Figure 2.8, callout 6).

> **Note**
>
> Activating an InfoObject also activates all inactive InfoObjects that are dependent on this InfoObject.

Figure 2.7 Select InfoObject(s) to Activate

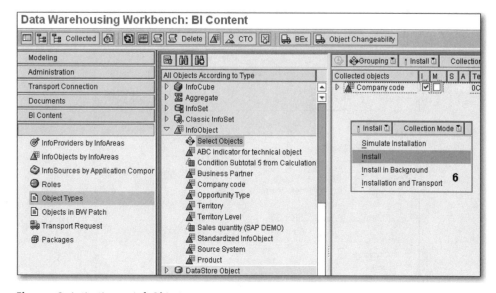

Figure 2.8 Activating an InfoObject

After you're done activating the SAP-supplied InfoObjects, you'll need to create and activate the custom InfoObjects needed for the case study, as outlined in Tables 2.4 and 2.7. Let's take a closer look at how to do this.

Steps to Create and Activate a Custom Characteristic InfoObject

We'll start by creating the InfoObject ZRES_PERS (Responsible Person), as illustrated in Figures 2.9 and 2.10. This InfoObject should be of the type Characteristic.

1. Open the **Edit InfoObject: Start** window using Transaction **RSD1**.
2. Under **Type**, select **Characteristic** (see Figure 2.9, callout 1).
3. In the text field next to the option **InfoObject**, enter the technical name of the InfoObject ("ZRES_PERS") and click the **Create** button (see Figure 2.9, callouts 2 and 3).
4. In the **Create Characteristic** dialog box, in the **Long description** text field, enter a description ("Responsible Person") and then click the **Enter** button (see Figure 2.9, callouts 4 and 5).

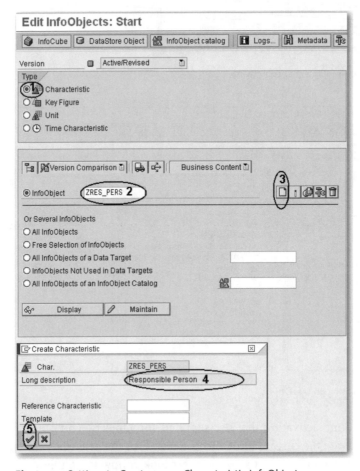

Figure 2.9 Settings to Create a new Characteristic InfoObject

5. On the **General** tab of the **Create Characteristic ZRES_PERS:Detail** window, specify the **Short description** ("Responsible Person"), **Data type** ("CHAR") and **Length** ("13") (see Figure 2.10, callouts 6, 7 and 8).

6. No attributes are required for this InfoObject, so you can click **Activate** (see Figure 2.10, callout 9).

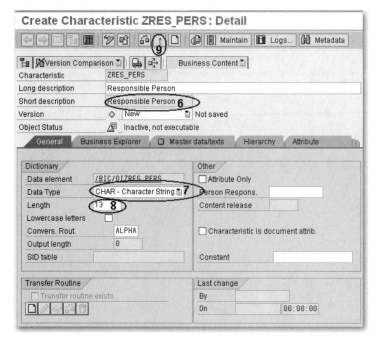

Figure 2.10 Activate a Custom InfoObject

The ZRES_PERS InfoObject is now saved and activated.

Using a similar process, you'll now need to create and activate the remaining required custom Key Figure InfoObjects, ZSLAMT_GC and ZCTAMT_GC. Let's get started.

Steps to Create a Custom Key Figure InfoObject

Note

The SAP-delivered unit currency InfoObject 0CURRENCY should have been activated before creating the custom Key Figures.

We'll now create a custom InfoObject of type Key Figure, as illustrated in Figures 2.11 and 2.12. The technical name of the InfoObject is ZSLAMT_GC:

1. Open the **Edit InfoObjects: Start** window using Transaction **RSD1**.

2. Under **Type**, select **Key Figure** (see Figure 2.11, callout 1).

3. In the text field next to the option **InfoObject**, enter the technical name of the InfoObject ("ZSLAMT_GC") and click the **Create** button (see Figure 2.11, callouts 2 and 3).

4. In the **Create Key Figure** dialog box, in the **Long description** text field, enter a description ("Sales amt — GC") and then click the **Enter** button (see Figure 2.11, callouts 4 and 5).

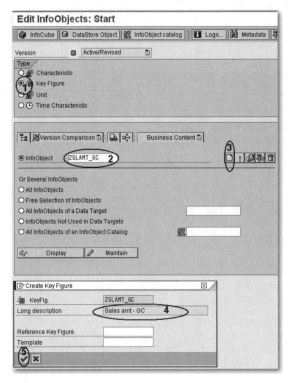

Figure 2.11 Settings to Create a New Custom Key Figure InfoObject

5. In the **Create Key Figure ZSLAMT_GC:ZSLAMT_GC Detail** window, enter a **Short decription** ("Sales amt — GC") (see Figure 2.12, callout 6).

6. On the **Type/unit** tab, select **Amount** and then select **CURR — Currency field, stored as DEC**. (see Figure 2.12, callouts 7 and 8).

7. According to the requirements, the InfoObject ZSLAMT_GC should be attached to the 0CURRENCY InfoObject. Thus, under **Currency/Unit of measure**, in the **Unit/Currency** field select **0CURRENCY** (see Figure 2.12, callout 9).

8. Click **Activate** (see Figure 2.12, callout 10). The ZSLAMT_GC InfoObject is now saved and activated.

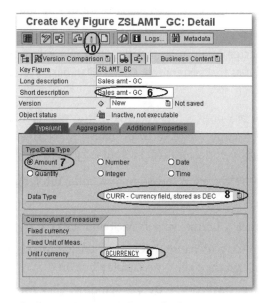

Figure 2.12 Settings to Create the Custom Key Figure InfoObject ZSLAMT_GC

You will now need to create the Key Figure InfoObject ZCTAMT_GC using the same steps 1 through 8, but using the appropriate information for the InfoObject ZCTAMT_GC. (see Figure 2.13).

Figure 2.13 Settings for the Custom Key Figure InfoObject ZCTAMT_GC

Steps to Populate the Master Data

The next step in the process is to load master data for the InfoObjects with the values listed in the reference table for the Characteristic values, as shown in Table 2.4.

As we've mentioned before, master data can be populated from a variety of sources: an SAP R/3 system, a flat-file system, an Oracle Database system using DB Connect, etc.

In this example, because there are only a few records in the master data table, we will enter the values for the Characteristics manually. Normally, however, the master data would be populated from a source system.

We will now manually enter the data for the company code InfoObject (0COMP_CODE), as illustrated in Figures 2.14 and 2.15:

1. Open the **Edit InfoObject: Start** window using Transaction **RSD1**.

2. Specify the InfoObject by entering its name ("0COMP_CODE") or selecting it from the dropdown list and then click the **Display** button.

3. In the **Display Characteristic 0COMP_CODE:Details** window, click **Maintain** to create or modify data for this InfoObject (see Figure 2.14, callout 1)

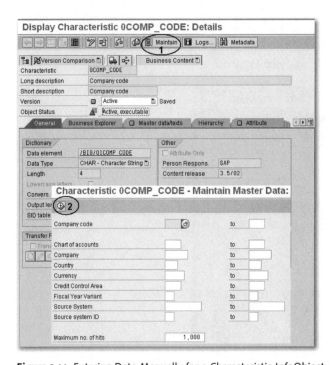

Figure 2.14 Entering Data Manually for a Characteristic InfoObject

4. In the **Characteristic 0COMP_CODE — Maintain Master Data:** window, click the **Execute** Button (see Figure 2.14, callout 2)

5. In the **Characteristic 0COMP_CODE — maintain master data: List** window, click **Create** to create a new record (see Figure 2.15 callout 3). Enter a value for the company code InfoObject ("20"), as listed in Table 2.4.

6. Click the **Enter** button (see Figure 2.15, callout 4) and then click the **Save** button (see Figure 2.15, callout 5).

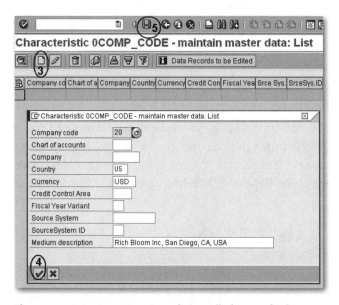

Figure 2.15 Inserting a New Record Manually for an InfoObject

7. Use steps 1 through 6 outlined here to insert master data for the other Characteristics listed in Table 2.4.

Steps to Apply the Hierarchy/Attribute Change Process

When you create a new record in the master data table, no action is necessary for the changes to become effective. Any changes to an existing record, however, require that you run the Apply Hierarchy/Attribute Change process, as listed here and illustrated in Figure 2.16.

1. Open the **Data Warehousing Workbench** using Transaction **RSA1**.

2. Select the option **Tools • Apply Hierarchy/Attribute Change** from the menu.

3. In the **Execute Hierarchy/Attribute Changes for Reporting** window, click **InfoObject List** to identify the Characteristic InfoObjects that have undergone a change since the last change run (see Figure 2.16, callout 1).

4. Select the InfoObjects for which the changes to data should apply and click **Save** (see Figure 2.16, callouts 2 and 3). InfoObjects that are displayed here, but are not selected for the change run, will not reflect the latest changes made to the data when reporting.

5. Once you click **Save**, a job name is automatically assigned by the system and you are taken back to the **Execute Hierarchy/Attribute Changes for Reporting** window.

6. Click the **Execute** button (see Figure 2.16, callout 4).

7. Click the **Refresh** button to confirm that the changes have been activated. The **Change Status** displays at the top of the table (see Figure 2.16, callout 5).

The Apply Hierarchy/Attribute Change process can be scheduled from this location to run at selected time periods or based on an event by clicking the **Selection** button (see Figure 2.16, callout 6) in the **Execute Hierarchy/Attribute Changes for Reporting** window and making the corresponding selections.

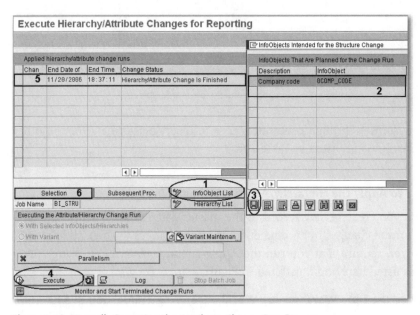

Figure 2.16 Manually Executing the Attribute Change Run Process

Subsequent events can be triggered following successful or unsuccessful completion of the change run.

2.9.2   Create InfoAreas

Now that you have created the InfoObjects, you will next create an InfoArea that will later contain InfoCubes. An InfoArea lets you group InfoProviders together. The following are the steps to create an InfoArea, as illustrated in Figure 2.17:

1. Open the **Data Warehousing Workbench** using Transaction **RSA1**.

2. Select the option **Modeling • InfoProvider**.

3. Right-click **InfoProvider** and select **Create InfoArea...**(see Figure 2.17, callout 1).

4. In the **Create InfoArea** section, in the **InfoArea** text field, enter the technical name for the **InfoArea** ("ZSALES") and in the **Long description** field, enter a description, ("Sales Management"). See Figure 2.17, callout 2.

5. Click **Enter** (see Figure 2.17, callout 3).

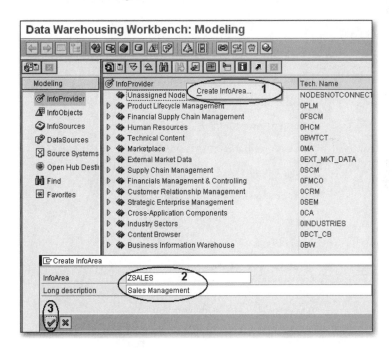

Figure 2.17 Create an InfoArea

2.9.3   Create InfoCubes

Now that you've created an InfoArea, you will create three InfoCubes under it. These include a Sales InfoCube for storing the actual sales and cost data, a Plan InfoCube for storing plan data, and a MultiProvider InfoCube that provides a unified view of the Sales InfoCube and Plan InfoCube. These are outlined in Table 2.8.

InfoCube	Description
ZSLS_ACT	Sales InfoCube
ZSLS_PLN	Plan InfoCube
ZSLS_CMB	Sales and Plan InfoCube (MultiProvider)

Table 2.8 InfoCubes for Creating a Financial Planning Application

Steps to Create a Sales InfoCube

This section explains how to create the Sales InfoCube based on the requirements listed earlier in Tables 2.4, 2.5, 2.6, and 2.7. The Dimensions and Key Figures used in the Sales InfoCube are shown in Table 2.9 and Table 2.10.

Dimensions	Characteristics
Financial Organization	Company Code (0COMP_CODE)
	Controlling Area (0CO_AREA)
	Cost Center (0COSTCENTER)
	Business Area (0BUS_AREA)
Sales Organization	Sales Organization (0SALESORG)
	Sales Office (0SALES_OFF)
	Distribution Channel (0DISTRCHAN)
	Sales Division (0DIVISION)
Version	Value Type (0VTYPE)
	Version (0VERSION)
Material	Material (0MATERIAL)
	Material Group (0MATL_GROUP)
Customer	Customer (0CUSTOMER)
Country	Country (0COUNTRY)
Time	Calendar Month (0CALMONTH)
	Calendar Year (0CALYEAR)

Table 2.9 Dimensions for the Sales InfoCube

Dimensions	Characteristics
Unit	Sales Quantity Unit (0D_UQTY)
	Currency (0CURRENCY)

Table 2.9 Dimensions for the Sales InfoCube (cont.)

Key Figures	Description
0D_QTY	Quantity
ZCTAMT_GC	Cost Amount in Goup Currency
ZSLAMT_GC	Sales Amount in Group Currency

Table 2.10 Key Figures for the Sales InfoCube

To create the Sales InfoCube, you create Dimensions, and assign Characteristic InfoObjects to Dimensions, and Key Figures to the Key Figure folder. This process is illustrated in Figures 2.18, 2.19, 2.20, 2.21, and 2.22. Let's get started:

1. Open the **Data Warehousing Workbench** using Transaction **RSA1**.

2. Select the option **Modeling • InfoProvider**.

3. Right-click the **Sales Management** InfoArea you created earlier and select **Create InfoCube** from the context menu (see Figure 2.18, callout 1).

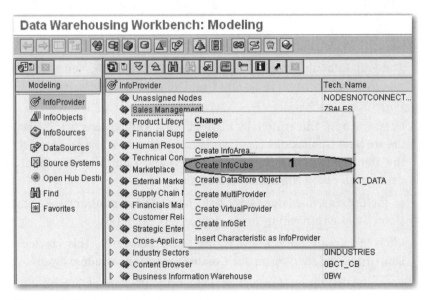

Figure 2.18 Creating an InfoCube — Part A

4. The **Edit InfoCube** window displays (see Figure 2.19). Enter the technical name of the InfoCube, ("ZSLS_ACT"), and a long description, ("Sales actual") into the text fields next to **InfoCube**. Make sure Standard InfoCube is selected under **InfoProvider Type**. Then click **Enter**. These steps are shown in Figure 2.19, callouts 2, 3, and 4.

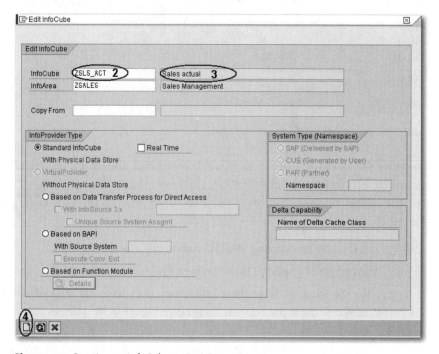

Figure 2.19 Creating an InfoCube — Part B

5. The **Edit InfoCube** window displays (see Figure 2.20). You will notice that the Data Package, Time, and Unit Dimensions are created automatically by the system.

6. Create a new Dimension by right-clicking **Dimensions** and selecting **Create New Dimensions** (see Figure 2.20, callout 5). The technical ID of the Dimension is automatically assigned and cannot be changed. The description of the Dimension can be changed.

7. In the **Create Dimensions** window, enter a **Description** for the Dimension ("Sales Organization") (see Figure 2.20, callout 6).

8. Click the **Create** button (see Figure 2.20, callout 7). This creates the Dimension and then opens the **Create Dimensions** window again.

9. Enter the description for the next Dimension ("Financial Organization").

10. Repeat steps 8 and 9 to create the remaining Dimensions for the Sales InfoCube that are specified in Table 2.9. They are:

   ▸ Version

   ▸ Material

   ▸ Customer

   ▸ Country

11. Click **Enter** when you are finished (see Figure 2.20, callout 8).

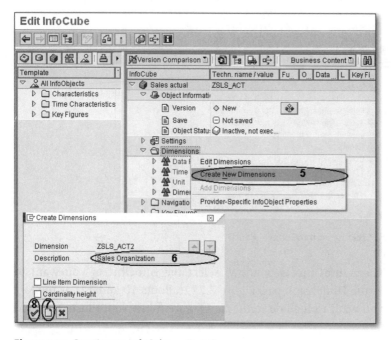

Figure 2.20 Creating an InfoCube — Part C

Note

You can create as many as 13 user-defined Dimensions in an InfoCube.

You have now created the Dimensions needed for the Sales InfoCube. The next task is to assign Characteristic InfoObjects to Dimensions and assign Key Figure InfoObjects to the Key Figure folder. Similar Characteristics are grouped under one Dimension. An InfoObject can be directly assigned to a Dimension or the Key Figure folder, using the **InfoObject Direct Input** option, as we'll show in the following steps.

1. Right-click the **Dimension** or **Key Figure** folder and choose **InfoObject Direct Input (**see Figure 2.21, callout 9).

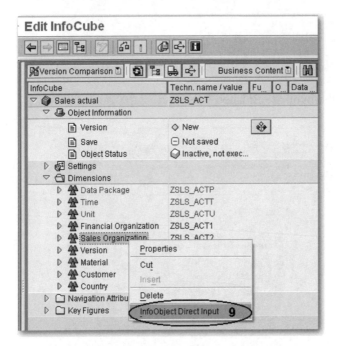

Figure 2.21 Creating an InfoCube — Part D

2. In the **Insert InfoObjects** window, select the InfoObjects you want to include in the Dimension (see Figure 2.22, callouts 10 and 11) or the Key Figures you want to include in the Key Figure folder (not illustrated) and click **Enter**).

Assign the following InfoObjects to the Dimensions:

▸ Dimension 1 (Sales Organization) — 0COMP_CODE, 0CO_AREA, 0COSTCENTER and 0BUS_AREA

▸ Dimension 2 (Financial Organization) — 0SALESORG, 0SALES_OFF, 0DISTRCHAN and 0DIVISION

▸ Dimension 3 (Version) — 0VTYPE and 0VERSION

▸ Dimension 4 (Material) — 0MATERIAL and 0MATERIAL_GRP

▸ Dimension 5 (Customer) — 0CUSTOMER

▸ Dimension 6 (Country) — 0COUNTRY

▸ Time Dimension — 0CALYEAR and 0CALMONTH.

Assign the following Key Figures to the Key Figure folder:

▶ 0D_QTY

▶ ZCTAMT_GC

▶ ZSLAMT_GC

For Key Figures that are of data type Quantity or Currency, the corresponding unit or currency measure associated with the Key Figure is automatically added to the Unit Dimension.

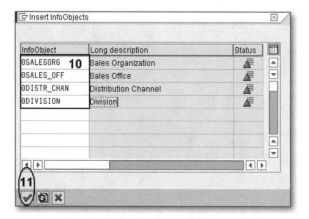

Figure 2.22 Creating an InfoCube — Part E

3. The InfoCube is now ready to be saved and activated. Click **Activate** to activate the InfoCube (see Figure 2.23, callout 12).

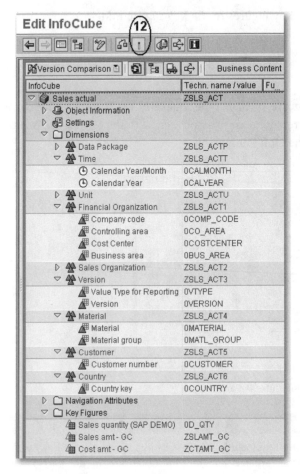

Figure 2.23 Activate the InfoCube

Now that you have created the Sales InfoCube, you will next create the Plan InfoCube.

Steps to Create a Plan InfoCube

In this section, we explain how to create the Plan InfoCube based on the case study requirements listed earlier in Tables 2.4, 2.5, 2.6, and 2.7. The Plan InfoCube is created in much the same way as the Sales InfoCube. The Plan InfoCube will, however, contain an additional InfoObject, ZRES_PERS. This InfoObject will be used in STS to control and monitor the planning process. Other than this difference, both of the InfoCubes contain the same Info-Objects. The Dimensions and Key Figures used in the Plan InfoCube are displayed in Table 2.11 and Table 2.12 respectively.

Dimensions	Characteristics
Financial Organization	Company Code (0COMP_CODE)
	Controlling Area (0CO_AREA)
	Cost Center (0COSTCENTER)
	Business Area (0BUS_AREA)
Sales Organization	Sales Organization (0SALESORG)
	Sales Office (0SALES_OFF)
	Distribution Channel (0DISTRCHAN)
	Sales Division (0DIVISION)
Version	Value Type (0VTYPE)
	Version (0VERSION)
Material	Material (0MATERIAL)
	Material Group (0MATL_GROUP)
Customer	Customer (0CUSTOMER)
Country	Country (0COUNTRY)
Responsible Person	Responsible Person (ZRES_PERS)
Time	Calendar Month (0CALMONTH)
	Calendar Year (0CALYEAR)
Unit	Sales Quantity Unit (0D_UQTY)
	Currency (0CURRENCY)

Table 2.11 Dimensions for the Plan InfoCube

Key Figures	Description
0D_QTY	Quantity
ZCTAMT_GC	Cost Amount in Goup Currency
ZSLAMT_GC	Sales Amount in Group Currency

Table 2.12 Key Figures for the Plan InfoCube

The following steps explain how to create the Plan InfoCube, as illustrated in Figures 2.24 and 2.25:

1. Open the **Data Warehousing Workbench** using Transaction **RSA1**.
2. Select the option **Modeling • InfoProvider**.

3. Right-click the InfoArea you created earlier (Sales Management) and select **Create InfoCube**.

4. Enter the technical name of the InfoCube ("ZSLS_PLN") and a long description ("Sales Plan") as shown in Figure 2.24, callouts 1 and 2. Because the structure of the Plan InfoCube is similar to that of the Sales InfoCube, we will use the structure used in the Sales InfoCube as a template to create the Plan InfoCube.

5. Select the Sales InfoCube (**ZSLS_ACT**) as the template for this InfoCube (see Figure 2.24, callout 3).

6. In the **InfoProvider Type** area, next to **Standard InfoCube**, select **Real Time** (see Figure 2.24, callout 4). This makes it possible to store plan data in the InfoCube via planning application interfaces.

7. Click **Create** (see Figure 2.24, callout 5).

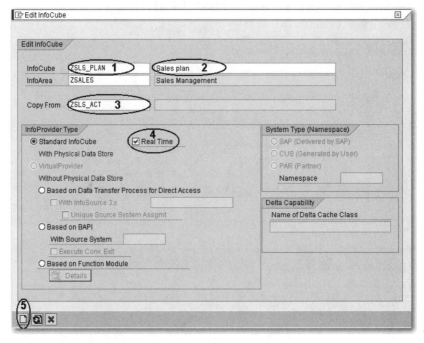

Figure 2.24 Create the Plan InfoCube — Part A

8. All of the InfoObjects are pre-selected and assigned to a Dimension similar to the definition of the Sales InfoCube.

9. Create an additional Dimension called Responsible Person in the Plan InfoCube and assign the InfoObject ZRES_PERS to the Dimension (see Figure 2.25, callout 6).

10. Click the **Activate** button to save and activate the Plan InfoCube (see Figure 2.25, callout 7).

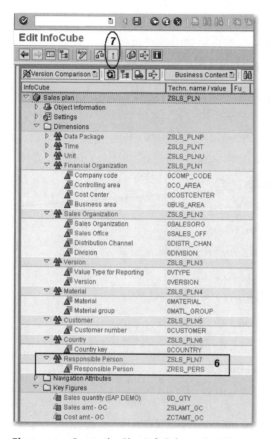

Figure 2.25 Create the Plan InfoCube — Part B

Steps to Create a MultiProvider Using Sales and Plan InfoCubes

A MultiProvider does not physically store data but instead provides a combined view of data from the InfoProviders used in its definition. A MultiProvider is necessary for our case study because one of the requirements for the planning application is to use the data in the Sales InfoCube as the source of data for planning.

The MultiProvider we'll create, called *Sales actual and plan*, will provide a unified view of the data in the Sales and Plan InfoCubes and will be used as the basis for configuring the planning application. The Dimensions and Key Figures used in the Sales Actual and Plan MultiProvider are shown in Table 2.13 and Table 2.14 respectively.

Dimensions	Characteristics
Financial Organization	Company Code (0COMP_CODE)
	Controlling Area (0CO_AREA)
	Cost Center (0COSTCENTER)
	Business Area (0BUS_AREA)
Sales Organization	Sales Organization (0SALESORG)
	Sales Office (0SALES_OFF)
	Distribution Channel (0DISTRCHAN)
	Sales Division (0DIVISION)
Version	Value Type (0VTYPE)
	Version (0VERSION)
Material	Material (0MATERIAL)
	Material Group (0MATL_GROUP)
Customer	Customer (0CUSTOMER)
Country	Country (0COUNTRY)
Time	Calendar Month (0CALMONTH)
	Calendar Year (0CALYEAR)
Unit	Sales Quantity Unit (0D_UQTY)
	Currency (0CURRENCY)

Table 2.13 Dimensions for the Sales Actual and Plan MultiProvider

Key Figures	Description
0D_QTY	Quantity
ZCTAMT_GC	Cost Amount in Goup Currency
ZSLAMT_GC	Sales Amount in Group Currency

Table 2.14 Key Figures for the Sales Actual and Plan MultiProvider

You'll now create a MultiProvider by performing the following steps, as illustrated in Figures 2.26, 2.27, 2.28, 2.29, and 2.30.

1. Open the **Data Warehousing Workbench** using Transaction **RSA1**.

2. Select the option **Modeling · InfoProvider**.

3. Right-click the InfoArea that you created earlier (**Sales Management**) and under which the MultiProvider will be created and select the context menu option **Create MultiProvider** (see Figure 2.26, callout 1).

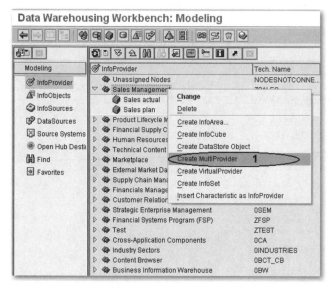

Figure 2.26 Create the Combined Sales and Plan MultiProvider — Part A

4. In the **Edit MultiProvider** dialog box, enter the **Technical Name** of the MultiProvider ("ZSLS_CMB") and the **Description** ("Sales actual and plan"). This step is shown in Figure 2.27, callouts 2 and 3).

5. Click **Create** to create the MultiProvider (see Figure 2.27, callout 4).

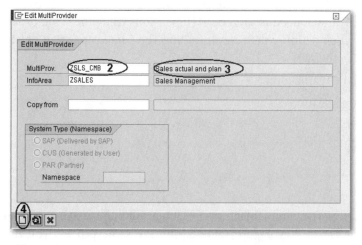

Figure 2.27 Create the Combined Sales and Plan MultiProvider — Part B

6. In the **MultiProvider: Relevant InfoProviders** dialog box, select the check boxes for the Sales and Plan InfoCubes to be used in the definition of the MultiProvider (see Figure 2.28, callout 5), and click **Enter** (see Figure 2.28, callout 6).

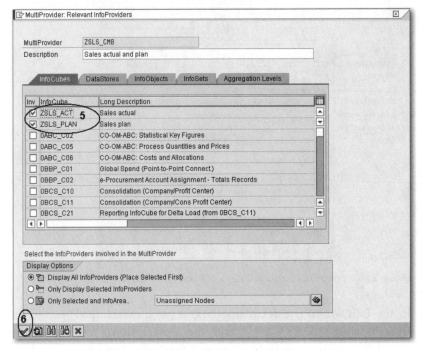

Figure 2.28 Create the Combined Sales and Plan MultiProvider — Part C

7. Configure the MultiProvider in the **Create MultiProvider** window (see Figure 2.29). You will need to create six Dimensions using the same process you used when defining the Sales InfoCube.The Dimensions you need to create are as follows:

   ▶ Financial Organization

   ▶ Sales Organization

   ▶ Version

   ▶ Material

   ▶ Customer

   ▶ Country

8. Assign Characteristic InfoObjects to the Dimensions and assign Key Figure InfoObjects to the Key Figure folder using the same process you used when defining the Sales InfoCube.

> **Note**
>
> Recall that a MultiProvider is an object that provides a unified view of the data in the underlying InfoProviders. Thus, after you assign Characteristic InfoObjects to the Dimensions and Key Figure InfoObjects to the Key Figure folder in the Multi-Provider, you will have to map the Characteristic InfoObjects and the Key Figure InfoObjects in the MultiProvider to the respective InfoObjects in the underlying InfoProviders. This process of mapping is also called Identification.

9. Click the **Identify Characteristic** icon (see Figure 2.29, callout 7). This opens the window where you can identify (map) all of the Characteristics contained in the MultiProvider to the InfoObjects in the underlying Info-Providers simultaneously. Note that you can also start the process of mapping an InfoObject individually by right-clicking it in the MultiProvider and selecting the **Identify (Assign)** option from the context menu.

10. In the **Identification of Participating Characteristics / Nav. Attr.** window, select (identify) the InfoObjects included in the MultiProvider (see Figure 2.30).

11. Click the **Identify Key Figures** icon to open the window where you will need to select (identify) the Key Figures (see Figure 2.29, callout 8) contained in the MultiProvider to the InfoObjects in the underlying InfoProviders. Note that this option is new in SAP NetWeaver BI 7.0.

12. Click the **Activate** button to save and activate the definition of the Sales actual and plan MultiProvider (see Figure 2.29, callout 9).

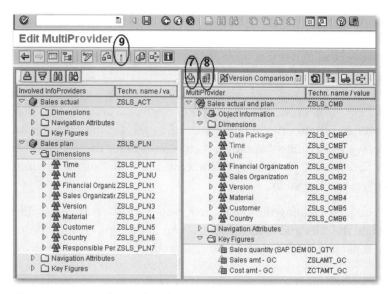

Figure 2.29 Create the Combined Sales and Plan MultiProvider — Part D

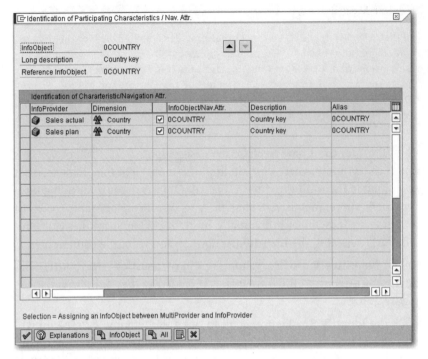

Figure 2.30 Create the Combined Sales and Plan MultiProvider — Part E

Now that we've created a MultiProvider, we will discuss the steps needed to create objects that are used to load data.

2.9.4 Create DataSources

A *DataSource* is an object that provides the data that will be loaded into Info-Providers in SAP NetWeaver BI. The actual source of the sales and cost data for our sample company, Rich Bloom, Inc. is an SAP R/3 system. The daily sales and cost data created in the SAP R/3 system is brought into the SAP NetWeaver BI system on a nightly basis. However, for the purposes of our example, we will assume that the sales and cost data for the year 2006 exists in a flat file. We will load the sales and cost data from this flat file into the SAP NetWeaver BI system.

Before you start creating the DataSource, you need to create a flat file that will contain the sales and cost data for the year 2006. This file must be in CSV (comma separated) format and has to contain the following columns:

▸ Company Code
▸ Cost Center

- Calendar Month
- Calendar Year
- Business Area
- Sales Organization
- Sales Office
- Sales Division
- Material
- Material Group
- Customer
- Country
- Sales amount
- Currency
- Cost Amount
- Quantity
- Unit of Measure

Then, enter data below the columns as shown in Figure 2.31. Name the file *us_salesdata.csv*, and save it to a directory called C:\Planning.

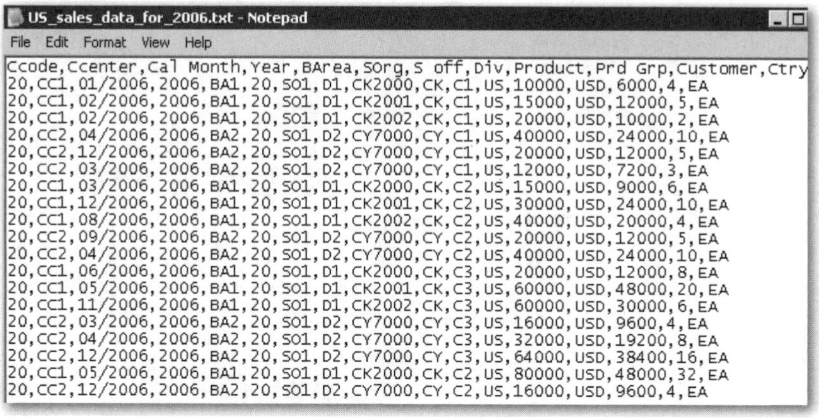
US_sales_data_for_2006.txt - Notepad
File Edit Format View Help

```
Ccode,Ccenter,Cal Month,Year,BArea,SOrg,S off,Div,Product,Prd Grp,Customer,Ctry
20,CC1,01/2006,2006,BA1,20,SO1,D1,CK2000,CK,C1,US,10000,USD,6000,4,EA
20,CC1,02/2006,2006,BA1,20,SO1,D1,CK2001,CK,C1,US,15000,USD,12000,5,EA
20,CC1,02/2006,2006,BA1,20,SO1,D1,CK2002,CK,C1,US,20000,USD,10000,2,EA
20,CC2,04/2006,2006,BA2,20,SO1,D2,CY7000,CY,C1,US,40000,USD,24000,10,EA
20,CC2,12/2006,2006,BA2,20,SO1,D2,CY7000,CY,C1,US,20000,USD,12000,5,EA
20,CC2,03/2006,2006,BA2,20,SO1,D2,CY7000,CY,C1,US,12000,USD,7200,3,EA
20,CC1,03/2006,2006,BA1,20,SO1,D1,CK2000,CK,C2,US,15000,USD,9000,6,EA
20,CC1,12/2006,2006,BA1,20,SO1,D1,CK2001,CK,C2,US,30000,USD,24000,10,EA
20,CC1,08/2006,2006,BA1,20,SO1,D1,CK2002,CK,C2,US,40000,USD,20000,4,EA
20,CC2,09/2006,2006,BA2,20,SO1,D2,CY7000,CY,C2,US,20000,USD,12000,5,EA
20,CC2,04/2006,2006,BA2,20,SO1,D2,CY7000,CY,C2,US,40000,USD,24000,10,EA
20,CC1,06/2006,2006,BA1,20,SO1,D1,CK2000,CK,C3,US,20000,USD,12000,8,EA
20,CC1,05/2006,2006,BA1,20,SO1,D1,CK2001,CK,C3,US,60000,USD,48000,20,EA
20,CC1,11/2006,2006,BA1,20,SO1,D1,CK2002,CK,C3,US,60000,USD,30000,6,EA
20,CC2,03/2006,2006,BA2,20,SO1,D2,CY7000,CY,C3,US,16000,USD,9600,4,EA
20,CC2,04/2006,2006,BA2,20,SO1,D2,CY7000,CY,C3,US,32000,USD,19200,8,EA
20,CC2,12/2006,2006,BA2,20,SO1,D2,CY7000,CY,C3,US,64000,USD,38400,16,EA
20,CC1,05/2006,2006,BA1,20,SO1,D1,CK2000,CK,C2,US,80000,USD,48000,32,EA
20,CC2,12/2006,2006,BA2,20,SO1,D2,CY7000,CY,C2,US,16000,USD,9600,4,EA
```

Figure 2.31 Sales and Cost Data for 2006 as a Flat File

Next, perform the following steps to create the DataSource, as illustrated in Figures 2.32, 2.33, and 2.34.

1. Open the **Data Warehousing Workbench** using Transaction **RSA1**.
2. Select the option **Modeling • Source Systems**.

3. Select and double-click a flat file source system for creating the Data-Source. We have used the **PC File System**. (see Figure 2.32, callout 1).

4. The **DataSource for** <*File System*> displays (in this case **PC_FILE PC File System**). Select any application component area, for example, **Non-SAP_ Sources**, and right-click and choose **Create DataSource** from the context menu (see Figure 2.32, callout 2).

5. In the **Create DataSource** window, enter the name of the **DataSource** ("ZSLS_FILE") as shown in Figure 2.32, callout 3, and then select **Transaction Data** from the **Data Type DataSource** dropdown list (see Figure 2.32, callout 4).

6. Click **Enter** (see Figure 2.32, callout 5).

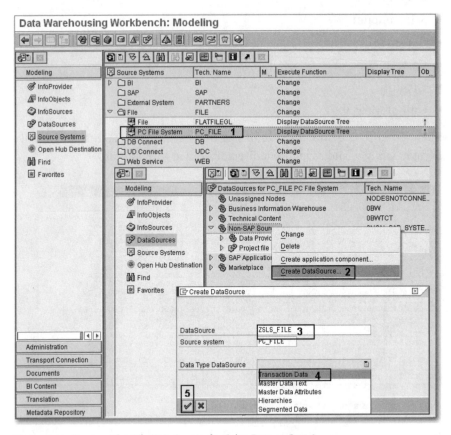

Figure 2.32 Create a Flat-File DataSource for Sales Data — Part A

7. On the **General Info** tab in the **Change DataSource** <*File Name*> window, enter the short ("Sales actual file"), medium ("Sales actual file") and long

("Sales actual file") descriptions for the DataSource. We will be using this DataSource to load sales and cost data for the year 2006 from a flat file.

8. On the **Fields** tab, you must enter the list of fields for which data exists in the flat file. The sequence you use is the same as that used for the data in the flat file. Instead of entering a field name, you can also enter the name of an InfoObject in the first row of the **Template InfoObject** column (see Figure 2.33, callout 6) that represents the field.

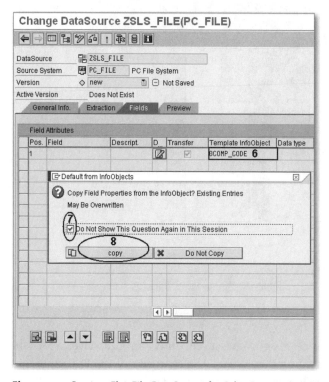

Figure 2.33 Create a Flat-File DataSource for Sales Data — Part B

9. After you enter the first InfoObject (0COMP_CODE) and press **Enter**, the **Default from InfoObjects** dialog box displays (see Figure 2.33). Select the option **Do Not Show This Question Again in This Session** and click **copy** (see Figure 2.33, callouts 7 and 8). This transfers all of the properties from the InfoObject to the corresponding field in the **Field** Column (see Figure 2.34 callout 9).

10. Continue to enter InfoObjects following the sequence of data coming from the flat file that contains the sales and cost data for 2006 by clicking the **Insert** button (see Figure 2.34 , callout 10) and entering the Info-Objects in the **Template InfoObject** column (see Figure 2.34, callout 11).

11. Click the **Activate** button to save and activate the DataSource (see Figure 2.34, callout 12).

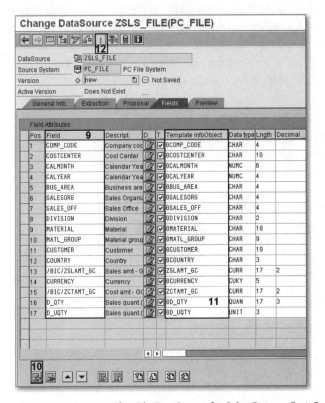

Figure 2.34 Create a Flat-File DataSource for Sales Data — Part C

Once the DataSource is activated successfully, an equivalent PSA table is automatically created by the system. The structure of the PSA table mirrors the structure of the file layout of the source data.

2.9.5 Create Transformations

With the new DTP for loading data in SAP NetWeaver BI, the data coming from a source system is loaded into the DataSource or PSA in its original form as sent from the source system. The DTP, however, lets you apply rules to modify the data coming from a DataSource before it is loaded into an Info-Provider.

At least one transformation is required before data reaches the data target. For our case study, we will use a single transformation of data from the PSA associated with the Sales DataSource to the Sales InfoCube.

Perform the following steps to create a transformation that will load data from the Sales DataSource created earlier into the Sales InfoCube, as illustrated in Figures 2.34, 2.35, 2.36, and 2.37:

1. Open the **Data Warehousing Workbench** using Transaction **RSA1**.

2. Select the option **Modeling • InfoProvider**.

3. Under the **Sales Management** InfoArea, right-click the **Sales actual** InfoCube and select the **Create Transformation** option from the context menu (see Figure 2.35, callout 1).

4. In the **Create Transformation** window, select the source of the transformation. Select the Object Type (**DataSource**), the DataSource (**ZSLS_FILE**), and the Source System (**PC_FILE**) (see Figure 2.35, callouts 2, 3, and 4).

5. Click **Enter** (see Figure 2.35, callout 5).

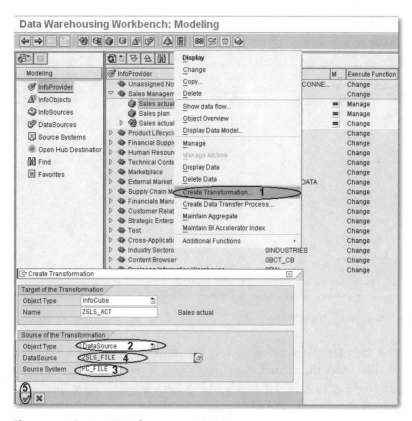

Figure 2.35 Create a Transformation — Part A

6. The **Transformation Create** window opens (see Figure 2.36). The system automatically proposes a mapping for the fields from the DataSource to

the InfoObjects in the **Sales actual** InfoCube. The proposal is based on the mapping of the InfoObjects in the **Template InfoObjects** column of the DataSource to the same InfoObject that exists as a Characteristic or Key Figure in the Sales actual InfoCube.

7. You'll notice that some of the InfoObjects in the Sales InfoCube are not mapped. This is because data for these InfoObjects is not available in the DataSource. Examples include **Distribution Channel**, **Controlling Area**, **Value Type**, and **Version**. These values have to be set directly in the transformation. For these cases, select the appropriate InfoObject in the **Rule Group: Standard Group** table, and double-click (see Figure 2.36).

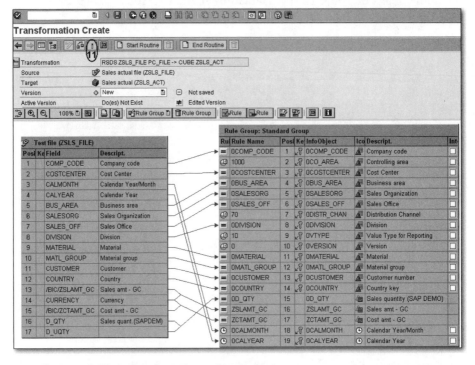

Figure 2.36 Create Transformation — Part B

8. In the **Rule Details** window, select **Constant** from the **Rule Type** drop-down list, enter the value for the InfoObject in the field next to **Constant Value** (see Figure 2.37, callouts 6 and 7). Set the following values:

   ▶ Distribution Channel = 70

   ▶ Controlling Area = 1000

   ▶ Value Type = 10 (Actual)

   ▶ Version = 00 (Actual)

9. Click **Transfer Values** (see Figure 2.37, callout 8).

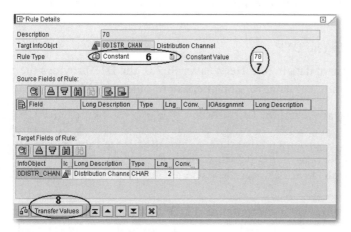

Figure 2.37 Create Transformation — Part C

10. The mapping between the source and target proposed by the system is not always perfect and may require manual changes. In this case, select the InfoObject in the **Rule Group: Standard Group** list in the **Transformation Create** window shown in Figure 2.36, and double-click it to open the **Rule Details** window. Use the − option to delete an existing mapping assignment from the source. Use the **+** option to make a new assignment (see Figure 2.38, callouts 9 and 10).

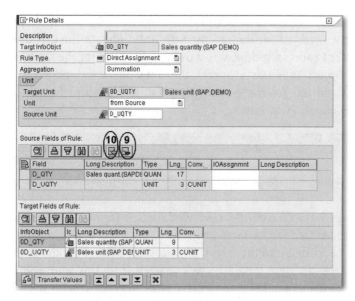

Figure 2.38 Create Transformation — Part D

11. After all mappings have been assigned, click the **Activate** button to save and activate the transformation object (see Figure 2.36, callout 11).

2.9.6 Create the DTP

In the new flow of data in SAP NetWeaver BI 7.0, the DTP provides the ability to extract and load data from one persistent object to another.

> **Note**
>
> It is important to understand that the transformation process we created earlier only provides the rules for the extraction and loading of data. The DTP then uses the transformation to actually load the data from one persistent area to another.

For our case study, we want to define a DTP that will extract data from the Sales actual file DataSource, use the transformation process we created earlier, and load the data into the Sales actual InfoCube.

Let's create a DTP by performing the following steps, as illustrated in Figures 2.39 and 2.40.

1. Open the **Data Warehousing Workbench** using Transaction **RSA1**.

2. Select the option **Modeling • InfoProvider**.

3. Under the **Sales Management** InfoArea, right-click the **Sales actual** InfoCube and select **Create Data Transfer Process** from the context menu (see Figure 2.39, callout 1).

4. We are creating a DTP that will load data from the Sales actual file Data-Source that we created earlier into the Sales InfoCube. In the **Creation of Data Transfer Process** window, select the source object for the DTP. Enter the source **Object Type** (**DataSource**), the **DataSource** we created earlier (**ZSLS_FILE**) and the **Source System** (**PC_FILE**) as shown in Figure 2.39, callouts 2, 3 and 4. Press **Enter**.

> **Note**
>
> A DTP can be created between a source and a target object only if a transformation process exists between the two objects.

5. In the **Change Data Transfer Process** window (see Figure 2.40), you need to select the **Extraction Mode**. If you select **Full**, all of the data from the source will be loaded into the target. If you select **Delta**, only the changes made since the last time the data was extracted from this source will be extracted into the target. Because we have sales and cost data for the 2006, we will use the Full Extraction Mode.

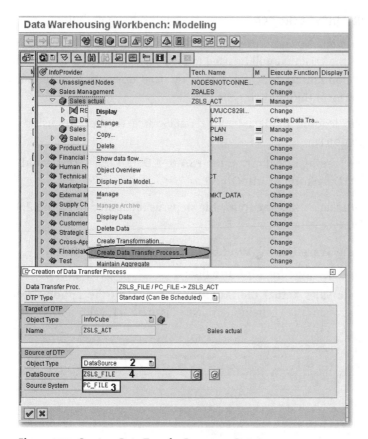

Figure 2.39 Create a Data Transfer Process — Part A

6. Click the **Activate** button to save and activate the DTP object (see Figure 2.40, callout 5).

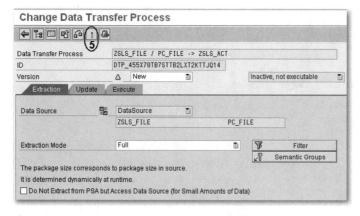

Figure 2.40 Create a Data Transfer Process — Part B

2.9.7 Create InfoPackages

In the previous steps we configured objects including the DataSource, Transformation, and the DTP that will be used to load Sales actual data to the Sales InfoCube. The configuration of the objects by itself does not load the data. You need to perform the following steps:

▶ Schedule the loading of data from a DataSource to the PSA using an InfoPackage object

▶ Schedule the loading of data from the PSA to a Data Target. This could be an InfoCube, DataStore, or InfoObject.

Create an InfoPackage using the following steps, as illustrated in Figure 2.41, 2.42, and 2.43.

1. Open the **Data Warehousing Workbench** using Transaction **RSA1**.

2. Select the option **Modeling · InfoProvider**.

3. Right-click the **Sales actual file** DataSource and select the option **Create InfoPackage...** from the context menu (see Figure 2.41, callout 1).

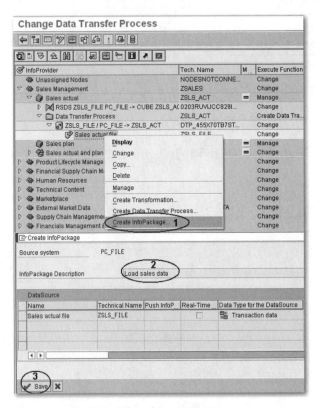

Figure 2.41 Create an InfoPackage — Part 1

4. In the **Create InfoPackage** window, enter the name of the InfoPackage ("Load sales data"), and click **Save** (see Figure 2.41, callouts 2 and 3).

5. In the **Scheduler (Maintain InfoPackage)** window, click the **Extraction** tab (see Figure 2.42, callout 4).

6. Choose the **Adapter** that determines whether the file you want to load exists on a local workstation or an SAP application server. Because our file exists on our PC, we will choose **Load Text-Type File from Local Workstation** from the dropdown list (see Figure 2.42, callout 5).

7. Enter the **Name of the File** ("C:\Planning\us_salesdata.csv") that contains the sales and cost data for 2006 (see Figure 2.42, callout 6).

8. Specify **Header Rows to be ignored** if you want the system to ignore header rows. Please refer to the Figure 2.40 for the layout of our file. Because the first row of the data contains the header, enter **Header Rows to be ignored** = 1 (see Figure 2.42, callout 7).

9. Next to **Data Format**, select **Separated with Separator (for Example, CSV)** from the dropdown list and next to **Data Separator**, enter a comma (,) as shown in Figure 2.42, callout 9.

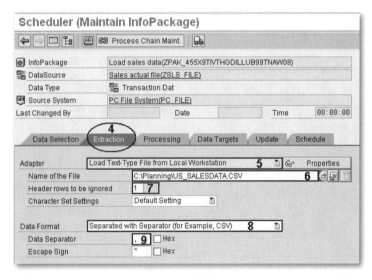

Figure 2.42 Create an InfoPackage — Part 2

10. Select **the Schedule** tab (see Figure 2.43, callout 10). Ensure the **Start Data Load Immediately** option is selected (see Figure 2.43, callout 11). Click **Start** (see Figure 2.43, callout 12). The data will now be extracted from the DataSource into the PSA Click the **Monitor** button to check the status of the extraction process (see Figure 2.43, callout 13).

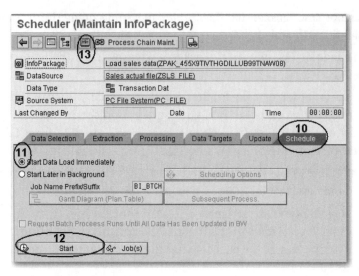

Figure 2.43 Executing an InfoPackage

11. The **Monitor — Administrator Workbench** window in Figure 2.44 shows the status of the data extracted from the flat-file DataSource into the PSA. If the data load is successful, the status of the load displays with a green traffic-light icon.

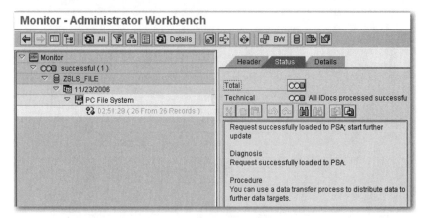

Figure 2.44 Monitoring the Status of InfoPackage

2.9.8 Load Data from the PSA to the Data Target

Now that you have loaded the data from the DataSource to the PSA, you are ready to schedule loading of data from the PSA to the Sales InfoCube using the DTP. The process applies the transformation when loading the data from the PSA to the data target.

1. Open the **Data Warehousing Workbench** using Transaction **RSA1**.

2. Select the option **Modeling • InfoProvider**.

3. Locate the DTP created earlier under the Sales InfoCube and double-click it (see Figure 2.45). The pane on the right displays the details of the DTP object.

4. Click the **Execute** tab, and then click the **Execute** button (see Figure 2.45, callout 1).

5. Click the **Monitor** button to check the status of the load (see Figure 2.45, callout 2).

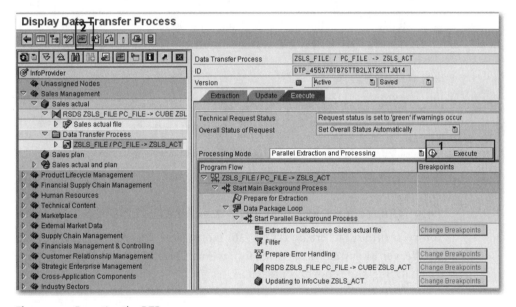

Figure 2.45 Executing the DTP

6. Return to the Data Warehousing Workbench by clicking the back-arrow button. Select the **Manage** option of the Sales InfoCube (see Figure 2.46, callout 3).

7. In the **InfoProvider Administration** window, select the **Requests** tab to see the requests that were loaded into the InfoCube (see Figure 2.46, callout 4).

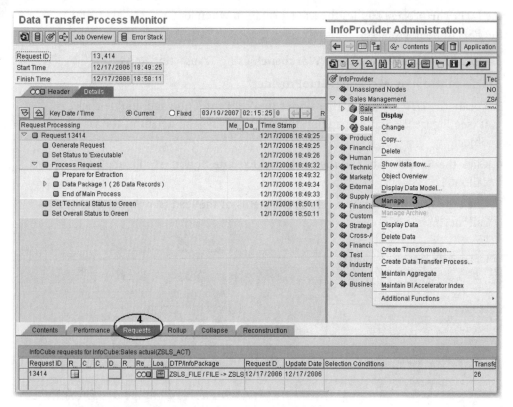

Figure 2.46 Monitor Data Transfer Execution Process

2.9.9 Reporting Data in SAP NetWeaver BI

You've seen how to create objects for storing and loading data in the SAP NetWeaver BI system. In this section, we will briefly discuss the tools used for analyzing and reporting the data.

The BEx Query Designer Tool

The BEx Query Designer tool is an add-on tool provided by SAP for analyzing data in SAP NetWeaver BI. You can use a query defined with this tool to report data from an InfoProvider in the following environments.

▶ **BEx Analyzer**

The BEx Analyzer tool is available to execute queries created in BEx Query Designer when you need to use Microsoft Excel features. The BEx Analyzer tool can be used to include a query defined in BEx Query Designer and run on the Microsoft Excel front end.

▶ **BEx Report Designer**

The BEx Report Designer was introduced in SAP NetWeaver BI 7.0. It provides a wide range of features for formatted reporting.

▶ **BEx Web Application Designer**

The BEx Web Application Designer is used to create Web applications. Web applications provide easy access to reports on the Web without having to install additional software on the desktop. Additionally, it provides integration of SAP NetWeaver BI reports with the SAP Enterprise Portal.

Organization of the BEx Query Designer

You can create a query in BEx Query Designer on any InfoProvider available for reporting. The BEx Query Designer in SAP NetWeaver BI 7.0 can be started using the following menu path from the desktop:

Start • Programs • Business Explorer • Query Designer

Selecting the Query Designer option unlocks new features introduced in NetWeaver BI 7.0. If the Query Designer for 3.x is installed on the desktop, an additional option displays, allowing you to invoke the Query Designer for this version. The following tabs, areas, and panes are available in the BEx Query Designer:

▶ **InfoProvider area**

The **InfoProvider** area lists the objects in the InfoProvider that you can use to create a query (see Figure 2.47, callout 1).

▶ **Filter tab**

The **Filter** tab displays by default, as shown in Figure 2.47. It consists of the following panes:

▷ **Characteristic Restrictions**

The **Characteristic Restrictions** pane (see Figure 2.47, callout 2A) is used to filter data in the query based on values of Characteristics. The restriction could be based either on a fixed set of values or on a variable used to enter or determine values of Characteristics during execution of a query.

▷ **Default Values**

The **Default Values** pane (see Figure 2.47, callout 2B) can also be used to filter the data in a query. When a user executes the query, these restrictions go into effect. However, the user has the option to change or delete these restrictions.

▶ **Properties pane**

The Properties pane displays one of two tabs: Properties (see Figure 2.47, callout 3A) and Tasks (see Figure 2.47, callout 3B).

  ▹ **Properties tab**

  The properties set in the Properties area, such as the descriptive name of a query, apply to the entire query.

  ▹ **Tasks tab**

  The Tasks area lets you set the properties of individual elements included in the query.

▶ **Messages area**

The Messages area (see Figure 2.47, callout 4) of the window displays messages generated by the BEx Query Designer tool. If error messages or warnings are generated when defining a query, the relevant messages are displayed so as to enable the query developer to correct the errors.

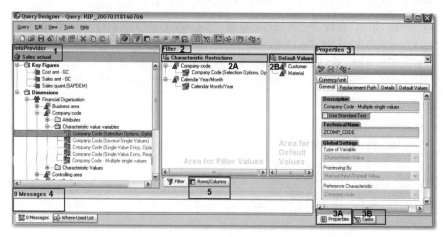

Figure 2.47 BEx Query Designer Filter Tab

▶ **Rows/Columns tab**

Click the Rows/Columns tab (see Figure 2.47, callout 5) to select it. The window shown in Figure 2.48 displays. The Rows/Columns Tab contains the following panes.

  ▹ **Free Characteristics**

  The Characteristics included in the Free Characteristic pane (Figure 2.48, callout 6A) are not displayed on the initial execution of a query but can be drilled down after execution.

▶ **Rows**

InfoObjects that need to be in rows during the initial execution of the query are entered in this pane (see Figure 2.48, callout 6C). Characteristics are normally included in this area.

▶ **Columns**

InfoObjects that need to be in columns during the initial execution of the query are entered in this pane (see Figure 2.48, callout 6B). Key Figures are normally included in this area.

▶ **Preview**

The Preview area (see Figure 2.48, callout 6D) gives a visual representation of output based on the definition of the query.

Through icons on the Rows/Columns tab, you can also access the following areas.

▶ **Conditions**

A condition (see Figure 2.48, callout 7) filters the results of the query based on quantitative information and applies to the entire query. For example, a condition can be defined to display the salesperson who has achieved sales above a specific dollar amount in a particular month.

▶ **Exception**

An exception (see Figure 2.48, callout 8) can be defined in a query to color-code the data in a report. Thresholds can be defined in the query to define these values. For example, an exception can be defined to color-code the data when the sales of a particular product exceed a specific dollar amount.

▶ **Tabular format**

This option can be used when data is to be displayed in a tabular format (see Figure 2.48, callout 9). All selected objects are displayed in the column part of the report.

▶ **Cell Editor**

The Cell Editor (see Figure 2.48, callout 10) is used when calculations are based on cell values of the report.

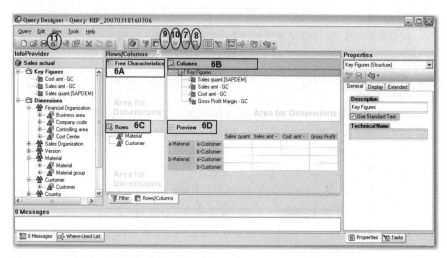

Figure 2.48 BEx Query Designer Row/Column Tab

Use of Variables in Queries

Variables are used in a query to dynamically restrict the data returned by the query. You may assign variables so that users can enter the selection during execution of a query, or so the selection will be entered automatically, based on ABAP code, a function also called a *user exit*.

The SAP BI system comes with a number of variables that are delivered as a part of SAP Business Content. In addition, you can create custom variables to meet a specific reporting requirement. The variables can be assigned to any Characteristic in the Characteristic Restrictions, Default Values, Free Characteristics, Row or Column panes of a query.

The following types of variables can be defined:

▶ **Characteristic**
Use this variable to restrict the Characteristic to a specific value or values.

▶ **Hierarchy**
Create this variable when a Characteristic contains hierarchy data and use it to filter data based on a specific hierarchy.

▶ **Hierarchy Node**

▶ Use this variable to restrict the data to a particular node in a hierarchy.

▶ **Text**
Use this variable to set the text value in query headings, column headings, and structural components. An example of a text variable is the title of a

query; for example, sales data for the year May 2004, where May 2004 represents the value coming from a text variable.

▶ **Formula**
Use this variable when performing computation on Key Figure values.

A processing type is assigned to each of the variables to show which method will be used to determine the value of the variable. The following processing types are available.

▶ **User input**
The value of variables will be entered by the user during the execution of the query.

▶ **Replacement path**
The value of variables is automatically set at runtime based on the setting defined in the variable.

▶ **SAP exit**
SAP provides code that is used to determine the value of SAP-supplied variables. This option applies to variables that are included in Business Content.

▶ **Customer exit**
The value of variables is coded by a developer in a non-SAP programming environment.

▶ **Authorization**
If a Characteristic is relevant to administering reporting authorization, the values can be determined based on the authorized values for the user.

Use of Key Figures in Queries

The Key Figures that are available in an InfoProvider can be added to the definition of a query for purpose of reporting. In addition, Key Figures can be used in queries in one of the following ways:

▶ **Restricted Key Figures**
Restricted Key Figures are used to restrict Key Figures based on the value of another Characteristic. For example, a Restricted Key Figure that determines the sales amount for calendar year 2007 can be determined by restricting the sales amount Key Figure to Calendar Year = 2007.

▶ **Calculated Key Figures**
Calculated Key Figures are used to compute formulas. For example, a Calculated Key Figure that determines the gross profit margin can be com-

puted by subtracting the cost amount from the sales amount. Computation can be done on Key Figures, Restricted Key Figures, or other calculated Key Figures.

2.9.10 Create a Query to Analyze Sales Data

Let's return to our case study. Now that you have loaded data into the Sales actual InfoCube, you can create a sample query to report data in this InfoProvider.

Follow these steps to create and execute a query, as illustrated in Figures 2.47, 2.48, 2.49, and 2.50:

1. Use the menu path **Start · Programs · Business Explorer · Query Designer** to open the BEx Query Designer.

2. On the toolbar, select the **Create Query** option and then select the **Sales actual** InfoCube as the **InfoProvider** for creating the query. Note that you can use drag-and-drop to include objects in the definition of the query.

3. Click **Filter** to display the Filter area.

4. Add the **Company code** and **Calendar Year/Month** InfoObjects to the Characteristic Restrictions pane on the **Filter** tab (use drag and drop).

5. Right-click the **Company code** Characteristic in the **Characteristic Restrictions** pane of the query. Click **Restrict** (see Figure 2.49, Callout 1).

6. This opens the **Select Values for** <*Characteristic*> dialog box. Next to **Show**, select **Variables** from the dropdown list (see Figure 2.49, Callout 2). The list shows all of the variables that are available for the Characteristic. If necessary, you can create a new variable for the Characteristic by clicking the **Create** icon (see Figure 2.49, Callout 3). For our case study, we will use a variable that already exists.

7. Under **Name**, select the SAP-supplied variable **0S_COCD** from the list (see Figure 2.49, Callout 4).

8. Click the blue arrow icon to select the variable for assignment (see Figure 2.49, Callout 5).

9. The variable is added to the **Selection** area (see Figure 2.49, Callout 6).

10. Click **OK** (see Figure 2.49, Callout 7).

11. Follow steps 5 to 10 to assign the variable **0I_CALMO** to the **Calendar Year/Month** Characteristic.

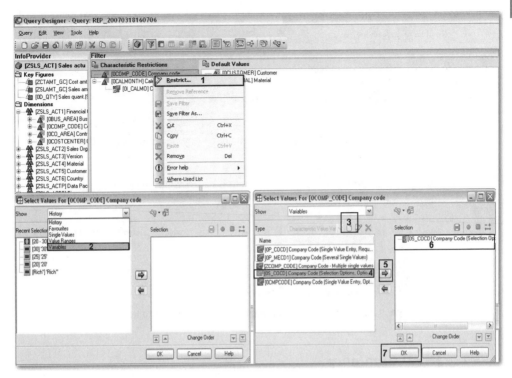

Figure 2.49 Assign a Variable to a Characteristic

12. Display the **Rows/Columns** area (see Figure 2.47, callout 5). Use drag and drop to add the InfoObjects **Material** and **Customer** from the **Sales actual** InfoProvider to the **Rows** section, as shown in Figure 2.48, callout 6C.

13. Using drag and drop, add **Sales Quant [SAPDEM]**, **Sales amt — GC**, and **Cost amt — GC** to the **Columns** section, as shown in Figure 2.48, callout 6B.

14. Enter a **Technical Name** and **Description** for the query using the **Properties** tab in the **Properties** pane of the window.

15. On the toolbar, click **Save**.

16. Execute the query by clicking **Execute** on the toolbar (see Figure 2.48, callout 11). The query will prompt you for a value for the Company Code and Calendar Month InfoObject. Select a value for company code. The results will be displayed as shown in Figure 2.50.

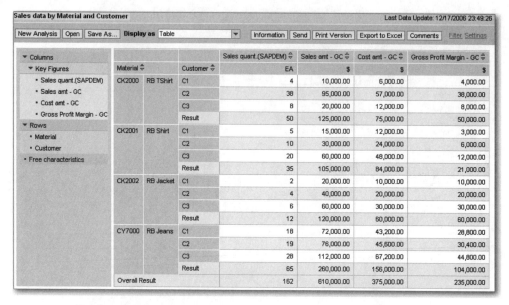

Figure 2.50 Result of Query — Sales Data by Material and Customer

2.10 Summary

In this chapter we introduced you to concepts and terminology used in the SAP NetWeaver BI Integrated Planning tool. We performed steps needed to configure objects used to store and load data. We examined the process of extracting, transforming, and loading data from a source system to data targets in the SAP NetWeaver BI system. Further, we explored options for reporting and analyzing the data.

In the next chapter, we will discuss the details of configuring a planning application using the SAP NetWeaver BI Integrated Planning tool.

In this chapter, we will show you how to configure a financial planning application using the SAP NetWeaver BI Integrated Planning tool. The case study introduced in Chapter 2 will serve as the basis for creating this application.

3 SAP NetWeaver BI Integrated Planning — Configuring a Financial Application

To begin this chapter, we'll recap the prerequisites for planning in SAP NetWeaver BI and introduce you to the Planning Modeler, a Web-based application used to configure a planning application in the SAP NetWeaver BI Integrated Planning tool. The chapter details the initial steps for creating a financial planning application using the Planning Modeler.

The next part of the chapter is devoted to the use of Planning Functions. Planning Functions are the heart of the planning tool in the SAP NetWeaver BI system and provide powerful features for creating and modifying data. We describe the different Planning Functions and the steps used to integrate these functions into a planning application. We also explain Planning Sequences and their role in planning, and how to use them to run multiple Planning Functions as one complete unit. We also discuss how to integrate Planning Sequences into Process Chains.

Subsequently, we explain how Characteristic Relationships can be used to develop a planning application. The dual role of Characteristic Relationships — enforcing data integrity and automatically deriving data — is explained through examples. We further discuss Data Slices and how they can protect plan data from being modified after it has been entered. Finally, we explain the role the Settings tab of an InfoProvider plays in planning and how the settings configured on this tab help determine time-dependent values used in planning.

3.1   SAP NetWeaver BI Integrated Planning Prerequisites

We learned in Chapter 2 that, starting with SAP NetWeaver BI 7.0, there are two options for planning in the SAP NetWeaver BI system: the SAP NetWeaver BI Integrated Planning tool and SAP BW BPS. In that chapter, we also discussed the advantages of using the SAP NetWeaver BI Integrated Planning tool when developing a new planning application. For our case study, we will use the SAP NetWeaver BI Integrated Planning tool to create the planning application.

The following is a summary of the prerequisites for planning in the SAP NetWeaver BI system:

▶ **Real-Time InfoCube**
You must have created at least one Real-Time InfoCube. When a Standard InfoCube is checked as Real-Time at creation, it becomes available for planning using planning objects. This InfoCube can be used to generate and modify data using planning objects in the SAP NetWeaver BI system. A Standard InfoCube that is not checked as Real-Time does not support generation or modification of plan data using the planning tools.

▶ **MultiProvider**
While plan data is always stored in a Real-Time InfoCube, you might need a planning application to reference data in an InfoProvider that is not a Real-Time InfoCube. For example, let us assume that an organization's sales data is maintained in a Standard InfoCube and that the plan data is maintained in a Real-Time InfoCube. In this case, you can define a Multi-Provider to include both the Standard InfoCube and the Real-Time InfoCube. You can then use this MultiProvider in the context of a planning application, and the planning objects can reference the data in both InfoCubes.

In Chapter 2, we showed you how to create a Standard InfoCube (ZSLS_ACT — Sales InfoCube) to store the actual sales and cost data, a Real-Time InfoCube (ZSLS_PLN — Plan InfoCube) to store the plan data, and a MultiProvider (ZSLS_CMB — Sales and Plan MultiProvider) to provide a combined view of the Sales InfoCube and the Plan InfoCube. In this chapter, we will use these InfoCubes to create a planning application.

▶ **Web Dynpro**
Before configuring a planning application using the SAP NetWeaver BI Integrated Planning tool, the Web Dynpro application must be installed

on the J2EE engine connected to the SAP NetWeaver BI system. This is usually done by the SAP Basis team.

> **Note**
>
> SAP OSS Notes 901022 and 919850 give additional information on how to install the application on the J2EE server.

Next, we'll discuss the Planning Modeler application you use to create planning objects.

3.2 SAP NetWeaver BI Integrated Planning and the Planning Modeler

The SAP NetWeaver BI Integrated Planning tool lets you create a planning application using one of two tools. They include:

- ▶ **Planning Modeler**
  The Planning Modeler provides a flexible approach to configuring planning objects and is suitable for developers.

- ▶ **Planning Wizard**
  The Planning Wizard uses a step-by-step approach which makes application creation easier. This option is suitable for beginners.

For the examples in this book, we will use the Planning Modeler exclusively.

Starting the Planning Modeler or Planning Wizard Application

To start the Planning Modeler or the Planning Wizard, you also have two options. You can start the SAP NetWeaver BI Integrated Planning tool from the SAP GUI using transaction **RSPLAN** (see Figure 3.1) and then click the **Start Modeler** or **Start Wizard** button. Alternatively, you can enter either application's URL directly into a Web browser.

The URL for launching the Planning Modeler is as follows:

*http://<J2EE_Server_IP_address:J2EE_server_domain_name>/logon/
logonServlet?redirectURL=/webdynpro/dispatcher/sap.com/
bi~plan~workbench1/Modeler*

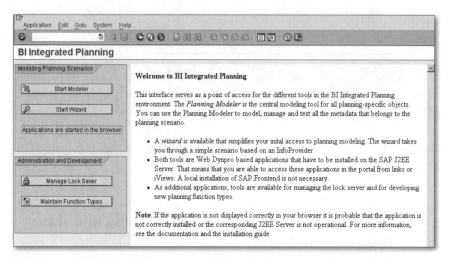

Figure 3.1 Execute Transaction RSPLAN to Launch the Planning Modeler on the Web

> **Note**
>
> Users can also be given the option of launching the Planning Modeler as an IView from the SAP Enterprise Portal.

The URL for launching the Planning Wizard is as follows:

http://<J2EE_server_domain_name:J2EE_server_port>/logon/logonServlet? redirectURL=/webdynpro/dispatcher/sap.com/bi~plan~workbench1/Wizard

3.2.1 Navigation in the Planning Modeler

When the Planning Modeler is launched, five tabs are displayed in the following order:

- ▶ InfoProvider
- ▶ Aggregation Levels
- ▶ Filter
- ▶ Planning Functions
- ▶ Planning Sequences

You select a tab by clicking it and configure planning objects in the same order as the tabs are displayed. On each of the tabs, the upper half of the screen is available for creating a new planning object or for maintaining an existing planning object. The lower half of the screen is used to configure detailed settings for the planning object selected in the upper half of the screen.

> **Note**
>
> By default, the InfoProvider tab is selected when the application is launched.

You are now ready to configure a planning application based on the case study requirements for our sample company, Rich Bloom, Inc. Let's get started.

3.3 Creating and Configuring a Planning Application

To start, let's take another look at Rich Bloom, Inc.'s planning goal. The company wants to use the actual sales and cost data for the year 2006 as the source of data for planning the *gross profit margin* in 2007. We prepared for this in Chapter 2 when we loaded the actual sales and cost data for 2006 into the Sales InfoCube. We also created a Real-Time Plan InfoCube to use exclusively for maintaining plan data through planning objects. Further, we configured a MultiProvider that includes the Sales InfoCube and Plan InfoCube objects to reference the actual sales and cost data for planning.

We will now create and configure a planning application that will plan for the sales of products and the cost of goods sold for the year 2007. The gross profit margin for the year will be calculated by subtracting the planned cost of goods sold from the planned sales of products. The ability to make this calculation will be the primary requirement for financial planning as we create the planning objects.

We will start configuring the planning application for our case study by launching the Planning Modeler application, using either of the methods described earlier. When you start the Planning Modeler, you're prompted to log in. Following a successful login to the system, the Planning Modeler interface opens with the InfoProvider tab selected. Let's now discuss the details of the configuration settings available on each Planning Modeler tab.

3.3.1 The InfoProvider Tab

Selecting the InfoProvider is the first step in creating a planning application using the SAP NetWeaver BI Integrated Planning tool. A Real-Time InfoCube or a MultiProvider that includes a Real-Time InfoCube can be selected for planning. In our scenario, we will select the Sales and Plan MultiProvider as the InfoProvider.

The following options are available for selecting the InfoProvider on the InfoProvider tab of the Planning Modeler (see Figure 3.2).

▸ You can use the dropdown list to the right of **Find** to specify the criteria for displaying the list of InfoProviders (see Figure 3.2, callout 1). You can also specify a selection criteria to filter the InfoProviders that will be displayed (see Figure 3.3 callout 2). Note that you can use wild cards (*) in the selection criteria.

▸ Clicking the **Start** button (see Figure 3.2, callout 3), displays — in the upper portion of the screen — a list of all Real-Time InfoCubes and Multi-Providers (InfoProviders) available in the SAP NetWeaver BI system (see Figure 3.2, callout 4).

▸ Clicking **Filter On** switches the display between **Filter On** and **Delete Filter**. With **Filter On** active, an area above the table is visible (see Figure 3.2, callout 5) where you can further filter the list of displayed InfoProviders. Selecting **Delete Filter** hides the filter area (see Figure 3.2, callout 6).

▸ Clicking the **Settings** button (see Figure 3.2, callout 7) opens a dialog box where you can specify the columns displayed in the InfoProvider list.

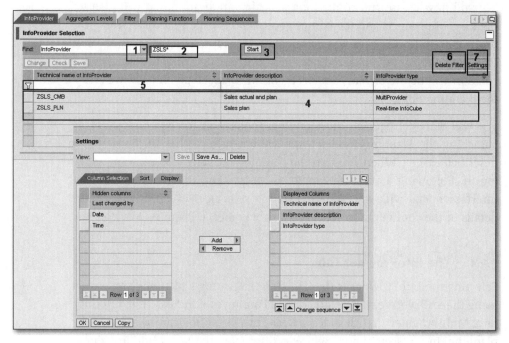

Figure 3.2 The InfoProvider tab of the Planning Modeler

▸ You select an InfoProvider from the list by clicking an entry displayed in the table (see Figure 3.3, callout 8).

▸ After you have selected an InfoProvider, several tabs are available in the lower area of the screen to define the planning settings for the InfoProvider (see Figure 3.3, callout 9).

Note

The button called **Change**, shown at the upper left of the screen in Figure 3.3, is available only if the object can be modified. If the object cannot be modified, the button is grayed out.

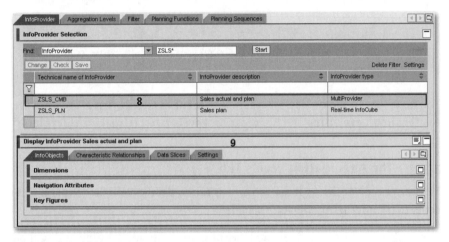

Figure 3.3 Selecting an InfoProvider on the InfoProvider Tab

We will select the Sales and Plan MultiProvider (ZSLS_CMB) that combines the data in the Sales InfoCube and Plan InfoCube (see Figure 3.3, callout 8) as the InfoProvider for the planning application.

As we mentioned earlier, the lower half of the screen displays the details of the InfoProvider selected and can be used to define planning settings (see Figure 3.3, callout 9). Four tabs are available: **InfoObjects**, **Characteristic Relationships**, **Data Slices**, and **Settings**. Let's look at each of these tabs in more detail.

▸ **InfoObjects**
Lists the InfoObjects that are available for the selected InfoProvider.

▸ **Characteristic Relationships**
Used to define the relationship in data. Can also be used to enforce data integrity or automatically derive the plan data based on this relationship.

▶ **Data Slices**
Used to protect the selected data from changes. For example, when a sales plan for a given period is approved by management, further changes may not be desired. In these cases, Data Slices can be defined to prevent further changes to the data.

▶ **Settings**
Used to set the date to be used when time-dependent InfoObjects are used in the InfoProvider.

We will discuss Characteristic Relationships in greater detail in Section 3.4, Data Slices in Section 3.5, and Settings in Section 3.6.

Note

The settings in the lower portion of the screen are configurable only for Real-Time InfoCubes, not MultiProviders.

The next step in the process of creating a financial application is creating the Aggregation Level using the Aggregation Levels tab. Let's take a closer look.

3.3.2 The Aggregation Levels Tab

Before we look at the Aggregation Levels tab in detail, we'll first explain concepts that underlie Aggregation Levels.

The *Aggregation Level* defines the level of granularity in planning and will be based on the planning requirements. An Aggregation Level is based on the InfoProvider that is selected for planning and identifies the necessary Characteristics and Key Figures for a given planning requirement. An Aggregation Level might only contain a subset of an InfoProvider's Characteristics and Key Figures that is necessary for a planning scenario.

You do not have to include all Characteristics or Key Figures of an InfoProvider in the Aggregation Level. For example, for sales planning, a company might decide to initially plan only at the product group level and not at the product level. Even though the InfoProvider that is used for planning might include the product Characteristic, it will not be necessary to include this Characteristic in the Aggregation Level.

After planning is completed, the company might apportion the plan data to different products based on a particular logic, such as prior-year sales data for the different products in the product group. This is an example of top-down planning, where planning is initially done on a higher-level Characteristic and later distributed to detailed-level Characteristics. The detailed-level Characteristics are not included in the Aggregation Level.

You can create more than one Aggregation Level for an InfoProvider selected for planning. An Aggregation Level does not physically store data but represents a logical view of data. It is equivalent to a *Virtual InfoProvider*.

You create planning objects based on the Aggregation Level. The data affected by the planning objects can only include InfoObjects included in the Aggregation Level. However, an exception to this rule exists when Characteristic Relationships are used to derive data. In that case, Characteristics don't have to be defined in the Aggregation Level because their values are derived. There are two types of Aggregation Level:

▶ **Simple Aggregation Level**
Based on a single Real-Time InfoCube.

▶ **Complex Aggregation Level**
Based on a MultiProvider that includes at least one Real-Time InfoCube.

Rules for Defining an Aggregation Level

When you define an Aggregation Level, you must observe the following rules.

▶ An Aggregation Level cannot be created based on another Aggregation Level.

▶ At least one Characteristic and Key Figure must be included in the Aggregation Level. If an InfoObject that contains a compounding key (higher level key) is included in the Aggregation Level, the compounding Characteristic must also be included in the Aggregation Level. For example, if you include the Plant Material InfoObject that includes the Plant as a compounding key to the Aggregation Level, then the Plant InfoObject is also automatically added to the Aggregation Level.

▶ The database aggregation for a Key Figure that is used for planning can only be one of the following: summation (SUM), minimum (MIN), or maximum (MAX). Key Figures that have database aggregations set to MIN or MAX can only be used for displaying data and cannot be used for modifying data in planning. When a Key Figure of type date or time is used in an Aggregation Level, it must be of data type Decimal (DEC).

▸ With Key Figures of type Currency or Unit that do not have a fixed currency or unit assigned to them, the Aggregation Level must contain the associated Currency or Unit Characteristic pertaining to those Key Figures.

▸ Non-cumulative and Reference Key Figures cannot be included in an Aggregation Level. Non-cumulative Key Figures cannot be aggregated with respect to any Characteristic. Examples of non-cumulative Key Figures are Account Balance and Inventory Balance. Reference Key Figures refer to another Key Figure and are used when eliminating internal business volume (sales within a company).

▸ Key Figures can be defined for exception aggregation with respect to another Characteristic. This definition determines how the value of the Key Figure is aggregated in reports. For example, the Date Key Figure can be defined to determine the minimum value based on the Time Characteristic. When an exception aggregation is defined for a Key Figure and if that Key Figure is included in an Aggregation Level, the Characteristic associated with the exception aggregation should also be included in the Aggregation Level.

You're now ready to look at the **Aggregation Levels** tab. It displays the Aggregation Levels for the InfoProvider selected on the **InfoProvider** tab. Alternatively, you can choose an Aggregation Level by selecting the appropriate filter criteria from the dropdown list located next to the **Find** button and entering search criteria. For our case study, we will select all Characteristics and Key Figures that are available in the Sales and Plan MultiProvider for the Aggregation Level.

Defining an Aggregation Level

Perform the following steps to create an Aggregation Level, as illustrated in Figures 3.4, 3.5, and 3.6:

1. Verify that on the **InfoProvider** tab, you selected the Sales and Plan MultiProvider.

2. Click the **Aggregation Levels** tab to select it (see Figure 3.4). This tab displays any Aggregation Levels already configured for the InfoProvider. Note that to select an Aggregation Level, you click the desired row in the table. Once an entry is selected, the details of the Aggregation Level are displayed in the lower half of the window.

3. We will be creating the first Aggregation Level for this InfoProvider. Click **Create** (see Figure 3.4, callout 1).

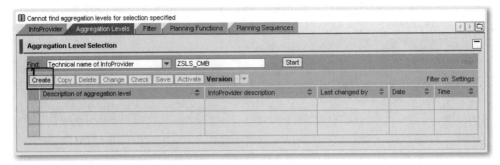

Figure 3.4 Creating an Aggregation Level — Part 1

4. The **Create Aggregation Level** dialog box displays. Enter a **Technical Name** ("ZSL_A_ALL") and a **Description** ("All characteristics and key figures") for the Aggregation Level, and click **Transfer** (see Figure 3.5, callouts 2, 3 and 4).

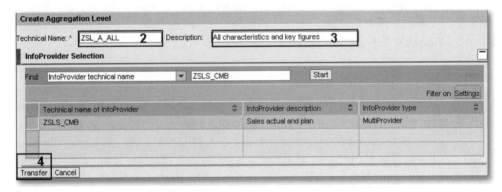

Figure 3.5 Creating an Aggregation Level — Part 2

5. The Characteristics for the InfoProvider display in the lower portion of the **Aggregation Levels** tab. If all of them are required, as they are for our case study, click **Select all** (see Figure 3.6, callout 5).

6. To see if the definition of the Aggregation Level is consistent, click **Check** (see Figure 3.6, callout 6).

7. Click **Save** (see Figure 3.6, callout 7).

8. Click **Activate** (see Figure 3.6, callout 8). The details of the activation are displayed in the top area of the Planning Modeler, above the tabs (see Figure 3.6, callout 9).

We have now created an Aggregation Level that includes all InfoObjects in the Sales and Plan MultiProvider. Next, we will create a Filter object using the Filter tab.

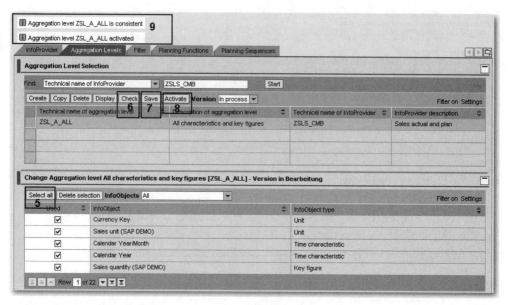

Figure 3.6 Defining the Aggregation Level Settings

3.3.3 The Filter Tab

Before we look at the Filter tab in detail, we'll first explain the concepts behind Filters. For a given planning requirement, not all data in the InfoProvider is required for planning. Therefore, Filters are set to restrict the data selected for planning in a planning application. They are used in the context of granular planning where user roles are the basis for developing the planning requirement.

Filters are always created based on an Aggregation Level. They are set on InfoObjects of type Characteristic, Time Characteristic, or Unit Characteristic. Filter values can be set with constants or dynamically through variables. Filters can also be set on hierarchy data.

When you use a Filter for manual planning or for modifying plan data using Planning Functions, the data is selected based on the Filter that will be used as the basis for planning. The planning objects that use a Filter cannot modify data that is not contained in the definition of the Filter.

If time-dependent data Characteristics are used in an InfoProvider, the date to be used can be set on the Filter tab. This setting will override the settings already made on the Settings tab for the InfoProvider.

Creating a Filter

Let's look at our sample company, Rich Bloom, Inc., to start creating a Filter. Recall that Rich Bloom, Inc. is headquartered in the U.S. and has two subsidiaries, one in the UK and one in Germany. Each company operates as an independent unit and is responsible for planning sales, cost, and gross profit margin data for its area of operations. Any planning that is done needs to be based on the respective subsidiary's company code, which is based on the location of operation.

Rich Bloom, Inc.'s sales people specialize in the company's various products: t-shirts, shirts, jackets, and jeans. When planning for sales and cost, each sales person will be responsible only for the products that fall under his or her area of specialization.

The company wants to create a Filter that will help the parent company and the subsidiaries plan for their respective locations. Further, the planning application should restrict users to plan data for the calendar year 2007. In addition, users should be restricted to plan data (Value Type = 20) and planning (Version = 1). Changes made to data should affect only the Plan InfoCube. The data in the Sales actual InfoCube will be used only as reference data in the planning application.

Based on these requirements, we will create a Filter that will include the following Characteristics:

▶ Company Code

▶ Calendar Year

▶ Value Type

▶ Plan Version

▶ InfoProvider

The value of the Characteristics will be set in the Filter to ensure that it meets users' planning requirements. Complete the following steps to create a Filter, as illustrated in Figures 3.7 and 3.8:

1. Click the **Filter** tab to select it and display any Filters that have already been configured for the Aggregation Level.

2. Click **Create** to start creating the first Filter on the Aggregation Level (see Figure 3.7, callout 1).

3. The **Create Filter** dialog box displays. Enter a **Technical Name** ("ZSL_F_CCD") and a **Description** ("Filter by Company Code"). These actions are shown in Figure 3.7, callouts 2 and 3.

4. Under **Aggregation Level Selection**, you can assign the Aggregation Level for the Filter. Select **Technical name of aggregation level** from the **Find** dropdown list to find the Aggregation Level (see Figure 3.7, callout 4). In the text field next to the dropdown list, you can choose to enter a wildcard that will be used to select the Aggregation Level. For our case study, we will leave this field blank (see Figure 3.7, callout 5).

5. Click **Start** (see Figure 3.7, callout 6). This will list all Aggregation Levels that meet the criteria entered. Select the Aggregation Level you want to use for the Filter ("All characteristics and key figures") as shown in Figure 3.7, callout 7.

6. Click **Transfer** (see Figure 3.7, callout 8).

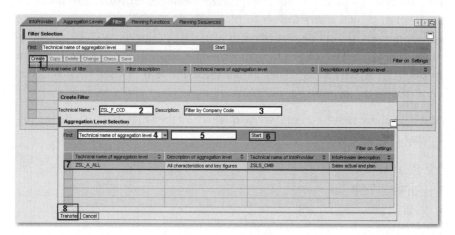

Figure 3.7 Creating a Filter

7. In the lower half of the screen, select the desired Characteristics for the Filter from the **Characteristics** dropdown list (see Figure 3.8, callout 9) and click **Add** (see Figure 3.8, callout 10).

8. Click **Input Help** (see Figure 3.8, callout 11). A dialog box opens that lists the values of the Characteristic. Select the value you want to use for the Filter and click **OK** (see Figure 3.8, callout 12). For our case study, select **Company Code = Rich Bloom Inc.**, **Calendar Year = 2007**, **Value type = 20**, **Version = 1**, **InfoProvider = Sales plan**. Note that you can select a fixed value or a variable and that the **Settings** tab can be used to set the value for time-dependent data.

9. Click **Save** (see Figure 3.8, callout 13) to save the Filter object.

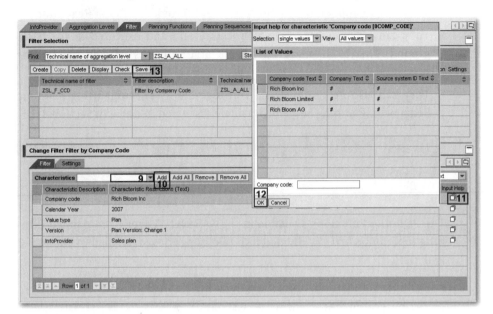

Figure 3.8 Defining Filter Settings

You have now created a Filter to restrict data based on the Company Code, Calendar Year, Value type, Version, and InfoProvider Characteristics. Before we continue, let's summarize the actions we've performed so far.

Summary of Actions Performed So Far

At this point, we have defined the basic settings for the planning application to meet the case study requirements. We identified the Sales and Plan MultiProvider as the InfoProvider for planning and created an Aggregation Level based on the MultiProvider by including all Characteristics of the Info-Provider. We also defined a Filter based on the Aggregation Level to restrict data based on the Company Code, Calendar Year, Value type, Version, and InfoProvider Characteristics.

In the next section, we will discuss the purpose of Planning Functions and explain how they can be used to meet some of the case study requirements.

3.3.4   The Planning Functions Tab

Planning Functions are at the heart of the SAP NetWeaver BI Integrated Planning tool and can be described as follows.

- ► They automate the generation and modification of data.
- ► They can be applied only to data in an InfoProvider of type Real-Time.
- ► They can be integrated into a Process Chain and executed in the background. This is advantageous when large volumes of data need to be processed.
- ► They can also be grouped and run together as one unit using Planning Sequences. Planning Sequences will be discussed in detail in Section 3.3.5.

> **Note**
>
> Note that, by and large, the SAP NetWeaver BI Integrated Planning tool and SAP BW BPS tools offer the same functionality for creating Planning Functions.

The Planning Functions available in the SAP NetWeaver BI Integrated Planning tool can be broadly divided into two categories, described in Tables 3.1 and 3.2:

- ► Multiple Standard Planning Functions (see Table 3.1)
- ► The Custom Planning Function (see Table 3.2)

Planning Function Type	Description
Copy	Lets you copy data from a source to a target. The source data is used as the reference data for copying.
Revalue	Used to increase or decrease the value of Key Figures based on a percentage or fixed value.
Delete	Used to delete Key Figure data.
Delete Invalid Combinations	A variation of the Delete Planning Function. Used in the context of Characteristic Relationships and deletes invalid combinations of data.
Repost	Enables you to move data from one Characteristic value to another.
Repost by Characteristic Relationship	A variation of the Reposting Planning Function. Used in the the context of Characteristic Relationships to move data based on relationships between Characteristics.
Distribute	Two variations exist: Distribution By Reference — the distribution is based on reference data. Distribution By Keys — the distribution is based on specified distribution keys.

Table 3.1 Standard Planning Functions

Planning Function Type	Description
Generate Combinations of Data	Used to generate the possible combinations of data for the associated Characteristics in an Aggregation Level and Filter. The data generated is based on the master data values for the Characteristics or based on Characteristic relationships defined in the underlying InfoProvider. The Key Figures associated with the Characteristic values that are generated by this function are set to zero when this Planning Function is executed.
Forecast	Used to automatically generate data based on a forecast method. Different methods of forecasting can be applied for generating the data.
Conversion	There are two types of Conversion functions: The Currency Translation Planning Function enables conversion of amounts from one currency to another. The Unit Conversion Planning Function enables conversion of quantities from one unit to another.
Formula	The Formula Planning Function can be used when the Standard Planning Functions can't meet a particular planning requirement. The formula language FOX provides a 4GL programming language to aid in generating and modifying plan data.

Table 3.1 Standard Planning Functions (cont.)

Planning Function Type	Description
Custom	Used when the Standard Planning Functions defined in Table 3.1 cannot meet a particular planning requirement. In this case, a customer specific Planning Function type can be implemented using an Advanced Business Application Programming (ABAP) class using transaction **RSPFL1**.

Table 3.2 The Custom Planning Function

Key Points about Planning Functions

The following definitions will enhance your understanding of Planning Functions.

▶ Planning Functions are used to generate and modify data based on certain rules. For example, you could develop a Planning Function that will use the data in the Sales InfoCube as reference data and copy it into a Plan InfoCube as the initial version of the plan. Subsequently, you could create other Planning Functions configured to conditionally apply additional rules to the initial plan, either increasing or decreasing the plan figures based on market conditions.

▶ Planning Functions are created on Aggregation Levels. They can be executed and tested by including them into a Planning Sequence. Planning Functions require that a Filter is specified in the Planning Sequence. We will discuss the use of Planning Sequences in detail in Section 3.3.5.

▶ Planning Functions can be integrated and executed within a planning application user interface. There are two ways to create a planning application user interface. One is to create the user interface using the BEx Analyzer and embed the application as a Microsoft Excel workbook. The other is to create a Web application user interface using the BEx Web Application Designer and execute it on the Web. We will create a complete planning application user interface using both of these methods in Chapter 4.

What Happens in the Background

Although the execution of a Planning Function is transparent to users, it will help you to understand its dynamics, outlined here:

1. Plan data that is to be modified using a Planning Function is selected from the database or the planning buffer. This plan data is also called transaction data. In addition, any reference data used by the Planning Function is also read.

2. The transaction data is grouped into subsets, if applicable. The Planning Function might be defined to change the values of certain Characteristics data. The system will use Characteristics that are not changed in the Planning Function for grouping. All of the data records that have the same Characteristic value will belong to a subset.

3. The Planning Function will be executed either all at once, or individually for each subset of data. For example, if you decide to use a Planning Function to change the values associated to all Characteristics, then there will be no grouping and the Planning Function will execute in one step. On the other hand, if you decide to use a Planning Function to leave the values associated to any Characteristic unchanged and only change the values of

Key Figures, then each record will form a subset and the Planning Function will execute in several steps. Note that each data subset can contain a different number of records based on the data selected.

We'll now define and work with different types of Planning Functions, starting with the Copy Planning Function.

The Copy Planning Function

Let's again look at Rich Bloom, Inc., our sample company. The company wants to use the actual sales and cost data from the year 2006 as the source for planning for the year 2007. You can create a Copy Planning Function to meet this requirement. This Planning Function will use the Sales and Plan MultiProvider that includes the Sales InfoCube and the Plan InfoCube as the InfoProvider. The data in the Sales InfoCube will be used as reference data. The Plan InfoCube will store the data generated by the Planning Function.

Creating and Configuring a Copy Planning Function

We will now use the Aggregation Level and the Filter we created earlier to create and configure the Copy Planning Function, as illustrated in Figures 3.9, 3.10, 3.11, and 3.12:

1. Click the **Planning Functions** tab to select it.

2. Click **Create** (see Figure 3.9, callout 1) to open the **Create Planning Function** dialog box (also shown in Figure 3.9). In the **Create Planning Function** dialog box, next to **Type**, select **Copy** from the dropdown list (see Figure 3.9, callout 2). Enter a **Technical Name** ("ZSL_P_COP"), and a **Description** ("Copy 2006 sales data as 2007 plan") for the Planning Function (see Figure 3.9, callouts 3 and 4).

3. Under **Aggregation Level Selection**, you can assign the Aggregation Level to be used by the Copy Planning Function. Select **Technical name of aggregation level** from the **Find** dropdown list to be used as the basis to find the Aggregation Level (see Figure 3.9, callout 5). In the text field next to the **Find** dropdown list, you can enter a wildcard to select the Aggregation Level. For our case study, we will leave this field blank (see Figure 3.9, callout 6).

4. Click **Start** (see Figure 3.9, callout 7). This will list all Aggregation Levels that meet the criteria entered. Select the Aggregation Level (**All characteristics and key figures**) to be used for the Planning function (see Figure 3.9, callout 8).

5. Click **Transfer** (see Figure 3.9, callout 9) to display the **Change Planning Function Copy 2006 sales data as 2007 — Characteristic usage** window, shown in Figure 3.10.

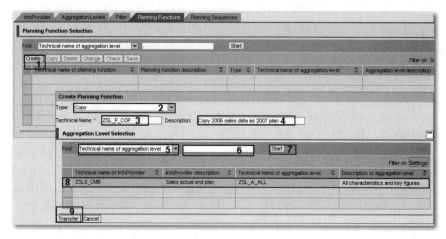

Figure 3.9 Creating a Copy Planning Function — Part 1

6. By default, the **For Characteristic Usage** field displays. Select the Characteristics that will be modified by the Planning Function by checking them in the **changed** column (see Figure 3.10, callout 10). For our case study, select the **Calendar Year/Month**, **Calendar Year**, **InfoProvider**, **Version**, and **Value Type for Reporting** Characteristics.

> **Note**
>
> If you need additional conditions to restrict the data affected by the Planning Function, you can select the Characteristics to which the conditions apply in the **used in conditions** column. Because we will be using the Copy Planning Function to copy all data from the Sales InfoCube to the Plan InfoCube, we will not make any selections here.

7. Click the **For Parameters** button (see Figure 3.10, callout 11) to display the area where you can set the Key Figure and Characteristic values you will use for copying the data.

8. Select **Select All Key Figures** (see Figure 3.11, callout 12) to specify that the Copy Function will copy data for all Key Figures from the Sales InfoCube to the Plan InfoCube. If you want the Planning Function to copy individual Key Figures, rather than all of them, you can select them manually by marking the appropriate checkboxes in the **changed** column.

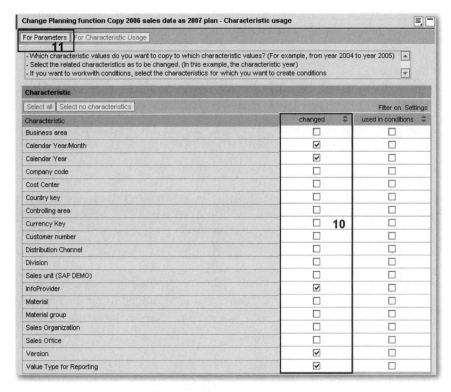

Figure 3.10 Creating a Copy Planning Function — Part 2

9. Click **Create row** (see Figure 3.11, callout 13) to start the process of specifying the **From** and **To** values the Copy Planning Function will use for the Characteristics.

10. Click **From Change** (see Figure 3.11, callout 14). The **Change characteristic selections** dialog box displays (see Figure 3.11, callout 15), where you can set the source data for the Copy function. To do so, select the appropriate value from the dropdown list available for each Characteristic. For our case study, select **Version = 0**, **Calendar Year = 2006**, **Calendar Year/Month = January 2006**, **InfoProvider = Sales actual**, and **Value Type for Reporting = 10**. This is also the reference data used by the Planning Function.

11. Click **To Change** (see Figure 3.11, callout 16) to display the **Change characteristic selections** dialog box. Select the appropriate target data values using the dropdown list available for each Characteristic. For our case study, select **Version = 1**, **Calendar Year = 2007**, **Calendar Year/Month = January 2007**, **InfoProvider = Sales Plan**, and **Value Type for Reporting = 20**.

Figure 3.11 Creating a Copy Planning Function — Part 3

> **Note**
>
> Note that the values of Charasteristics generated or modified by a Planning Function should contain a value that is selectable by in the Filter object.

12. Repeat steps 9 thru 11 to identify the corresponding source and target data for the different Characteristics that are changed using the Planning Function. Figure 3.12, callout 17 shows a portion of the settings defined for the Copy Planning Function.

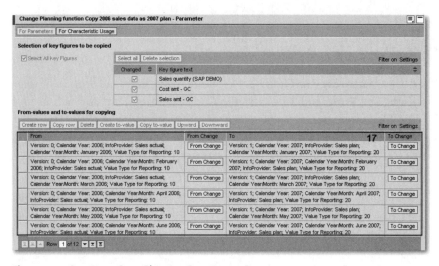

Figure 3.12 Creating a Copy Planning Function — Part 4

13. The definition of the Planning Function is now complete. Click **Check** in the upper area of the Planning Function window. (You can see the **Check** button — grayed out — in Figure 3.9; it doesn't become available until later in the process.) This ensures that the Planning Function has been defined correctly.

14. Click **Save** (again, shown grayed out in Figure 3.9) to save the changes.

We have now defined a Copy Planning Function to copy the actual sales and cost data for the year 2006 to the plan data for the year 2007. In the next section, we will examine how to create a Revaluation Planning Function.

The Revaluation Planning Function

Let's return to Rich Bloom, Inc.'s current situation. The company is experiencing good demand for its products in the Shirts group and wants to use this fact as an opportunity to increase prices by 5%. The company is expected to maintain the planned sales quantity even after increasing prices.

We can use the standard Revaluation Planning Function for revaluing the plan data for the products in the Shirts group. Costs are expected to remain the same for the plan period. As a result, the changes to the data should affect only the sales amount.

A Revalue Planning Function does not affect Characteristic values in the Info-Provider. It affects only Key Figures. For our planning requirement, we will use the Revalue Planning Function to revalue the sales amount Key Figures. Additional conditions can be configured to restrict changes to the data to only the selected Material Group (Shirts).

Use the following steps to create a Revaluation Planning Function, as illustrated in Figures 3.13, 3.14, 3.15, and 3.16:

1. Click the **Planning Functions** tab to select it (if necessary).

2. Click **Create** to open the **Create Planning Function** dialog box (see Figure 3.13, callout 1). Next to **Type**, select **Revaluation** from the dropdown list (see Figure 3.13, callout 2). Enter a **Technical Name** ("ZSL_P_REV"), and a **Description** ("Revalue sales amount") for the Planning Function (see Figure 3.13, callouts 3 and 4).

3. Under **Aggregation Level Selection**, you will be able to assign the Aggregation Level to be used by the Revaluation Planning Function. Choose **Technical name of aggregation level** from the dropdown list (see Figure 3.13, callout 5) to use as the criterion for finding the Aggregation Level. In the next text field, you can optionally enter a wildcard to be used to select the Aggregation Level. For our case study, we will leave this field blank (see Figure 3.13, callout 6).

4. Click **Start** (see Figure 3.13, callout 7). This will list all Aggregation Levels that meet the criteria entered. Select the Aggregation Level **All characteristics and key figures** (see Figure 3.13, callout 8).

5. Click **Transfer** (see Figure 3.13, callout 9) to display the **Change Planning function Revalue sales amount** — **Characteristic usage** window, shown in Figure 3.14. Two areas, **For Parameters** and **Characteristic Usage**, are available to configure the settings for the Planning Function.

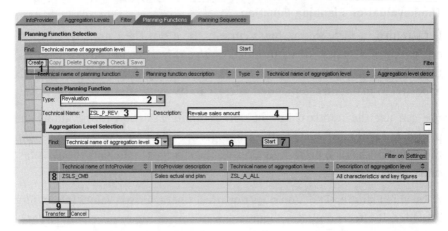

Figure 3.13 Creating a Revaluation Planning Function — Part 1

6. By default, the **For Characteristic Usage** area displays. In this area you select the Characteristics used to filter data when executing a Planning Function. Because we will be revaluating the price for all products that fall under the Shirts group, select **Material group** in the **used in conditions** column (see Figure 3.14, callout 10).

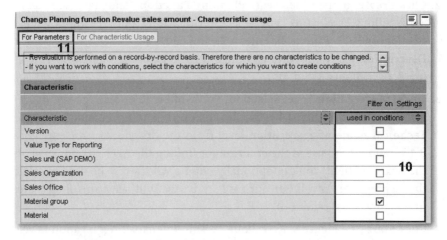

Figure 3.14 Creating a Revaluation Planning Function — Part 2

7. Click the **For Parameters** button (see Figure 3.14, callout 11) to display the **Selected Condition** and **Associated Parameter Record** tabs (see Figure 3.15).

8. On the **Associated Parameter Record** tab, you can select whether the Revalue Planning Function should apply a uniform percentage to all Key Figures or apply different percentages to individual Key Figures (see Figure 3.15, callout 12). When **Individual percentages** is selected, you specify the percentage values to use for the different Key Figures. You can also specify a formula variable here to dynamically determine the revaluation factor. For our case study, set the **Sales amt — GC** Key Figure to be increased by 5 % (see Figure 3.15, callout 13).

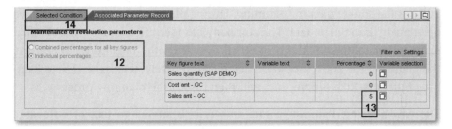

Figure 3.15 Creating a Revaluation Planning Function — Part 3

9. Click the **Selected Condition** tab (see Figure 3.15, callout 14). If, in the **For Characteristic Usage** area, you have identified Characteristics to filter the data further when executing the Planning Function, the values are selected by clicking the icon at the end of the row for the Characteristic, as shown in Figure 3.16, callout 15. For our case study, select the Shirts group (**Material group**).

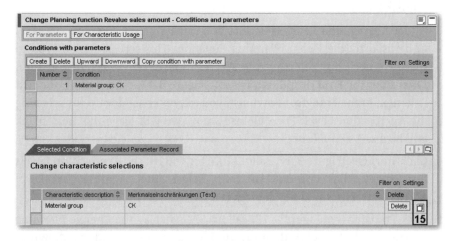

Figure 3.16 Creating Revaluation Planning Function — Part 4

10. Click **Save** (shown grayed out in Figure 3.13) to save the Planning Function.

You have now seen how to create a Revalue Planning Function to revalue plan data. In the next section, we will examine how to create a Planning Function to delete planning data using our sample company, Rich Bloom, Inc.

The Delete Planning Function

Rich Bloom, Inc. has started the process of planning sales, cost, and gross profit margin for calendar year 2007 and has used the actual sales data of 2006 as the source data for planning. During planning, several changes have been made to the plan data. The company has identified issues with the plan data and wants to start the process all over from the beginning. Therefore, the plan data for 2007 should be deleted completely, using the Delete Planning function. Rich Bloom, Inc. will then restart the planning process.

The way a Delete Planning Function works is similar to that of a Revalue Planning Function. Also, the Delete Planning Function does not affect Characteristic values; it affects only Key Figures. Use the following steps to create the Delete Planning Function, as illustrated in Figures 3.17 and 3.18:

1. Click the **Planning Functions** tab to select it.

2. Click **Create** to open the **Create Planning Function** dialog box (see Figure 3.17). Next to **Type**, select **Delete** from the dropdown list (see Figure 3.17, callout 1). Enter a **Technical Name** ("ZSL_P_DEL"), and a **Description** ("Delete plan data for 2007") for the Planning Function (see Figure 3.17, callouts 2 and 3).

3. Under **Aggregation Level Selection**, you can assign the Aggregation Level to be used by the Delete Planning Function. This screen enables you to specify criteria for selecting the Aggregation Level. Select **Aggregation Level** from the **Find** dropdown list (see Figure 3.17, callout 4). In the text field next to the **Find** dropdown list, you can enter a wildcard for selecting the Aggregation Level. For our case study, we will leave this field blank (see Figure 3.17, callout 5).

4. Click **Start** (see Figure 3.17, callout 6). This will list the Aggregation Levels that meet the criteria entered. Select the Aggregation Level **All characteristics and key figures** (see Figure 3.17, callout 7).

5. Click **Transfer** (see Figure 3.17, callout 8) to display the **Change Planning function — Delete plan data for 2007 — Parameter** window, shown in Figure 3.18. Two areas, **For Characteristic Usage** and **For Parameters** are available to configure the settings for the Planning Function.

By default, the **For Characteristic Usage** area displays. The Characteristics for restricting the data when executing the Planning Function can be selected on this tab. Because we want to delete all plan data, we will not make any selections.

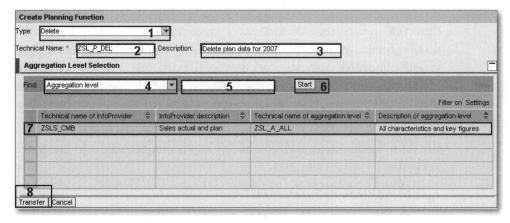

Figure 3.17 Creating a Delete Planning Function — Part 1

6. Click the **For Parameters** button to display the area where you can select the Key Figures you want the Delete Planning Function to delete. For our case study, select **Select All Key Figures** to set the plan values of all Key Figures to zero (see Figure 3.18, callout 9).

7. Click **Save** to save the Planning Function.

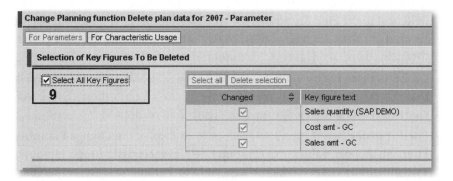

Figure 3.18 Creating a Delete Planning Function — Part 2

You have now seen how to use the Delete Planning Function to delete data. In the next section, we will use our case study to see how to create a Planning Function to repost planning data.

The Repost Planning Function

Rich Bloom, Inc. has planned sales and cost data for calendar year 2007 using the actual sales and cost data for the year 2006 as the source for planning. Further, all customers in the Sales InfoCube were copied to the Plan InfoCube using the Copy Planning Function.

However, one of Rich Bloom, Inc.'s customers was recently bought by another company. In the past, Rich Bloom, Inc. has been selling its products to both companies. Now, the sales data for the customer who was bought has to be reposted to the other company. The Repost Planning Function can be used for this purpose. Note that the Repost Planning Function does not affect Key Figure values. It affects only Characteristic values.

Use the following steps to create the Repost Planning Function, as illustrated in Figures 3.19, 3.20 and 3.21:

1. Click the **Planning Functions** tab to select it.

2. Click **Create** to open the **Create Planning Function** dialog box (see Figure 3.19). Next to **Type**, select **Repost** from the dropdown list (see Figure 3.19, callout 1). Enter a **Technical Name** ("ZSL_P_REP"), and a **Description** ("Repost values for customer") for the Planning Function (see Figure 3.19, callouts 2 and 3).

3. Under **Aggregation Level Selection**, you can assign the Aggregation Level to be used by the Delete Planning Function. This screen enables you to specify criteria for selecting the Aggregation Level. Select **Aggregation Level** from the **Find** dropdown list (see Figure 3.19, callout 4). In the text field next to the **Find** dropdown list, you can optionally enter a wildcard to be used to select the Aggregation Level. For our case study, we will leave this field blank (see Figure 3.19, callout 5).

4. Click **Start** (see Figure 3.19, callout 6). This will list all Aggregation Levels that meet the criteria entered. Select the Aggregation Level **All characteristics and key figures** (see Figure 3.19, callout 7).

5. Click **Transfer** (see Figure 3.19, callout 8) to display the **Change Planning Function Repost values for customer — Characteristic usage** window. Two areas, **For Characteristic Usage** and **For Parameters**, are available to configure the settings for the Planning Function.

6. By default, the **For Characteristic Usage** area displays. Select the Characteristic(s) that will be used to select data in the Repost Planning Function. For our case study, select the **Customer number** Characteristic in the **changed** column (see Figure 3.20, callout 9).

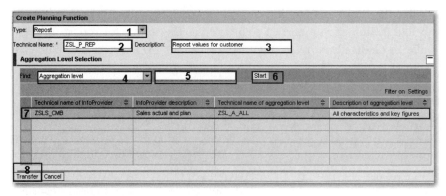

Figure 3.19 Creating a Repost Planning Function — Part 1

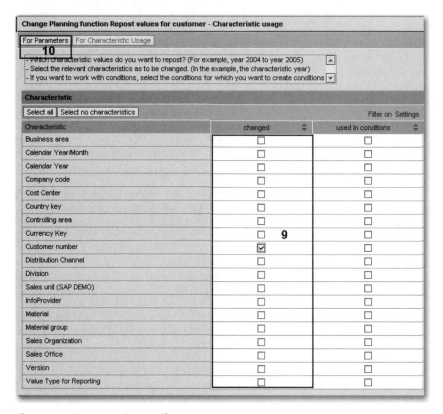

Figure 3.20 Creating a Repost Planning Function — Part 2

7. Click the **For Parameters** button (see Figure 3.20, callout 10) to display the area where you can select the Key Figures for which the reposting should be effective (see Figure 3.21, callout 11). For our case study, select **Select All Key Figures**.

8. Click the **From Change** button (see Figure 3.21, callout 12) to select the value **Customer number: C1** to be used as the source for reposting. Click the **To Change** button (see Figure 3.21, callout 13) to select the value **Customer number: C3** as the target for reposting.

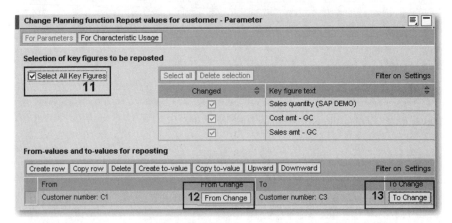

Figure 3.21 Creating a Repost Planning Function — Part 3

9. Save the Planning Function.

You have now seen how to use the Repost Planning Function to repost plan data from one customer to another. In the next section, we will look into creating a Planning Function that apportions plan data that is planned at a higher level to a more granular level, based on a distribution factor.

The Distribution by Key Planning Function

At this point, you already know how to use the Repost Planning Function to post plan data from one customer to another. You can also achieve the same results using the Distribution by Key Planning Function. In this case, the data from one customer is distributed to another customer by specifying a factor for distribution. The Distribution by Key Planning Function is more versatile than the Repost Planning Function because it lets you specify the distribution factor when a source Characteristic is distributed to several target values.

The Distribution by Key Planning Function can be used for different planning scenarios. For example, sales and cost data might be initially planned at the calendar year level and not at the calendar month level. But it might be decided to apportion the sales data to the various calendar months. Based on historical trends of sales data, the values might need to be distributed using a certain ratio. This ratio is defined as a distribution factor in the Distribution by Key Planning Function. When the Planning Function is executed, the Key Figure values are distributed from one Characteristic value to another, based on the distribution factor specified.

Using the same scenario as earlier, where two of Rich Bloom, Inc.'s customers have merged and sales data needs to be reposted from one company to another, perform the following steps to create the Distribution by Key Planning Function. These steps are illustrated in Figures 3.22, 3.23 and 3.24:

1. Click the **Planning Function** tab to select it.

2. Click **Create** to open the **Create Planning Function** dialog box (see Figure 3.22). Next to **Type**, select **Distribution by Keys** from the dropdown list (see Figure 3.22, callout 1). Enter a **Technical Name** ("ZSL_P_DBK"), and a **Description** ("Distribute values for customer — Key") for the Planning Function (see Figure 3.22, callouts 2 and 3).

3. Under **Aggregation Level Selection**, you can assign the Aggregation Level to be used by the Delete Planning Function. This screen allows you to specify a criteria for selecting the Aggregation Level. Select **Aggregation Level** from the **Find** dropdown list (see Figure 3.22, callout 4). In the text field next to the **Find** dropdown list, you can optionally enter a wildcard to be used to select the Aggregation Level. For our case study, we will leave this field blank (see Figure 3.22, callout 5).

4. Click **Start** (see Figure 3.22, callout 6). This will list all Aggregation Levels that meet the criteria entered. Select the Aggregation Level **All characteristics and key figures** (see Figure 3.22, callout 7).

5. Click **Transfer** (see Figure 3.22, callout 8) to display the **Change Planning Function Distribute values for customer — Key — Characteristic usage** window, shown in Figure 3.23. Two areas, **For Characteristic Usage** and **For Parameters,** are available to configure the settings for the Planning Function.

6. In the **For Characteristic Usage** area, select the Characteristic that is to be changed using the Distribution by Key Planning Function. For our case study, select the **Customer number** in the **changed** column (see Figure 3.23, callout 9).

7. Click the **For Parameters** button (see Figure 3.23, callout 10). In the **For Parameters** area, you can select the Key Figures to which the distribution should apply (see Figure 3.24, callout 11). For our case study, select **Select All Key Figures**.

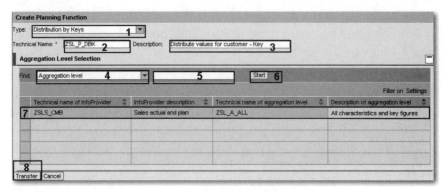

Figure 3.22 Creating a Distribution by Key Planning Function — Part 1

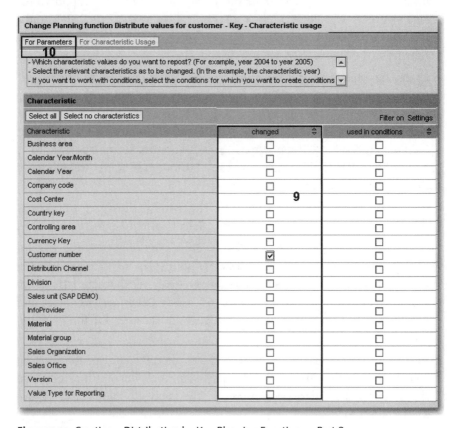

Figure 3.23 Creating a Distribution by Key Planning Function — Part 2

8. Click the **From Change** button to select the value **Customer number: C1** to be used as the source for the distribution by key (see Figure 3.24, callout 12). Click the **To Change** button to select the value **Customer number: C3**

to be used as the target for distribution by key (see Figure 3.24, callout 13). Because you are going to apportion all the plan data from customer C1 to customer C3, you will set the distribution factor to 1 (see Figure 3.24, callout 14).

Please note that you can distribute a single value to multiple values using a factor. A variable can also be used to dynamically determine the distribution factor. If you need to apportion the plan data from one Characteristic value to multiple Characteristic values, you can create additional rows to specify a new set of **From** and **To** values for distribution.

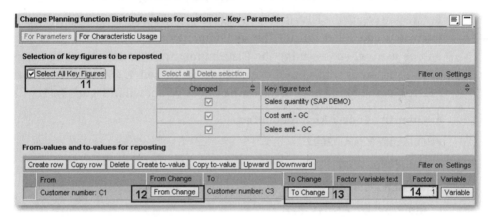

Figure 3.24 Creating a Distribution by Key Planning Function — Part 3

9. Save the Planning Function.

You have now seen how to distribute values using the Distribution by Key Planning Function. In the next section, we will show you how to create a Planning Function to distribute planning data by reference.

The Distribution by Reference Planning Function

You use a Distribution by Reference Planning Function when existing data, usually historical, will be used as reference data to distribute values. The system generates the combination of Characteristics that correspond to the reference data.

This Planning Function is similar to the Distribute by Key Planning Function, but reference data rather than plan data is used as the basis for distribution. The reference values you'll select for distribution should exist in the InfoProvider. If reference data does not exist, a message will be displayed, indicating that reference data cannot be found when executing this Planning Function.

To look at our case study again, Rich Bloom, Inc. is planning data at the Material level. But in some cases, it's easier to initially plan at the Material Group level. After the plan data is created at this level, it can be distributed to the Material level based on reference data. In the following example, we will distribute the plan data for the calendar month January 2007 that was initially planned at the Material Group level to the Material level based on actual sales for the calendar month January 2006.

Preparing for the Distribution by Reference Planning Function

Before you create the Distribution by Reference Planning Function, you need to create a new Filter called **Filter by Company Code and Month**. This Filter will be used when executing the Distribution by Reference Planning Function. Using steps similar to those outlined in Section 1.3.3, create the new Filter with the following Characteristic values, as shown in Figure 3.25:

▶ **Company Code = Rich Bloom Inc.**

▶ **Calendar Year = 2007**

▶ **Value type = 20**

▶ **Version = 1**

▶ **InfoProvider = Sales plan**

▶ **Calendar Year/Month = January 2007**

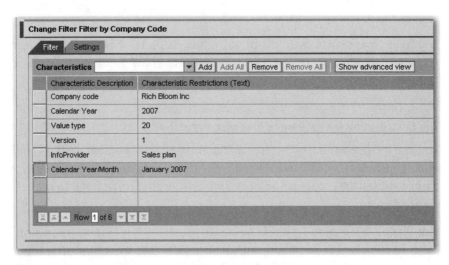

Figure 3.25 Defining a Filter for the Distribution by Reference Planning Function

Perform the following steps to create the Distribution by Reference Planning Function for our case study, as illustrated in Figures 3.26, 3.27, and 3.28:

1. Click the **Planning Function** tab to select it.

2. Click **Create** to open the **Create Planning Function** dialog box (see Figure 3.26). Next to **Type**, select **Distribution by Reference** from the dropdown list (see Figure 3.26, callout 1). Enter a **Technical Name** ("ZSL_P_DBR"), and a **Description** ("Distribute based on reference data — material") for the Planning Function (see Figure 3.26, callouts 2 and 3).

3. Under **Aggregation Level Selection**, you can assign the Aggregation Level to be used by the Distribution by Reference Planning Function. This screen allows you to specify a criteria for selecting the Aggregation Level. Select **Aggregation Level** from the **Find** dropdown list (see Figure 3.26, callout 4). In the text field next to the **Find** dropdown list, you can optionally enter a wildcard to be used to select the Aggregation Level. For our case study, we will leave this field blank (see Figure 3.26, callout 5).

4. Click **Start** (see Figure 3.26, callout 6). This will list all Aggregation Levels that meet the criteria entered. Select the Aggregation Level **All characteristics and key figures** (see Figure 3.26, callout 7).

5. Click **Transfer** (see Figure 3.26, callout 8) to display the **Change Planning Function Distribute based on reference data — material — Characteristic usage** window, shown in Figure 3.27. Two areas, **For Characteristic Usage** and **For Parameters,** are available to configure the settings for the Planning Function.

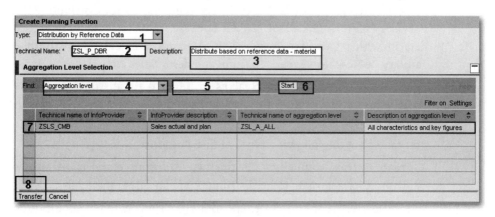

Figure 3.26 Creating a Distribution by Reference Planning Function — Part 1

6. By default, the **For Characteristic Usage** area displays. Select the Characteristic that is to be changed using the Distribution by Reference Planning

Function (see Figure 3.27, callout 9). For our case study, we will choose the **Material**, by selecting it in the **changed** column.

7. Click the **For Parameters** button (see Figure 3.27, callout 10). In the **For Parameters** area, select the Key Figures for which the distribution should occur (see Figure 3.28, callout 11). For our case study, we will select **Select All Key Figures**.

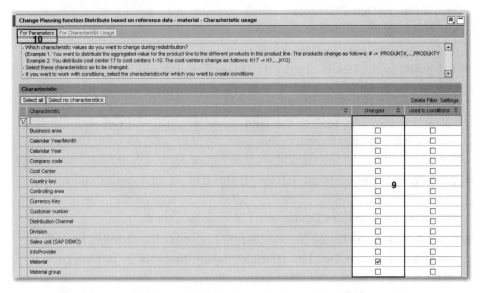

Figure 3.27 Creating a Distribution by Reference Planning Function — Part 2

8. Click the **Change** button to select the reference values for distributing the data (see Figure 3.28, callout 12). For our case study, we will use reference data in which **Calendar Year = 2006, Version = 0, Calendar Month = January 2006, Value Type = 10, InfoProvider = Sales Actual**.

9. Specify the source and target values to be used for distribution in the **From-values and to-values for distribution** area (see Figure 3.28, callout 13).

You can select the following types of distributions:

▷ **Create Entries Manually** — In this case, the source and target values for the Characteristic to be distributed are specified manually.

▷ **Top-Down Distribution** — There are two options when using this type of distribution: **Distribute All** and **Only Distribute "Not Assigned (#)."** When using the **Distribute All** option, all values are distributed. When using the **Only Distribute "Not Assigned (#)"** option, only the values that are unassigned are distributed.

For our case study, for the **From-values and to-values for distribution**, select **Top-Down Distribution** and **Distribute All**.

10. Save the Planning Function.

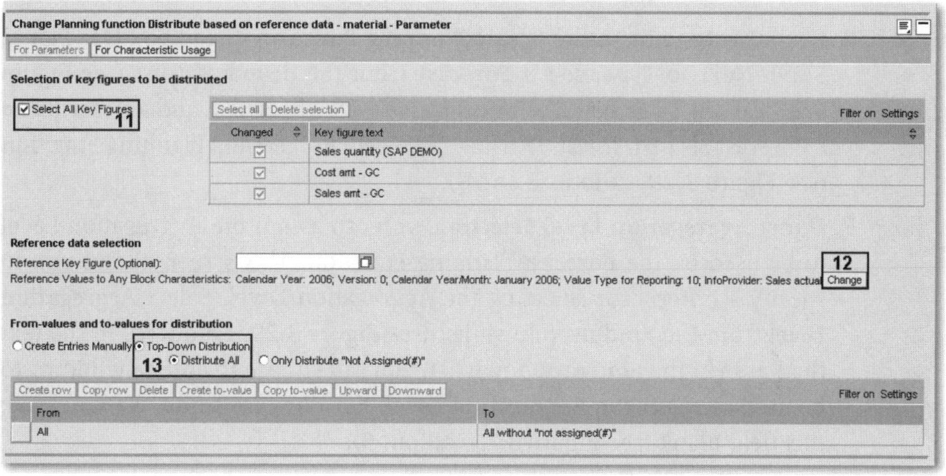

Figure 3.28 Creating a Distribution by Reference Planning Function — Part 3

You have now seen how to distribute values using the Distribution by Key Planning Function. In the next section, we will show you how to create a Planning Function to generate a forecast.

The Forecast Planning Function

A forecast is a prediction based on past performance and an analysis of expected business conditions. It helps you establish policies that let you manage financial, production and workforce needs more effectively. The Forecast Planning Function uses existing data from a prior period to predict the expected outcome based on a Time Characteristic along with reference data. Historical data is usually used for this purpose. As an example, sales data for 2006 can be used as reference data to forecast sales data for 2007. If data already exists for the forecast period, you need to delete the data before executing the Forecast Planning Function.

Different forecasting strategies are available with this Planning Function:

► Average, Moving Average
► Weighted Moving Average
► Linear Exponential Smoothing
► Linear Regression

Use the following steps to create a Forecast Planning Function that will use the Average forecast strategy to derive the forecast, as illustrated in Figures 3.29, 3.30, and 3.31.

1. Click the **Planning Functions** tab to select it.

2. Click **Create** to open the **Create Planning Function** dialog box (see Figure 3.29). Next to **Type**, select **Forecast** from the dropdown list (see Figure 3.29, callout 1). Enter a **Technical Name** ("ZSL_P_FOR"), and a **Description** ("Forecast sls plan for 2007 using 2006 actuals") for the Planning Function (see Figure 3.29, callouts 2 and 3).

3. Under **Aggregation Level Selection**, you can assign the Aggregation Level to be used by the Forecast Planning Function. This screen allows you to specify a criteria for selecting the Aggregation Level. Select **Aggregation Level** from the **Find** dropdown list (see Figure 3.29, callout 4). In the text field next to the **Find** dropdown list, you can choose to enter a wildcard to be used to select the Aggregation Level. For our case study, we will leave this field blank (see Figure 3.29, callout 5).

4. Click **Start** (see Figure 3.29, callout 6). This will list all Aggregation Levels that meet the criteria entered. Select the Aggregation Level **All characteristics and key figures** (see Figure 3.29, callout 7).

5. Click **Transfer** (see Figure 3.29, callout 8) to display the **Change Planning Function Forecast sales for 2007 based on 2006 — Characteristic usage** window shown in Figure 3.30. Two areas, **For Characteristic Usage** and **For Parameters,** are available to configure the settings for the Planning Function.

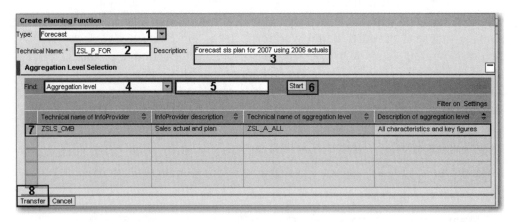

Figure 3.29 Creating a Forecasting Planning Function — Part 1

6. By default, the **For Characteristics** area displays. Select **Calendar Year/Month** from the **Time Characteristics for Forecast** dropdown list (see Figure 3.30, callout 9).

7. Click the **For Parameters** button (see Figure 3.30, callout 10).

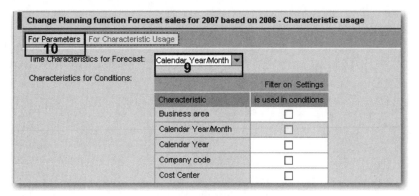

Figure 3.30 Creating a Forecast Planning Function — Part 2

8. In the **For Parameters** area, select the Key Figures you want to forecast (see Figure 3.31, callout 11). For our case study, select **Select All Key Figures**.

9. In the **Forecast Data** area, next to **Forecast Period**, click **Change** (see Figure 3.31, callout 12) and select the period for which the forecast data is to be generated. This will open a window where you can enter the forecast period. For our case study, select **Calendar Year/Month: January 2007 — December 2007**.

10. In the **Historic Data** area, next to **Past Period**, click the **Change** button (see Figure 3.31, callout 13) to select the period to be used as the historical basis for creating the forecast. This will open a window where you can enter the historical basis for creating a forecast. For our case study, select **Calendar Year/Month: January 2006 — December 2006**.

11. In the **Historic Data** area, next to **Historic Data Filter, click** the **Change** button to select a Filter that will be used for the forecast. This will open a window where you can enter the values for the historic data filter. For our case study, specify **Calendar Year = 2006, Version = 0, Value Type = 10 and InfoProvider = Sales actual** (see Figure 3.31, callout 14).

12. In the **Forecast Procedure** area, select **Average** from the **Forecast Strategy** dropdown list (see Figure 3.31, callout 15).

13. Save the Planning Function.

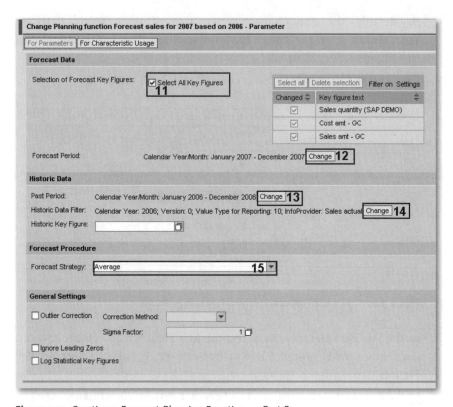

Figure 3.31 Creating a Forecast Planning Function — Part 2

You have now seen how to generate data using the Forecast Planning Function. In the next section, we will show you how to create a Formula Planning Function.

The Formula Planning Function

You use a Formula Planning Function when you can't use a Standard Planning Function to accomplish a planning requirement. You can also use a Formula Planning Function when you need to combine more than one Standard Planning Function and execute these functions one after the other. This might result in improved execution times and optimization of the process.

The Formula Planning Function lets you use a fourth generation language (4 GL) called Formula Extension (FOX) formula language to code the planning requirements. This provides additional flexibility when configuring a planning requirement by letting you write the logic for the Planning Function.

Starting with SAP NetWeaver BI 7.0, the FOX language lets you call SAP functions. Thus, you can use the FOX language in conjunction with Formula Planning Functions to develop a Custom Planning Function to meet any requirement.

FOX is a simple, easy-to-use programming language and is similar to the coding structure and constructs available in a 4GL language. Table 3.3 describes its features.

FOX Feature	Description
Condition statements	IF and ENDIF statements can be used to execute code conditionally.
Loop constructs	WHEN and DO statements are used to repeat the execution of a block of statements while or until a condition remains true.
Local variable	Variables can be declared and used in the code.
Operators	Standard operators (=, >, <) can be used to indicate the type of operation.
Assignments	A variable value can be set or assigned. The value to the right of the operator is used to set the variable values to the left of the operator.
Statement delimiter	Every statement in FOX ends with a period.

Table 3.3 Key Features of the FOX language

Note
SAP has provided extensive documentation on the use of the FOX language in Formula Planning Functions. The syntax and examples can be accessed from the area in the system provided for entering the formula code in the Formula Planning Function.

We will now show you how you can combine the Copy and Revalue Planning Functions into a single Planning Function using the Formula Planning Function, as illustrated in Figures 3.32, 3.33, and 3.34:

1. Click the **Planning Functions** tab to select it.

2. Click **Create** to open the **Create Planning Function** dialog box (see Figure 3.32). In the **Create Planning Function** dialog box, next to **Type**, select **Formula** from the dropdown list (see Figure 3.32, callout 1). Enter a **Technical Name** ("ZSL_P_FOX"), and a **Description** ("Copy and revalue data using Formula") for the Planning Function (see Figure 3.32, callouts 2 and 3).

3. Under **Aggregation Level Selection**, you can assign the Aggregation Level to be used by the Formula Planning Function. This screen allows you to specify a criteria for selecting the Aggregation Level. Select **Aggregation Level** from the **Find** dropdown list (see Figure 3.32, callout 4). In the text field next to the **Find** dropdown list, you can enter a wildcard to be used to select the Aggregation Level. For our case study, we will leave this field blank (see Figure 3.32, callout 5).

4. Click **Start** (see Figure 3.32, callout 6). This will list all Aggregation Levels that meet the criteria entered. Select the Aggregation Level **All characteristics and key figures** (see Figure 3.32, callout 7).

5. Click **Transfer** (see Figure 3.32, callout 8) to display the **Change Planning Function Copy and Revalue data using formula — Parameter** window, shown in Figure 3.33. Two areas, **For Characteristic Usage** and **For Parameters,** are available to configure the settings for the Planning Function.

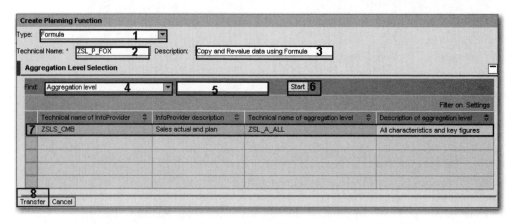

Figure 3.32 Creating a Formula Planning Function — Part 1

6. Click the **For Characteristic Usage** button (see Figure 3.33, callout 9). This displays the Characteristics Usage area. Select the Characteristic you want to change using the Formula Planning Function (see Figure 3.34, callout 10). For our case study, choose the **Calendar Year**, **Calendar Year/Month**, **InfoProvider**, **Version**, and **Value Type for Recording**.

7. Click the **For Parameters** button (see Figure 3.34, callout 11) to return to the previous screen. In the **Formula** section (see Figure 3.33, callout 12), include the code that follows this text . This code copies the sales and cost data for the year 2006 as plan data for the year 2007 and revalues the sales amount by 5 %.

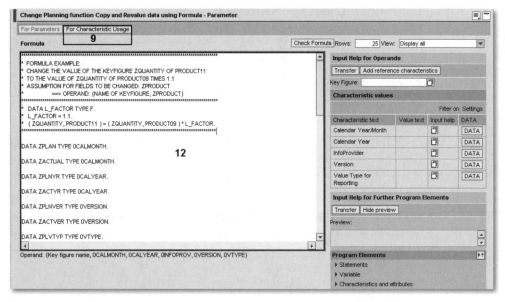

Figure 3.33 Creating a Formula Planning Function — Part 2

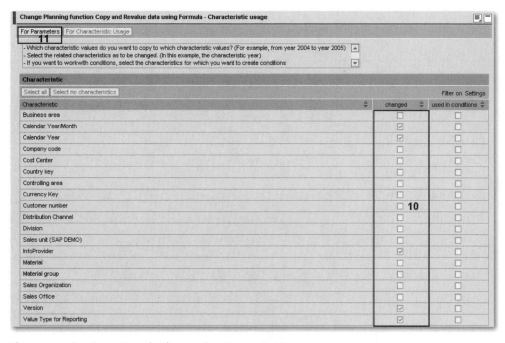

Figure 3.34 Creating a Formula Planning Function — Part 3

```
*    FORMULA EXAMPLE: (The following example appears in the
*    Formula section)
***************** BEGIN EXAMPLE ******************************
*    CHANGE THE VALUE OF THE KEYFIGURE ZQUANTITY OF PRODUCT11
*    TO THE VALUE OF ZQUANTITY OF PRODUCT09 TIMES 1.1

*    ASSUMPTION FOR FIELDS TO BE CHANGED: ZPRODUCT
*                    ==> OPERAND: {NAME OF KEYFIGURE, ZPRODUCT}
************************************************************
*    DATA L_FACTOR TYPE F.
*    L_FACTOR = 1.1.
*    { ZQUANTITY, PRODUCT11 } = { ZQUANTITY, PRODUCT09 } * ⮐
     L_FACTOR.
************************************************************
***************** END EXAMPLE *******************************

DATA ZPLAN TYPE OCALMONTH.
DATA ZACTUAL TYPE OCALMONTH.
DATA ZPLNYR TYPE OCALYEAR.
DATA ZACTYR TYPE OCALYEAR.
DATA ZPLNVER TYPE OVERSION.
DATA ZACTVER TYPE OVERSION.
DATA ZPLVTYP TYPE OVTYPE.
DATA ZACVTYP TYPE OVTYPE.
DATA ZCTR TYPE I.

ZPLNVER = '001'.
ZACTVER = '000'.
ZPLVTYP = '020'.
ZACVTYP = '010'.
ZPLNYR = '2007'.
ZACTYR = '2006'.
ZPLAN = '200701'.
ZACTUAL = '200601'.

  DO.
    ZCTR = ZCTR + 1.

    IF ZCTR > 1.

       ZPLAN = TMVL(ZPLAN,1).
       ZACTUAL = TMVL(ZACTUAL,1).

    ENDIF.
```

```
{ZSLAMT_GC,ZPLAN,ZPLNYR,ZSLS_PLN,ZPLNVER,ZPLVTYP} =
{ZSLAMT_GC,ZACTUAL,ZACTYR,ZSLS_ACT,ZACTVER,ZACVTYP} * ⤶
1.05.

{ZCTAMT_GC,ZPLAN,ZPLNYR,ZSLS_PLN,ZPLNVER,ZPLVTYP} =
  {ZCTAMT_GC,ZACTUAL,ZACTYR,ZSLS_ACT,ZACTVER,ZACVTYP} .
  {OD_QTY,ZPLAN,ZPLNYR,ZSLS_PLN,ZPLNVER,ZPLVTYP} =
  {OD_QTY,ZACTUAL,ZACTYR,ZSLS_ACT,ZACTVER,ZACVTYP}.

IF ZCTR = 12.
  EXIT.
ENDIF.

ENDDO.
```

8. Save the Formula Planning Function.

You have now seen how you can use a Formula Planning Function to integrate multiple standard Planning Functions (e.g., Copy and Revalue) into one Planning Function. In the next section, we will show you how to create a Custom Planning Function.

The Custom Planning Function

A Custom Planning Function is used when a Standard Planning Function cannot be used to accomplish a planning requirement. The Custom Planning Function lets you use the ABAP programming language to satisfy complex planning requirements.

> **Note**
>
> The Custom Planning Function is different from the Formula Planning Function in that the Custom Planning Function uses the ABAP programming language to develop the Planning Function, whereas the Formula Planning Function uses the FOX language.

A Custom Planning Function is helpful to use under the following circumstances.

▶ A complex planning requirement must be satisfied

▶ Database table access is required

▶ Using ABAP is necessary

> **Note**
>
> You should be aware that using FOX with a Formula Planning Function does not offer the same flexibility as using ABAP with a Custom Planning Function.

Let's look again at our sample company, Rich Bloom, Inc. The company is planning to offer a promotional price on a few products for the plan period. The promotional products are maintained in a custom table named ZMATERIAL. The company has begun its planning process for 2007 and wants to offer a 5% reduction in sales price on the products maintained on this table. The Planning Function should adjust the sales revenue amount and decrease it by 5% for the products maintained in the custom table.

Follow these steps to create both a Custom Planning Function Type that will be referenced in the Custom Planning Function, and the Custom Planning Function, as illustrated in Figures 3.35, 3.36, 3.37, and 3.38:

1. Create a custom class called ZCL_PRD_PROM using Transaction SE24.
2. Select the **Interfaces** tab of the class (see Figure 3.35, callout 1) and enter the interface "IF_RSPFLA_SRVTYPE_IMP_EXEC" (see Figure 3.35, callout 2).
3. Click **Enter**.

> **Note**
>
> The interface IF_RSPFLA_SRVTYPE_IMP_EXEC_REF can be used when reference data is used.

4. Select the **Methods** tab (see Figure 3.35, callout 3). The interface IF_RSPFLA_SRVTYPE_IMP_EXEC includes three methods, one that can be executed on initialization, one on actual execution, and one after execution.

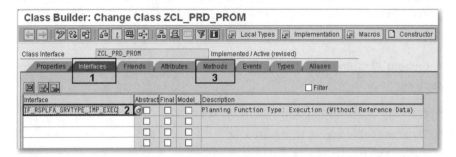

Figure 3.35 Creating a Custom Planning Function — Part 1

5. Double-click the **IF_RSPFLA_SRVTYPE_IMP_EXEC~EXECUTE** method (see Figure 3.36, callout 4). In the text box of the dialog box **Class Builder: Class ZCL_PRD_PROM** that then opens (see Figure 3.36, callout 5), enter the code that follows this step:

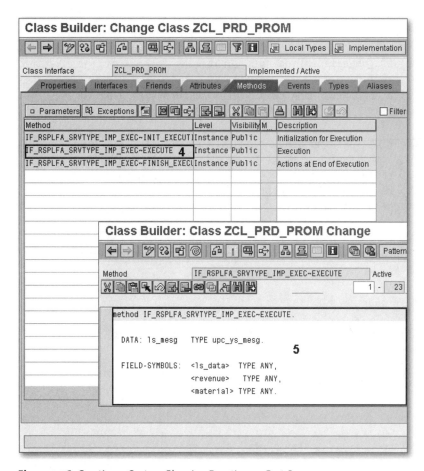

Figure 3.36 Creating a Custom Planning Function — Part 2

```
method IF_RSPLFA_SRVTYPE_IMP_EXEC~EXECUTE.
 DATA: ls_mesg TYPE upc_ys_mesg.

 FIELD-SYMBOLS: <ls_data> TYPE ANY,
 <revenue> TYPE ANY,
 <material> TYPE ANY,
 <ws_material> TYPE ANY.
data: prom_mat_tab type table of zmaterial.
```

```
* Identify the products that are on promotion and store it
* in an internal table
select material from zmaterial
  into table
  prom_mat_tab.

* Loop through the data

loop at c_th_data assigning <ls_data>.

  assign component '0MATERIAL' of structure <ls_data> TO
  <material>.

* Check whether the product on data record is classified
* as promotional.
  read table prom_mat_tab
  with key material = <material>
  assigning <ws_material>.


* If product is classified as promotional, reduce revenue
* by 5%

  if sy-subrc = 0.

  ASSIGN COMPONENT 'ZSLAMT_GC' OF STRUCTURE <ls_data> TO
  <revenue>.

  <revenue> = ( <revenue> * 95 ) / 100.

  endif.

  endloop.

endmethod.
```

6. Click the **Activate** button to activate the class.

7. Using transaction **RSPLF1**, create a **Function Type** ("ZSL_P_CUS") and **Description** ("Recalculate plan sales based on promotions"). In the **Class** text box, enter "ZCL_PRD_PROM" (see Figure 3.37, callout 6).

8. Activate the Planning Function Type.

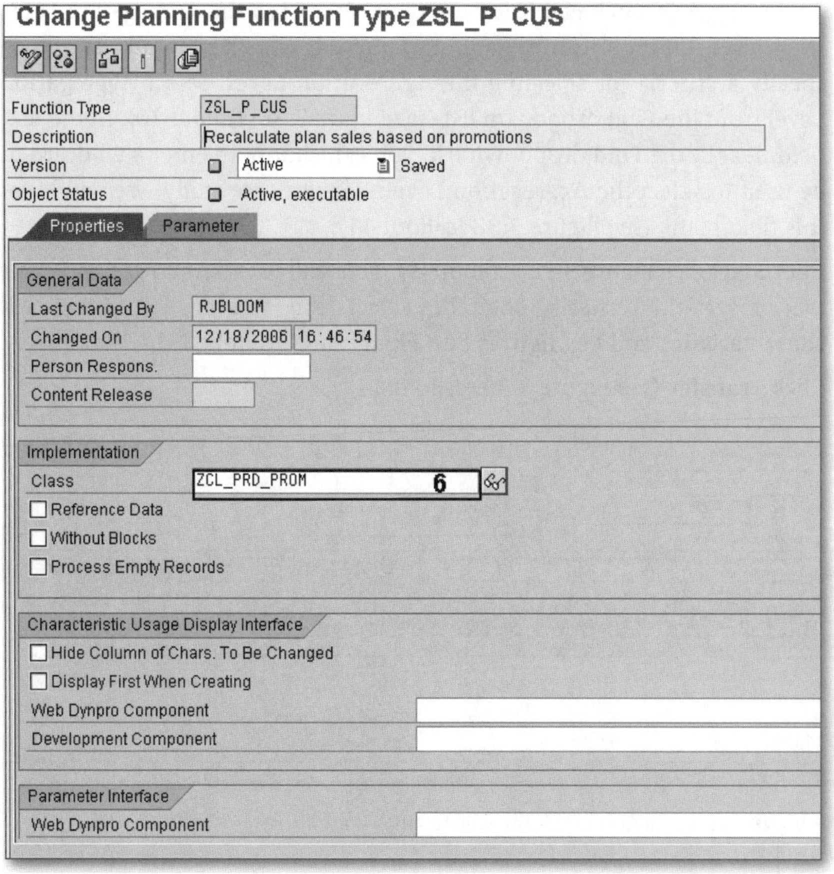

Figure 3.37 Creating a Custom Planning Function — Part 3

We have now created a Custom Planning Function Type that uses a class to reduce the planned sales amount by 5 % for products maintained in the table ZMATERIAL. Next, we will use the Planning Modeler to create a Planning Function based on the Planning Function Type created in the previous steps. Proceed as follows:

1. Click the **Planning Functions** tab.

2. Click **Create** to open the **Create Planning Function** dialog box (see Figure 3.38). Next to **Type**, select **Recalculate plan sales based on promotion** from the dropdown list (see Figure 3.38, callout 7). Enter a **Technical Name** ("ZSL_P_CPF"), and a **Description** ("Adjust plan data rev for products on promotion") for the Planning Function (see Figure 3.38, callouts 8 and 9).

3. Under **Aggregation Level Selection**, you can assign the Aggregation Level to be used by the Custom Planning Function. This screen allows you to specify a criteria for selecting the Aggregation Level. Select **Aggregation Level** from the **Find** dropdown list (see Figure 3.38, callout 10). In the text field next to the **Find** dropdown list, you can choose to enter a wildcard to be used to select the Aggregation Level. For our case study, we will leave this field blank (see Figure 3.38, callout 11).

4. Click **Start** (see Figure 3.38, callout 12). This will list all Aggregation Levels that meet the criteria entered. Select the Aggregation Level **All characteristics and key figures** (see Figure 3.38, callout 13).

5. Click **Transfer** (see Figure 3.38, callout 14).

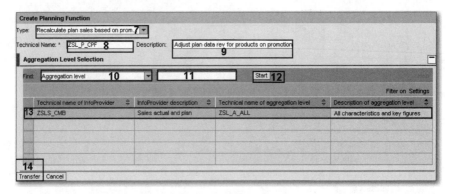

Figure 3.38 Creating a Custom Planning Function — Part 3

6. Save the Custom Planning Function.

You have now seen how to use a Custom Planning Function to read data from a custom table and to adjust plan revenue based on ABAP code in a custom class. Next, we'll show you how to create a Currency Translation Planning Function.

The Currency Translation Planning Function

The Currency Translation Planning Function is used when a Key Figure of type Currency must be converted from one currency to another. The converted amount can be stored in the same Key Figure or in a different Key Figure.

For example, Rich Bloom, Inc.'s operations are spread over several countries. Each location uses the local currency for executing business transactions in that country. If company transactions need to be analyzed and reported in one global currency, it will be necessary to convert the amounts from the local currencies to the global currency using the Currency Planning Function. The global currency is usually the currency used at the company headquarters; in Rich Bloom, Inc.'s case that is US dollars. This conversion might be required, for example, to meet statutory reporting requirements.

The Currency Translation type is used to convert an amount from one currency to another. It can be configured using transaction **RSCUR**. For this configuration, you have to specify the source currency, target currency, time reference, and exchange rate type.

Before we configure a Currency Translation Planning Function, we will configure a Currency Translation type to convert an amount to US dollars, as illustrated in Figure 3.39:

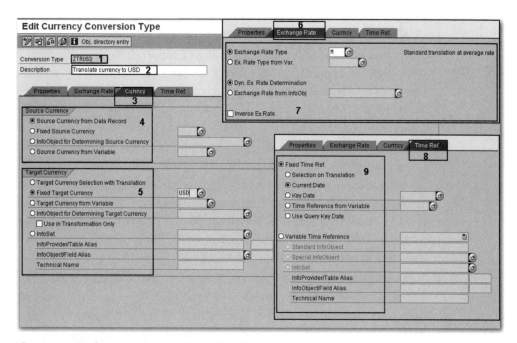

Figure 3.39 Configuring a Currency Transaction Type

1. Execute transaction **RSCUR** to open the **Edit Currency Conversion Type** window. Enter the technical name of the **Conversion Type** ("ZTRUSD") and a **Description** ("Translate currency to USD") (see Figure 3.39, callouts 1 and 2).

2. Click the **Currncy** tab (see Figure 3.39, callout 3). Set the **Source Currency** to **Source Currency from Data Record** (see Figure 3.39, callout 4). Set the

Target Currency to **Fixed Target Currency** equal to "USD" (see Figure 3.39, callout 5).

3. Select the **Exchange Rate** tab (see Figure 3.39, callout 6). Set the **Exchange Rate Type** to "M" (**Standard translation at average rate**) and select **Dyn. Ex. Rate Determination** (see Figure 3.39, callout 7). The exchange rate is normally maintained in the SAP R/3 system and transferred to the SAP NetWeaver BI system on a periodic basis.

4. Select the **Time Ref.** (see Figure 3.39, callout 8) tab and set **Fixed Time Ref.** to **Current Date** (see Figure 3.39, callout 9). This setting will calculate the conversion amount based on the exchange rate as of the date the Planning Function is executed.

We will now create the Currency Translation Planning Function, as illustrated in Figures 3.40, and 3.41:

1. Click the **Planning Function** tab to select it.

2. Click **Create** to open the **Create Planning Function** dialog box (see Figure 3.40). Next to **Type**, select **Currency Translation** from the dropdown list (see Figure 3.40, callout 1). Enter a **Technical Name** ("ZSL_P_TRC"), and a **Description** ("Translate currency") for the Planning Function (see Figure 3.40, callouts 2 and 3).

3. Under **Aggregation Level Selection**, you can assign the Aggregation Level to be used by the Currency Translation Planning Function. This screen allows you to specify a criteria for selecting the Aggregation Level. Select **Aggregation Level** from the **Find** dropdown list (see Figure 3.40, callout 4). In the text field next to the **Find** dropdown list, you can enter a wildcard to be used to select the Aggregation Level. For our case study, we will leave this field blank (see Figure 3.40, callout 5).

4. Click **Start** (see Figure 3.40, callout 6). This will list all Aggregation Levels that meet the criteria entered. Select the Aggregation Level **All characteristics and key figures** (see Figure 3.40, callout 7).

5. Click **Transfer** (see Figure 3.40, callout 8) to display the **Change Planning Function Translate Currency — Parameter** window, shown in Figure 3.41.

6. Two areas, **For Characteristic Usage** and **For Parameters,** are available to configure the settings for the Planning Function.

7. In the **For Characteristic Usage** area, the InfoObjects of the Currency type are automatically selected. Select the Currency InfoObjects that contain the currencies of the Key Figure that needs to be translated; for example,

0CURRENCY. If you want to use conditions, select the Characteristics for which you want to create them.

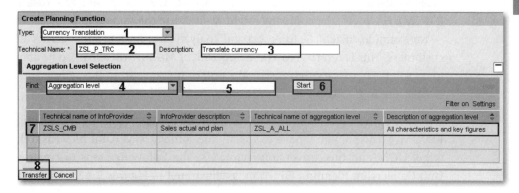

Figure 3.40 Creating a Currency Translation Planning Function — Part 1

8. In the **For Parameters** area, click **New row** (see Figure 3.41, callout 9). Specify the **Target Key Figures** "ZSLAMT_GC" (callout 10), **Source Key Figures** "ZSLAMT_GC" (callout 11) and the **Currency Translation Type** "Translate currency to USD" (callout 12) to be used for converting the Key Figures from the source currency to the target currency.

Figure 3.41 Creating a Currency Translation Planning Function — Part 2

9. Save the Currency Translation Planning Function.

You have now seen how a Currency Translation Planning Function can be used to convert an amount from a source currency to a target currency by using the Currency Translation Planning Function. We'll next show you how to create a Unit Conversion Planning Function.

The Unit Conversion Planning Function

The Unit Conversion Planning Function is used to convert a Key Figure of type Unit from one unit to another. The converted quantity can be stored in the same Key Figure or another Key Figure.

For example, Rich Bloom, Inc. sells the same products to various customers using different units of measure, such as "Dozen" or "Each". The unit of measure used to sell a product is referred to as the *Selling Unit of Measure* (SUOM). However, the company might want to use the same unit of measure — for example, "Each" — to report and analyze sales for a product across all customers. This is referred to as the *Base Unit of Measure* (BUOM). To be able to do so, it is necessary to translate the unit of measure from the Selling Unit of Measure to the Base Unit of Measure.

The Unit Conversion Planning Function can be configured using transaction **RSUOM**. To do so, you'll have to specify the source UOM (Unit of Measure), target UOM and the conversion factor. Use the following steps to create a Unit Conversion Planning Function, as illustrated in Figures 3.42, and 3.43:

1. Click the **Planning Function** tab to select it.

2. Click **Create** to open the **Create Planning Function** dialog box (see Figure 3.42). Next to **Type**, select **Unit Conversion** from the dropdown list (see Figure 3.42, callout 1). Enter a **Technical Name** ("ZSL_P_CVU"), and a **Description** ("Unit Conversion") for the Planning Function (see Figure 3.42, callouts 2 and 3).

3. Under **Aggregation Level Selection**, you can assign the Aggregation Level to be used by the Unit Conversion Planning Function. This screen enables you to specify criteria for selecting the Aggregation Level. Select **Aggregation Level** from the **Find** dropdown list (see Figure 3.42, callout 4). In the text field next to the **Find** dropdown list, you can enter a wildcard for selecting the Aggregation Level. For our case study, we will leave this field blank (see Figure 3.42, callout 5).

4. Click **Start** (see Figure 3.42, callout 6). This will list all Aggregation Levels that meet the criteria entered. Select the Aggregation Level **All characteristics and key figures** (see Figure 3.42, callout 7).

5. Click **Transfer** (see Figure 3.42, callout 8) to display the **Change Planning Function Unit conversion — Parameter** window shown in Figure 3.43. Two areas, **For Characteristic Usage** and **For Parameters,** are available to configure the settings for the Planning Function.

6. In the **For Characteristic Usage** area, the InfoObjects of type Unit are automatically selected. Select the Unit InfoObjects that contain the units of the Key Figure that needs to be converted; for example, 0UNIT. If you want to use conditions, select the Characteristics for which you want to create them.

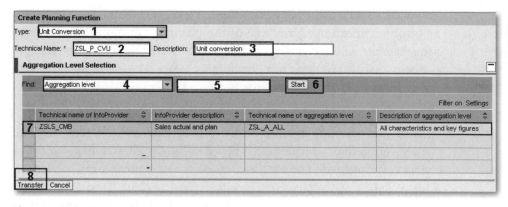

Figure 3.42 Creating a Unit Conversion Planning Function — Part 1

7. In the **Parameters** area, click **New Row** (see Figure 3.43, callout 9). Specify the **Target Key Figures** (see Figure 3.43, callout 10), **Source Key Figures** (see Figure 3.43, callout 11) and the **Unit Conversion Type** (see Figure 3.43, callout 12) to be used for converting the Key Figures from the source unit to the target unit.

8. Save the Unit Conversion Planning Function.

Figure 3.43 Creating a Unit Conversion Planning Function — Part 2

You have now seen how a Unit Conversion Planning Function can be used to convert a quantity from a source UOM to a target UOM by using the Unit Conversion type.

We're now done looking at how different types of Planning Functions are used to meet the needs of a planning application. Next, let's look at the details of creating and using Planning Sequences to execute multiple Planning Functions at once.

3.3.5 The Planning Sequences Tab

The Planning Sequence tab in the Planning Modeler is used to create and maintain *Planning Sequences*. Planning Sequences are used to execute several Planning Functions consecutively. That is, when Planning Functions are grouped into a Planning Sequence, they are executed as one unit. If there is an error when executing any one of the Planning Functions in a Planning Sequence, the whole Planning Sequence fails. Note that it is *not* possible to perform a partial execution of a Planning Sequence. The following are advantages of using a Planning Sequence:

- **Automation**
  Users don't have to execute Planning Functions one at a time. Instead, they can define a Planning Sequence to group all Planning Functions together that need to be executed.

- **Error elimination**
  When Planning Functions are executed one by one by users, they might inadvertently make mistakes. These can include:
  - Selecting an incorrect Filter
  - Executing the Planning Functions in the incorrect order
  - Forgetting to execute a Planning Function

  These problems can be avoided when using a Planning Sequence.

- **Background processing**
  A Planning Sequence can be run in the background. This is especially useful for executing Planning Functions that have long runtimes. For example, Planning Functions will fail when executed directly (in the foreground) if the execution time exceeds the threshold set in the system. If so, you can execute the Planning Function as a global Planning Sequence in the background as a batch job.

- **Integration into Process Chains**
  A Planning Sequence can be integrated into a Process Chain and configured to run after completion of specific steps in the chain. This lets you execute Planning Sequences based on workflow processes.

- **Integration into Planning Applications**
  A Planning Sequence can be integrated and executed inside a planning application.

Planning Sequence Steps

Two different types of steps can be included into a Planning Sequence:

- **Input Template**
  In this type, an Aggregation Level/Filter is specified. It is used to view the results after executing a Planning Function included in a Planning Sequence.

▶ **Planning Function**
   In this type, a Planning Function and the associated Aggregation Level/Filter are specified.

If a Filter or Planning Function includes a variable that is ready for input, a variable screen displays when executing the Planning Sequence. You will have to enter the values for the selection. Alternatively, you can assign variants which contain the values for the selection.

Trace Mode in Planning Sequences

Trace mode provides a step-by-step breakdown of a Planning Function's execution. This can be helpful when a Planning Function does not work as expected and you need to view the details of how the Planning Function was executed.

The details are shown based on block numbers. Clicking a block provides detailed information on how the Planning Function obtained the resulting data. Four tabs are available to analyze the trace. They are:

▶ **Data Before**
   Displays the data before the execution of a Planning Function.

▶ **Data After**
   Displays the data after the execution of Planning Function.

▶ **Reference Data**
   Displays the reference data, if any, used by the Planning Function.

▶ **Data Comparison**
   Displays the before and after data of the Planning Function's execution. This is used for comparison purposes.

In the next section, we will show you how to define a Planning Sequence.

Creating a Planning Sequence

Using the following steps, you will now add the Copy Planning Function and the Revaluation Planning Function to a Planning Sequence, as illustrated in Figures 3.44 and 3.45:

1. Click the **Planning Sequences** tab to select it (see Figure 3.44, callout 1).

2. Click **Create** (see Figure 3.44, callout 2) to open the **Create Planning Sequence** dialog box. Enter the **Technical Name** ("ZSL_S_CRV") and **Description** ("Copy and Revalue plan data") for the Planning Sequence and click the **Transfer** button (see Figure 3.44, callouts 3, 4 and 5).

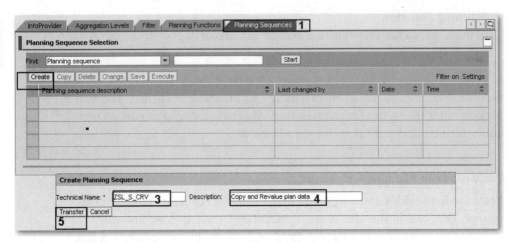

Figure 3.44 Creating a Planning Sequence — Part 1

3. For our case study, we will include two steps in the Planning Sequence: the Copy Planning Function and the Revalue Planning Function. Click **Add step for planning function** to include a Planning Function in the Planning Sequence (see Figure 3.45, callout 6).

4. Select the **Aggregation Level (All characteristics and key figures)**, **Filter (Filter by Company Code)** and **Planning Function (Copy 2006 sales data as 2007 plan)** as a step in the Planning Sequence (see Figure 3.45, callout 7).

5. Use steps 3 and 4 to add the Revalue Planning Function. Figure 3.45, callout 8 shows the results of this action.

6. You can test the steps in the Planning Sequence individually by selecting each step in the lower area of the screen and clicking the **Execute** button. If a detailed trace is required, click the **Execution with trace** button.

7. If you wish to execute all steps in the Planning Sequence as a whole, one after another, you can do so by clicking the **Execute** button in the upper area of the screen.

8. Click the **Save** button to save the Planning Sequence (see Figure 3.45, callout 9).

When executing a Planning Sequence, any manual changes performed to data can be saved permanently. Now that you know how to create a Planning Sequence, we will show you in the following section how to integrate a Planning Sequence into a Process Chain.

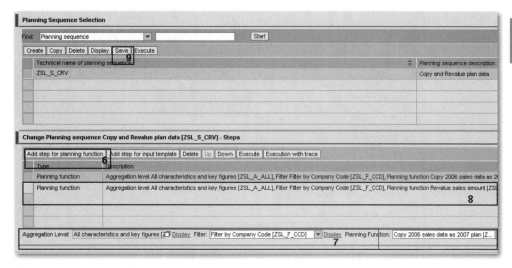

Figure 3.45 Creating a Planning Sequence — Part 2

Integrate a Planning Sequence into a Process Chain

A Process Chain is the scheduling tool provided in the SAP NetWeaver BI system. It can be used to schedule different tasks in the background in a particular sequence. Use the following steps to integrate a Planning Sequence into a Process Chain, as illustrated in Figures 3.46, 3.47 and 3.48:

1. Using transaction **RSPC**, start creating a Process Chain and include the Start Process. The Start Process is the first step in any Process Chain. The Start Variant of the Start Process determines the time when the Process Chain should be executed and can be set to be executed on demand, based on a date and time, or based on an event.

2. Click the linked-chain button to display the Process Types in the left pane of the Process Chain (see Figure 3.46, callout 1).

3. Under **Other BW Processes**, select the **Execute Planning Sequence** process type and drag it into the Process Chain that is displayed in the right pane (see Figure 3.46, callout 2).

4. The **Insert Execute Planning Sequence** dialog box opens. Click the **Create Variant** icon (see Figure 3.46, callout 3).

5. The **Execute Planning Sequence** dialog box opens. Enter a **Process Variants** name ("ZSALES_PLN") and **Long description** ("Execute planning sequence to copy and revalue data") for the variant (see Figure 3.46, callouts 4 and 5).

6. Click **Enter** (see Figure 3.46, callout 6).

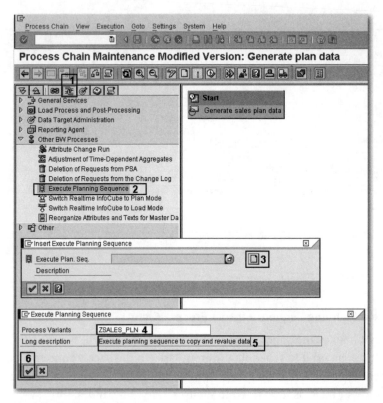

Figure 3.46 Integrating a Planning Sequence into a Process Chain — Part 1

7. In the **Process Maintenance: Execute Planning Sequence** window that now opens, select the **Planning Sequence ZSL_S_CRV**, (see Figure 3.47, callout 7). If the Planning Sequence includes variables, the variant to be used for the Planning Sequence is also set on this screen. If variables are used in the Filter or Planning Function for the selected Planning Sequence, a variant that specifies the value for the variables is set. The variant for the Planning Sequence is created in the Planning Modeler.

8. Save the variant by clicking the **Save** button (see Figure 3.47, callout 8). Use the green arrow to return to the Process Chain definition.

9. Save and activate the Process Chain (see Figure 3.48, callout 9). The Process Chain will be triggered according to the definition in the Start variant. When the Process Chain runs, the Planning Sequence is executed in the background.

You have now seen how to use a Process Chain to automate the creation of plan data for an organization. In the next section, we will look at using Characteristic Relationships in a planning application.

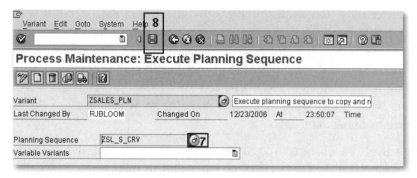

Figure 3.47 Integrating a Planning Sequence into a Process Chain — Part 2

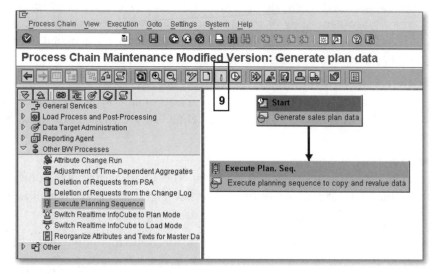

Figure 3.48 Definition of a Process Chain Including a Planning Sequence

3.4 Characteristic Relationships

The relationship between Characteristics in a Real-Time InfoCube is defined by Characteristic Relationships. For example, let's assume that the customer and sales organization Characteristics are included in an InfoCube used for storing plan data. Customer C1 belongs to sales organization S1, Customer C2 belongs to sales organization S2, and so on. There is a relationship between the Characteristics of the customer and the sales organization. The planning tool in SAP NetWeaver BI lets you define the relationship between these Characteristics.

Characteristic Relationships promote the integrity of data stored in a Real-Time InfoCube. By defining relationships, you enforce the validity of data. This is particularly helpful when there are complex associations between Characteristics and when there is a greater likelihood for user-related errors during manual entry of data. Characteristic Relationships help to reduce errors when users perform manual planning or when they use Planning Functions to maintain data.

The value of a Characteristic in planning can be checked, derived or proposed based on the Characteristic Relationship, as follows:

▶ **Check**
The system can check the validity of the data for characteristic relationships when generating or maintaining plan data. In the example we discussed earlier, the check will ensure that customer C1 is assigned only to sales organization S1 and not to sales organization S2.

▶ **Derive**
The data for a target Characteristic can be automatically derived based on the value of a source Characteristic defined in a Characteristic Relationship.

▶ **Propose**
Plan data can be generated based on the Characteristic Relationships defined between Characteristics. The Key Figure fields are not filled in when Characteristic Relationships are used to generate plan data.

Characteristic Relationships can be set to be used with or without derivation, as follows:

▶ **With Derivation**
Use this setting to derive the value of the target Characteristic based on the source Characteristic(s). The target Characteristic must exist in the InfoCube. When using this option, the target Characteristic should also be included in the Aggregation Level.

▶ **Without Derivation**
Use this setting to check the valididity of the combination of values of Characteristics used to enter plan data. If the data that is entered does not match the definition, an error message displays. It is important to note that combination checks will be done only on new records. Data that existed in the InfoCube before the Characteristic Relationship was created may not be valid based on the new relationships. Such records can continue to exist, but they are not checked. Existing data that fails the combi-

nation check cannot be changed. The data will, however, be displayed in the layout.

The basis of a Characteristic Relationship can be one of the following:

► **Attribute**
This type is selected when the target Characteristic is an attribute of the source Characteristic. The attribute value is used to either check, derive, or propose the value of a target Characteristic. In this case, both the source Characteristic and the target Characteristic should belong to the InfoCube.

► **Data Store**
The data records in the Data Store are used for defining the relationship. When using the Data Store for checking, derivation, or proposal, the keys of the Data Store should be included as source Characteristics in the InfoCube.

► **Hierarchy**
This type is based on a hierarchy created in the BI system. Only one source Characteristic and one target Characteristic can be used for this option. The source and target Characteristics should be in the selected hierarchy. A hierarchy must exist including the source and target Characteristic. A typical example of this is a hierarchical display of the relationship between Material and Material Group. A number of Materials are displayed under a Material Group in a hierarchical format.

► **Exit**
The relationship is defined using a custom ABAP class. The class should implement the interface IF_RSPLS_CR_EXIT. The interface includes three methods: propose, check, and derive. A corresponding method is coded based on the type of relationship that is required.

The Characteristic Relationship for a Real-Time InfoCube used in BI Integrated planning is set on the InfoProvider tab of the Planning Modeler.

To look at our sample company again, Rich Bloom, Inc. uses Cost Center and Business Area InfoObjects in the Plan InfoCube. The Business Area InfoObject is an attribute of the Cost Center InfoObject. The values for Business Area are dependent on Cost Center. During planning, the values of Business Area need to be derived from the Cost Center InfoObject.

Perform the following steps to configure a Characteristic Relationship, as illustrated in Figure 3.49:

1. On the **InfoProvider** tab of the Planning Modeler, select the InfoProvider for planning (**Plan InfoCube**). For setting Characteristic Relationships, the InfoProvider should always be a Real-Time InfoCube.

2. Select the **Characteristic Relationship** tab (see Figure 3.49, callout 1).

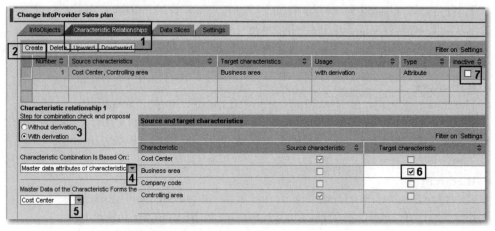

Figure 3.49 Creating a Characteristic Relationship

3. Click the **Create** button (see Figure 3.49, callout 2).

4. Select **Characteristic relationship 1** to be **With Derivation** (see Figure 3.49, callout 3). For our case study, we will use the Cost Center master data to derive the Business Area. The Cost Center is the source Characteristic and Business Area is the target Characteristic.

5. Select the Characteristic combination to be based on **Master data attributes of characteristic** (see Figure 3.49, callout 4).

6. When selecting the attribute as the basis for defining the combination check, select the **Cost Center** as the source InfoObject (see Figure 3.49, callout 5). Select **Business area** as the target Characteristic (see Figure 3.49, callout 6).

7. Save the Characteristic Relationship by clicking the **Save** button on the InfoProvider tab. The definitions take effect immediately.

8. If you want to deactivate a Characteristic Relationship, select the **Inactive** checkbox (see Figure 3.49, callout 7).

Please note the following when defining Characteristic Relationships.

▸ The Characteristic Relationship plays an important role when the association and relation between business entities will be considered in the planning process to check, derive, or propose combinations of data.

▶ Characteristic Relationships can be created only on a Real-Time InfoCube. If Characteristic Relationships are defined on a Real-Time InfoCube, the relationship is enforced on all MultiProviders that include that InfoCube.

▶ When Characteristic Relationships are defined, it takes additional time to process the data. To that extent, performance is affected by the choice whether to use Characteristic Relationships for combination checks or for automatically deriving the data. This has to be taken into account when making a decision to use Characteristic Relationships.

▶ If a Characteristic is set to be derived using the relationship, the Characteristic should not be included in the Input Enabled Query or Planning Function. An Input-Enabled query is a query used for manual planning. If the Characteristic is included in the Input-Enabled query, the derivation will not work.

▶ Data that exists in an InfoCube before the Characteristic Relationship is defined might not conform to the defined relationship. The Planning Function "Delete Invalid combinations of data" is available to delete any data that does not satisfy the current Characteristic Relationships. The Planning Function "Repost Invalid Combinations" will repost data based on the current Characteristic Relationship.

In this section, you have seen the benefits and usage of Characteristic Relationships in a planning application. In the next section, we will discuss how to use Data Slices.

3.5 Data Slices

In the SAP NetWeaver BI Integrated Planning tool, a user responsible for planning can make changes to the plan data through an Input-Enabled query. The user can also modify the data using Planning Functions. In some cases, you may need to restrict changes to data for a set of Characteristic values. For example, after the planning process is completed and approved by management for a given period, the data may have to be locked against any changes. The Data Slice planning object helps in meeting this objective.

When a Data Slice is created, the data records that are selected based on its definition are prevented from being changed. In this scenario, you can't change the data through manual entry or through Planning Functions. If a user tries to make changes to a plan that is protected by a Data Slice, an error message displays.

195

A Data Slice is created with respect to an InfoProvider identified for planning and it is defined on the InfoProvider tab of the Planning Modeler. A Data Slice can be created using selections entered manually by specifying fixed values, or by a variable to dynamically determine the values. A variable provides more flexibility and can be used continuously without making changes to planning objects.

A Data Slice can also be implemented based on a user-exit. When a Data Slice is created in this way, the user-exit determines the logic to select data that needs to be protected against changes. In this case, a custom ABAP class for interface IF_RSPLS_DS_EXIT should be implemented. When a Data Slice is created and saved, it is automatically activated. However, a Data Slice can be deactivated at any time.

Let's once again take a look at our sample company, Rich Bloom, Inc. The company has completed the process of planning sales data for 2007 and management has approved the data. It has also been decided that the data for this period should be locked so that no further changes can be made. To meet this requirement, you'll create a Data Slice using the following steps, as illustrated in Figures 3.50 and 3.51:

1. On the **InfoProvider** tab of the Planning Modeler, select the InfoProvider for planning (**Plan InfoCube**). The InfoProvider should be a Real-Time InfoCube for configuring Data Slices.

2. Select the **Data Slices** tab (see Figure 3.50, callout 1).

3. Click the **Create** button (see Figure 3.50, callout 2).

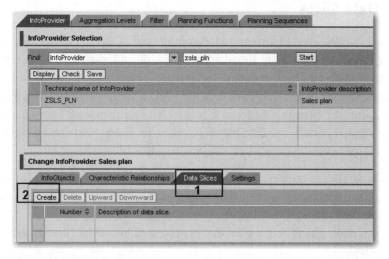

Figure 3.50 Creating a Data Slice — Part 1

4. Enter a description ("Disallow changes to Plan data for Calendar Year 2007") for the Data Slice (see Figure 3.51, callout 3).

5. Select the type for implementing **Data Slice 1** (see Figure 3.51, callout 4). For our case study, choose **for a selection** from the **Data Slice Is Based On** dropdown list.

6. Set the value(s) to be used by the Data Slice definition (see Figure 3.51, callout 5). If needed, you can use a variable to specify the values. For our case study, set the value of Calendar Year to 2007.

7. Save the Data Slice by clicking the **Save** button on the InfoProvider tab. The Data Slice is activated automatically on saving.

8. If you want to deactivate the Data Slice, check the **Inactive** check box (see Figure 3.51, callout 6) and save the changes.

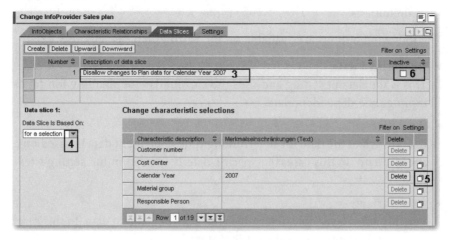

Figure 3.51 Creating a Data Slice — Part 2

Please note the following when defining Data Slices:

▸ Data Slices can be created only on a Real-Time InfoCube. If Data Slices are defined on a Real-Time InfoCube, the lock is enforced on all MultiProviders that include that InfoCube.

▸ When a Data Slice is created based on a selection, changes are prevented in the data records for the selection.

▸ When a Data Slice is created based on a user exit, changes are prevented in the data records for the selection that is implemented in the user exit.

▸ If a Data Slice is defined and no selection or logic is defined in the user exit, then change is prevented for all records in the underlying InfoProvider. It is important to ensure that selections or logic is valid when defining a Data Slice.

In this section, we have seen the benefits and usage of Data Slices in a planning application. In the next section, we will discuss the options available on the InfoProvider **Settings** tab.

3.6 Settings

When a Real-Time InfoCube contains time-dependent data, the basis for determining the time-dependent data for planning is configured on the **Settings** tab of an InfoProvider. The settings apply only to Real-Time InfoCubes and any MultiProviders that contain the Real-Time InfoCube(s) in their definitions.

The following options are available on the **Settings** tab (see Figure 3.52).

▶ **Unspecified date**
  This is the default setting and uses the current date of planning for determining time-dependent data.

▶ **fixed date**
  Use this when the date for determining time-dependent data is based on a specific date. In this case, the specific date is entered in the setting's text field.

▶ **from variable**
  Use this when a variable determines the time-dependent data. In this case, the variable is entered in the setting's text field.

This tab also contains the maximum number of records that can be generated when using the Planning Function **Generate Combinations** to generate data. The default is **50,000** records.

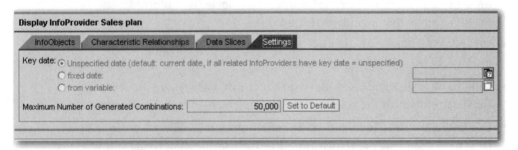

Figure 3.52 Time Dependency Settings

3.7   Summary

In this chapter, based on the requirements of our case study, you have completed the initial steps of configuring a planning application, created Planning Functions to meet the requirements for planning, learned about Planning Sequences, and seen how they can be integrated into a Process Chain. You've also analyzed the use of Characteristic Relationships, Data Slices, and Settings that are specific to an InfoProvider.

You now have the objects you need to create a complete planning application user interface, which you will do in Chapter 4. You will also make the interface available to users. The main objective in developing the application will be to plan for the gross profit margin, based on planned sales and cost information.

This chapter walks you through the development of a complete planning application user interface that will meet the requirements of the case study that was detailed in Chapter 2. This chapter will also describe the various tools available for building a user planning application in the SAP NetWeaver BI system.

4 SAP NetWeaver BI Integrated Planning — User Interface

We'll begin this chapter by introducing the range of tools available to users for planning and reporting in the SAP NetWeaver BI system. Next, we will illustrate the steps in defining an Input-Enabled Query for creating and modifying the plan data, using the planning objects created in Chapter 3.

Subsequently, we will discuss the steps for creating a planning application user interface using the BEx Analyzer tool. More specifically, we'll show you how to integrate the Input-Enabled Query we will create in this chapter and the planning objects we created in Chapter 2 into a Microsoft Excel workbook.

Later in the chapter, we will describe the steps for creating a planning application user interface on the Web. The BEx Web Application Designer tool is used for this purpose. Finally, we illustrate the steps to create a query that will meet the key requirement of Rich Bloom, Inc. to analyze the planned gross profit margin. We will see how the plan data created using the planning application can be used to plan the gross profit margin. Let's start by looking at the different options available for reporting using the BEx suite of tools and Visual Composer.

4.1 Reporting Tools in SAP NetWeaver BI

The SAP BI system provides a range of tools that enable planning and reporting. They are:

▶ BEx Query Designer
▶ BEx Analyzer

- BEx Web Application Designer
- BEx Report Designer
- Visual Composer

Lets look at each of these tools in more detail.

4.1.1 BEx Query Designer

The BEx Query Designer is the tool that is used to create queries in the SAP NetWeaver BI system. A query is used for analyzing data. Some of the key features of the BEx Query Designer include variables, drill-down capabilities, conditions, exceptions, Input-Enabled Queries, the ability to use information broadcasting, and enabling queries for use with third-party applications. Let's look at each of these features in more detail.

Variables

A variable can be defined to restrict the data returned when a query is executed. Different types of variables are supported and can be used based on the requirements of a query. The variable that prompts for user input when executing a query is the most common type of variable used to restrict the data returned by a query.

Drill-Down Capabilities

When a user executes a query, all of the data required for analysis may not be needed at once. The Characteristics that are absolutely required for analysis when a query is executed are included in the **Rows** area of the query. The Characteristics that may be used optionally for analysis are included in the **Free Characteristics** area. The Characteristics included in the Free Characteristics area can be used for analysis as drill-down Characteristics after the query is executed.

Conditions

A condition is used to restrict data returned by a query, based on quantitative information. For example, a condition can be defined to display only the top ten customers, based on sales revenue.

Exceptions

An exception is defined in a query to help analyze the data better. The exception allows for color-coding of the data returned by a query. The color-coding helps users to grasp visually the meaning of data. The color-coding displayed in the output of a query can be used to recognize deviations in data from the standard norm and can help with timely decision-making.

Input-Enabled Query

A special type of query called Input-Enabled Query can be defined for the purpose of planning. A query developed as an Input-Enabled Query can be used for manually creating or modifying plan data. This type of query can be based on the planning objects created using the SAP NetWeaver BI Integrated Planning tool.

Information Broadcasting

A query can be defined to include the Information Broadcasting feature for distributing data. The Information Broadcasting function provides the settings for determining when a query should be executed and how the output of a query should be distributed. The results of a query can be distributed via various channels, such as email, printer, or SAP Enterprise Portal. Users have considerable flexibility in choosing the format for sending the output of a query. Available formats include HTML, online link, and PDF.

Information Broadcasting lets users distribute reports in a timely manner. In addition, Process Chains provide the ability to trigger a process to execute a query and distribute the data as defined in the Information Broadcasting setting.

Enabling queries for Third-Party Applications

A query created in the BEx Query Designer can be enabled for use in third-party applications and used in those applications as the source of data. For example, a query created in the BEx Query Designer can be used in the Crystal Reports application to generate formatted reports.

The SAP Enterprise Portal is a platform supplied by SAP that helps companies to unify business processes by allowing users to access up-to-date information from different systems used by an enterprise. This is the recommended option for deploying the reports created in the SAP NetWeaver BI system to users on the Web. Starting with SAP NetWeaver 7.0, the use of SAP Enterprise Portal is mandatory to use any of the new capabilities available in this release when reporting on the Web. We will now see how the BEx Analyzer tool can be used to deploy a query created in the BEx Query Designer to users.

4.1.2 BEx Analyzer

Many users work with Microsoft Excel software for reporting and analysis. SAP has taken this into consideration when building the software to report data in SAP NetWeaver BI. The BEx Analyzer tool helps users report and analyze data using features available in Microsoft Excel.

The BEx Analyzer tool must be installed as an add-on — along with the SAP GUI — on a user's computer before it can be used to create and execute queries in the SAP NetWeaver BI system. When the BEx Analyzer tool is used, the query is executed and displayed in a Microsoft Excel workbook, which provides users Microsoft Excel features for reporting and analyzing the data.

Use of workbooks is particularly helpful when executing queries related to financial data. The data can be easily integrated and exported to other Microsoft Excel documents in the context of analysis and decision-making. We will now see how the BEx Web Application Designer is used for developing reports from anywhere, using the Internet.

4.1.3 BEx Web Application Designer

The BEx Web Application Designer is used when queries will be deployed on the Web. Queries developed in the BEx Query Designer can be integrated into a Web template using this tool.

One of the significant advantages of using the BEx Web Application Designer for developing reports is that users can run the applications directly on the Web. No special software needs to be installed on users' computers. The only prerequisite for executing applications on the Web is that users should be able to access the Web.

The BEx Web Application Designer in SAP NetWeaver 7.0 provides a sophisticated interface for reporting by allowing users to develop dashboards for presenting key performance indicators (KPIs). All the features that are available when using the BEx Analyzer for reporting are also available when using the BEx Web Application Designer. The BEx Web Application Designer also lets you distribute reports using Information Broadcasting.

The Web template created in the BEx Web Application Designer can be used as the basis for reporting data as an iView in the SAP Enterprise Portal. An iView is an application that can be deployed on a Web page. The application can be sourced from different systems: SAP R/3, SAP CRM, SAP NetWeaver BI, etc.

Prior to SAP NetWeaver 7.0, the Web application server was primarily used as the basis for deploying Web applications developed in the SAP NetWeaver BI system. The SAP Enterprise Portal was not mandatory for deploying the Web application. In SAP NetWeaver 7.0, the SAP Enterprise Portal is required to use any of the new capabilities available in this release when reporting on the Web. The new features introduced in the BEx Web Application Designer can be used when developing the Web templates.

> **Tip**
>
> The output of a query on the Web can be displayed as a PDF document. This is a new feature introduced in SAP NetWeaver 7.0.

You will now see how you can use the BEx Report Designer for developing formatted reports.

4.1.4   BEx Report Designer

The BEx Report Designer is a new tool introduced in SAP NetWeaver 7.0 to meet the requirements of formatted reporting. One of the main limitations when using the BEx tools prior to SAP NetWeaver 7.0 was the complexity and limited functionality for creating formatted reports. Even though the Web application provided for features to create formatted reports, they required additional customization and did not fully satisfy all of the user requirements. Users sometimes needed third-party software to develop formatted reports.

The above limitations led SAP to create the BEx Report Designer, an exclusive tool for formatted reporting. It is especially useful when the generated reports are to be sent to customers or vendors in a particular format and when the BEx Analyzer and the BEx Web Application Designer tools cannot fully satisfy this requirement. Next, we will look into how Visual Composer can be used to integrate information from multiple systems.

4.1.5 Visual Composer

The data used by an enterprise might be in different systems: SAP R/3, SAP CRM, Oracle, Informix, etc. The data from these systems may need to be presented as a homogenous report. Visual Composer can be used in this case to bring data from multiple systems and present in a single interface.

Visual Composer uses the SAP Enterprise Portal for defining and executing reports. A Visual Composer report is defined and saved as an iView in the SAP Enterprise Portal and made available to users.

Note
SAP plans to use Visual Composer extensively in future releases as a key vehicle for reporting. The features available in the BEx Web Application Designer are also expected to be made available in Visual Composer.

In this section, we briefly discussed the different tools available for reporting data and explained features offered by the BEx suite of tools and Visual Composer. In the next section, we will create a query that will be used as the basis for manually creating and modifying plan data.

4.2 Creating an Input-Enabled Query for Planning

With the introduction of BI Integrated Planning in SAP NetWeaver 7.0, a new feature of the BEx Query Designer is the Input-Enabled Query. An Input-Enabled Query is used only in the context of a planning application. It makes it possible to create and modify data in a Real-Time InfoCube.

One of the objectives that our model company, Rich Bloom, Inc., would like to achieve using the SAP NetWeaver BI Integrated Planning tool is to make available a complete planning application that would help the sales force to plan data for 2007. One of the requirements is to create a query that can be used for entering the plan data. Although the actual sales data for 2006 will be used as reference data for planning for 2007, the company expects to make manual changes to reflect the demand for the period.

In Chapter 2, we discussed the steps to create a query using the BEx Query Designer. We will now use the same steps to create a query that will be used for planning. The query created for this requirement will be enabled for user input. The following steps are used to create an Input-Enabled Query:

1. Launch the BEx Query Designer tool from your PC using the menu path **Start • Programs • Business Explorer • Query Designer.** The BEx Query Designer toolbar displays. Click **Create** on the toolbar to display the **New Query: Select Infoprovider** dialog box.

2. The next step is to select an InfoProvider for the query from the list displayed in the dialog box. An Input-Enabled Query should be created based on an InfoProvider of type Aggregation Level. The Aggregation Level is created using the Planning Modeler. For our case study, select the Aggregation Level (**[ZSL_A_ALL]**, **All characteristics and Key Figures**) (see Figure 4.1, callout 1).

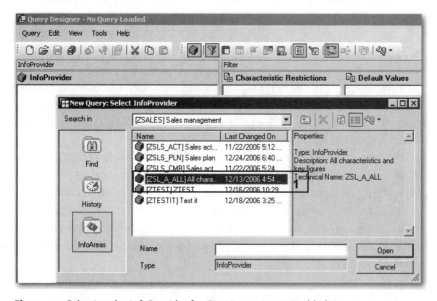

Figure 4.1 Selecting the InfoProvider for Creating an Input-Enabled Query

3. The **Query Designer — Query:** *<technical name>* screen displays, showing the **Filter** tab. In the **Characteristic Restrictions** area, include the Characteristics that will be used as the basis for filtering the data returned by the query. When a Characteristic is included in this area, you must specify a type of restriction for the Characteristic. The restriction can be based on variables or fixed values (see Figure 4.2, callout 2). The restrictions that are set here are permanent and cannot be changed during navigation of the query. For our case study, set the following restrictions:

- ▸ Company Code = 20 (Rich Bloom, Inc.)
- ▸ Sales Office = S01 (US sales office)

- Country = US (USA)
- Controlling Area = 1000 (Rich Bloom)
- Distribution Channel = 70 (Direct Distribution)
- InfoProvider = ZSLS_PLN (Sales plan)
- Value Type = 20 (Plan)
- Version = 01 (Plan Version: Change 1)
- Currency = USD (United States Dollar)
- Sales Unit = EA (Each)
- Sales Organization = 20 (Rich Bloom Inc, San Diego,CA,USA)

Note

The restrictions for the Input-Enabled Query can also be based on a Filter planning object. If a Filter planning object is configured for the Aggregation Level that is used by a query, then the Filter object can be seen under a separate folder along with the Dimension and Key Figure folders. Users can drag and drop the Filter planning object from the folder to the Characteristic Restrictions area.

4. Next, you can include restrictions in the **Default Values** area of the query. The Characteristics included in the **Default Values** area can be used for specifying temporary Filters for the query; that is, those that can be changed while navigating the query. The Characteristics included here can also be included in the Free Characteristics area or the Rows area of the query. For our case study, we will not set any restrictions directly in the **Default Values** area.

Note

You will notice that in Figure 4.2, callout 3, Characteristics are included in the Default Values area. This is because Characteristics included in the Row or Column areas of the query, as we will do in the next step, are automatically added to the Default Values area.

5. Click the **Rows/Columns** tab (see Figure 4.2, callout 4).

6. Identify the Characteristics and Key Figures to be used in the **Free Characteristics**, **Rows** and **Columns** areas. The Characteristics included in the **Free Characteristics** area (see Figure 4.3, callout 5) are not displayed immediately but are available for drill-down after the query is executed.

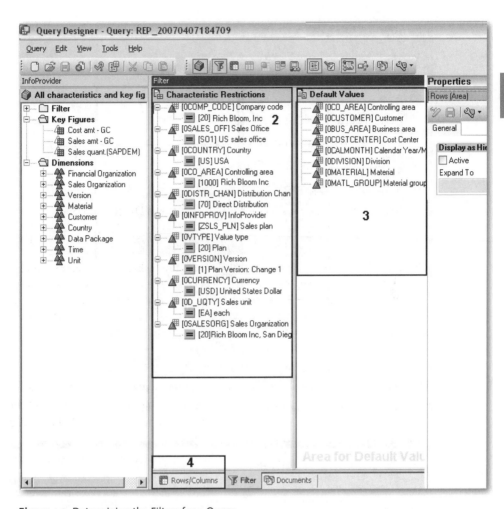

Figure 4.2 Determining the Filters for a Query

For our case study, in the **Free Characteristics** area, we will include the Controlling Area Characteristic and in the **Rows** area of the query, include **Material group**, **Calendar Year/Month**, **Material**, **Division**, **Business area**, **Cost Center** and **Customer Characteristics** (see Figure 4.3, callout 6).

7. The Key Figures are usually included in the **Columns** area of the query (see Figure 4.3, callout 7). For our case study, include the planned **Quantity**, **Sales amt — GC** and **Cost amt — GC** Key Figures.

8. Next, you'll need to set the properties of the query. For our case study, we'll set the query to be an Input-Enabled Query. To do so, on the **Extended** tab of the **Properties** pane of the query, select the **Start Query in Change Mode** checkbox (Figure 4.4, callout 8 and 9).

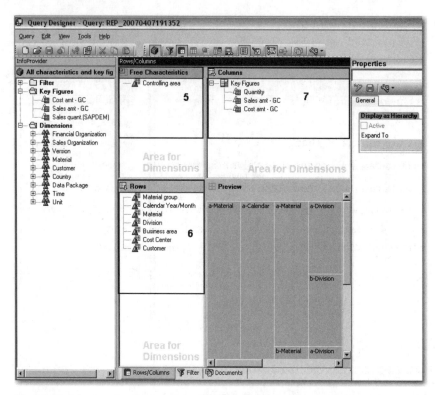

Figure 4.3 Selecting the Characteristics and Key Figures for the Query

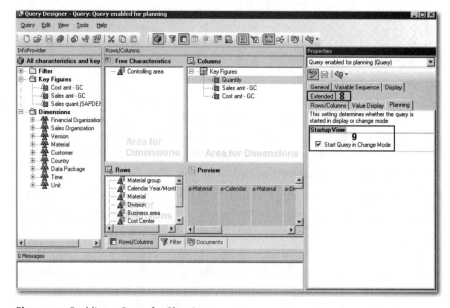

Figure 4.4 Enabling a Query for Planning

9. Next, you will need to set the properties of Characteristics and Key Figures. Click the individual Characteristics or Key Figures in the **Columns** or **Rows** pane and configure the desired settings in the Properties pane.

You need to set the property for the Key Figures for which the data can be changed (or cannot be changed) by the query. The following options are available:

▸ **Data cannot be changed**

▸ **Data can be changed using planning functions**

▸ **Data can be changed using user entries or planning functions**

For our case study, on the **Planning** tab for the selected Key Figure (see Figure 4.5, callouts 10 and 11), set **Quantity**, **Sales amt — GC** and **Cost amt — GC** to be changed using user entries or planning functions.

Note

SAP NetWeaver 7.0 provides advanced features to select multiple Characteristics and Key Figures at once. This is useful when a property setting applies to more than one Characteristic or Key Figure.

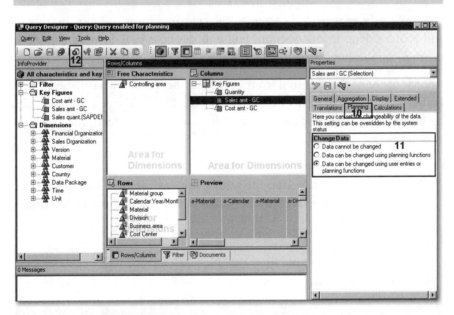

Figure 4.5 Enabling a Key Figure for Changes to Data

10. Save the query by specifying a technical name and description for the query. The query can be tested by selecting the **Query Execute** button (see Figure 4.5, callout 12).

You have now created an Input-Enabled Query for planning. The Input-Enabled Query will be integrated into a planning application and made available to users. The planning application will contain all of the planning requirements listed by Rich Bloom, Inc. in the case study.

> **Note**
>
> When a user maintains plan data using an Input-Enabled Query, all of the Characteristic and Key Figure values pertaining to each of the rows will be written to the Plan InfoCube. It is important that the design of the Input-Enabled Query ensures that for each row entered, the values of all Characteristics in the Aggregation Level are uniquely identified.

In the next section, we will see how to create a planning application using the BEx Analyzer tool.

4.3 Creating a Planning Application User Interface Using the BEx Analyzer

The BEx Analyzer provides a Microsoft Excel-based front end to plan, report and analyze data. In this section, you will see how to develop a complete planning application using the BEx Analyzer tool.

Launch the BEx Analyzer tool from your PC using the menu path **Start • Programs • Business Explorer • BEx Analyzer**. The BEx Analyzer add-on should be installed on the computer for this purpose. The BEx Analyzer provides two toolbars:

▶ **Analysis**
The Analysis toolbar is used for setting the environment to report data, maintain Microsoft Excel workbooks and execute queries and Microsoft Excel workbooks.

▶ **Design**
The Design toolbar is used for designing a Microsoft Excel workbook or a planning application.

> **Note**
>
> A workbook is a Microsoft Excel spreadsheet that contains the results of executing a query.

We will now discuss the different options available on the **Analysis** toolbar.

4.3.1 Analysis Toolbar

The Analysis Toolbar contains eight options, as shown in Figure 4.6. Let's look at each option in more detail.

Figure 4.6 Analysis Toolbar in the BEx Analyzer

Open

Click **Open** (see Figure 4.6, callout 1) to open a query or workbook in the BEx Analyzer.

Save

Click **Save** (see Figure 4.6, callout 2) to display the **Save Workbook**, **Save Workbook As** and **Save View** options. The **Save** option allows you to save the current workbook displayed in the Analyzer. The **Save Workbook As** option is used for saving the workbook in a different name. The **Save View** option is used for saving the current state of the workbook as a view.

Refresh/Pause Refresh

Click **Refresh/Pause** (see Figure 4.6, callout 3) to toggle between Refresh and Pause. A refresh requests current data from the system for an active workbook. If Refresh has been clicked, clicking it again will pause the refreshing of current data.

Change Variable Values

Click **Change Variable Values** (see Figure 4.6, callout 4) to change the values of the variables that are used in a query associated with the workbook. When a workbook includes a query that uses variables, these variables are processed and the **Select Value for Variable** screen displays for any variables that allow user input.

Tools

Click **Tools** (see Figure 4.6, callout 5) to gain access to other BEx tools or launch the Planning Modeler. The following sub-menus are available:

▶ **Create New Query**
Lets you create a new query using the BEx Query Designer.

▶ **Edit Query** *<Query Name>*
Lets you edit the query associated with the current workbook. The *<Query Name>* represents the query associated with the current workbook.

▶ **BEx Information Broadcaster**
Lets you use the broadcast features to pre-calculate and distribute workbooks.

▶ **Planning Modeler**
Lets you launch the Web-based application for creating and maintaining planning objects when using the BI Integrated Planning tool.

▶ **BEx Report Designer**
Lets you design and execute formatted reports.

▶ **BEx Web Analyzer**
Lets you perform ad hoc analysis of data in InfoProviders on the Web.

Global Settings

Click **Global Settings** (see Figure 4.6, callout 6) to configure settings for all of the objects maintained in the BEx Analyzer. To do so, you have four tabs available.

▶ **Behavior**
The **Behavior** tab lets you configure the following settings:

  ▷ **Maximum number of Objects in Local History**
  Lets you control the display of the number of queries and workbooks recently opened or edited in the History sub-menu option. The number of entries in this list is based on this setting.

  ▷ **Display System Name in Local History**
  Lets you display the system name of queries and workbooks when listing the history information.

  ▷ **Log on with Attached SAP GUI**
  Lets you receive messages from the server.

  ▷ **Legacy Version from Easy Access Menu**
  Lets you launch the 3.x version of BEx Analyzer when using the RRMX transaction.

  ▷ **Launch Analyzer When Excel Starts**
  Lets you start the BEx Analyzer when Microsoft Excel is launched.

▶ **Select Default Workbook**
Lets you set the default workbook where the output of a query is to be displayed.

▶ **Trace**
Let you collect information for a BEx Analyzer session. The information in trace files can be used for further analysis when encountering issues with the BEx Analyzer.

▶ **Statistics**
Lets you log performance data associated with executing queries.

Connect/System Information

Click **Connect/System Information** (see Figure 4.6, callout 7) to display the SAP NetWeaver BI system to which you are connected. This item can also be used to connect to or disconnect from a system.

Application Help

Click **Application Help** to display two sub-menus:

▶ **Application Help**
Provides detailed help on the BEx Analyzer tool.

▶ **About**
Displays the version of the BEx Analyzer that is being used.

We can now discuss the different options available in the **Design** toolbar.

4.3.2 Design Toolbar

The Design toolbar, as shown in Figure 4.7, is used to design a workbook or a planning application. The Design toolbar is a new feature in SAP NetWeaver 7.0 and provides the same set of tools available in the BEx Web Application Designer. The output of the data when using the BEx Analyzer displays in a workbook.

Figure 4.7 Design Toolbar in the BEx Analyzer

The Design toolbar contains thirteen options. Let's look at each option in more detail:

Design Mode

Click **Design Mode** (see Figure 4.7, callout 1) to toggle between Design mode and Analysis mode. Design mode is used to design a workbook or a planning application. Analysis mode is used to execute a workbook or a planning application.

Analysis Grid

Click and drag the **Analysis Grid** item (see Figure 4.7, callout 2) into a workbook to display the results of a query in a tabular format. This is the most commonly used option and is used to display the output of a query. The **Analysis Grid** item can also be inserted into a workbook by selecting a cell in the workbook and then clicking **Analysis Grid**. More than one **Analysis Grid** item can be included in a workbook.

The properties of an **Analysis Grid** item can be set by right-clicking it and choosing one of the following tabs that relate to the display of the results of a query:

▶ **General**
  The following settings can be configured on this tab.

  ▷ **Data Provider**
    Lets you set the source of data for the Analysis Grid item. A query can be set as a Data Provider. The results of the query selected in the Data Provider are displayed in the workbook.

  ▷ **Range**
    Lets you set the size and the location where the item is to be displayed in the workbook.

  ▷ **Use Formulas**
    Lets you set any cell that displays in the Analysis Grid to be replaced by a formula developed using formula feature in Microsoft Excel.

  ▷ **Adjust Print Area**
    Lets you automatically adjust the Print Area for the Analysis Grid item in the workbook.

  ▷ **Enable Cell Protection**
    This property is used in the context of planning and lets you protect cells that are not defined as modifiable in a query from being changed in the workbook.

▶ **Apply Formatting**
Lets you format results displayed in a workbook. When the checkbox for this property is deselected, all formatting for the workbook is turned off. De-selecting this option may help to improve performance.

▶ **Allow Navigation**
This property is set to allow navigation for the Analysis Grid item. If this option is de-selected, the context menu is not available and further navigation is not possible for the item. You cannot use drag-and-drop functionality in this case.

▶ **AutoFit**
Lets you set the cells of the Analysis Grid item to expand and display the full width of the data.

▶ **Display Sort Icons**
Lets you sort the Characteristics and Key Figures in the Analysis Grid in ascending and descending order. The **Sort** icon displays along with the description for the header columns when this option is enabled.

▶ **Display Hierarchy Icons**
This property is useful when displaying data in a hierarchical format. It lets you expand and collapse the hierarchical data.

▶ **Clipping**
Lets you set scrolling for horizontal or vertical data in the table.

▶ **Associated Chart**
Lets you display the chart associated with the data displayed in an Analysis Grid.

Navigation Pane

Click **Navigation Pane** (see Figure 4.7, callout 3) to further filter and drill down through the results of the execution of a query in a workbook. The navigation pane is associated with a Data Provider and lets you navigate by the Characteristics and Structures contained in the Data Provider.

Filter List

Click **Filter List** (see Figure 4.7, callout 4) to display the active filters for the Characteristics selected in this list.

Button

Click **Button** (see Figure 4.7, callout 5) to enable the execution of a command in a workbook. Commands are a new feature introduced in SAP NetWeaver 7.0 and enable users to define a wide range of functions in the report. The commands help to enhance the user experience when executing the report.

Dropdown Box

Click **Dropdown Box** (see Figure 4.7, callout 6) to select data that is displayed in a workbook. This option is typically used to select data that is displayed in the Analysis Grid item. A Data Provider is associated with the Dropdown Box item, and a Characteristic included in the Data Provider is chosen as a Characteristic for selection.

You can use three tabs to set the properties of the Dropdown Box. They are the **General** tab, the **Dimensions** tab, and the **Target Data Providers** tab.

- **General**
  Used to set the following properties of the Dropdown Box:
  - Data Providers to be used as the basis for the item
  - Range to set the size and location of the item
  - Label for the item
- **Dimensions**
  Used to set the Characteristic for the Dropdown Box. In addition, the Read Mode can be specified on this tab. The Read Mode determines the data displayed in the filter. Three options are possible for displaying the data.
  - **Posted Values**
    The values that are in the fact table of the InfoProvider for the Characteristic are displayed.
  - **Dimension Table**
    The values on the Dimension tab of the InfoProvider for the Characteristic are displayed.
  - **Master data Table**
    The values that are in the master data for the Characteristic are displayed.
- **Target Data Provider**
  Used to set the Data Providers that will be affected when a selection is made in the Dropdown Box. When a selection is made in the Dropdown Box, all Web items associated with the Target Data Provider will be filtered based on the selection.

Checkbox Group

Click **Checkbox Group** (see Figure 4.7, callout 7) to display a list of all values for a Characteristic and allow users to select multiple values.

Radio Button Group

Click **Radio Button Group** (see Figure 4.7, callout 8) to display a list of all values for a Characteristic and allow users to select one of the values.

List of Conditions

Click **List of Conditions** (see Figure 4.7, callout 9) to display the conditions that are associated with a query as a list. The conditions are defined in the query. Users will be able to activate and deactivate the conditions in the workbook.

List of Exceptions

Click **List of Exceptions** (see Figure 4.7, callout 10) to display the exceptions associated with a query as a list. The Exceptions are defined in the query. Users will be able to activate and deactivate the exceptions in the workbook.

Text Design

Click **Text Design** (see Figure 4.7, callout 11) to display information about a query displayed in the workbook. Properties such as the author of the query, query description, or InfoProvider can be displayed.

Messages

Click **Messages** (see Figure 4.7, callout 12) to display messages associated when executing a query inside a workbook. Options are available to display warning, success, and informational messages.

Workbook Setting

Click **Workbook Setting** (see Figure 4.7, callout 13) to display the settings for the workbook. Among the settings available here are those that enable you to refresh the workbook and process the variable screen when opening the workbook.

4.3.3 Steps to Create a Planning Application User Interface Using the BEx Analyzer Tool

You have now seen the functions that are available in the BEx Analyzer Analysis and Design toolbars. Next, we will explore the usage of these design elements in our planning application.

Looking once again at our sample company, Rich Bloom, Inc., we know that the company wants to create a complete planning application to plan for the gross profit margin. In Chapter 3, we created several Planning Functions that could be used in the planning application. In Section 4.2, we created an Input-Enabled Query that will be used for planning. Let's now create a planning application using the BEx Analyzer tool.

Preparing the BEx Analyzer Tool for Security

Before you can begin to create a Planning Application using the BEx Analyzer, you need to configure security settings, as shown in the following steps and illustrated in Figure 4.8:

1. Launch the BEx Analyzer tool from your PC using the menu path **Start • Programs • Business Explorer • BEx Analyzer**.

2. Select **Tools •Macros • Security**.

3. Ensure that macros can be executed in BEx Analyzer by verifying that the option **Trust access to Visual Basic Project** is enabled (see Figure 4.8, callout 1). If it is not, enable it now and click **OK**.

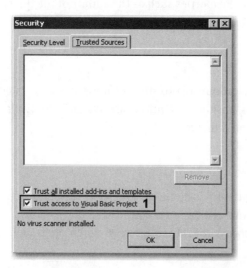

Figure 4.8 Security Settings to Execute Workbooks in the BEx Analyzer

Configuring the Properties for the Analysis Grid Item

Once you have configured the security settings in the BEx Analyzer, the next task is to configure the Properties for the **Analysis Grid** item, as described in the following steps and illustrated in Figure 4.9:

1. The Design mode is automatically enabled. Select a cell on the workbook and click the **Analysis Grid** item in the Design toolbar (see Figure 4.9, callout 2). This adds the item to the workbook.

2. Next, you will set the properties for the **Analysis Grid** item. Right-click the item and select **Properties** (see Figure 4.9, callout 3).

3. You will first assign an Input-Enabled Query as Data Provider for the **Analysis Grid** item. On the **General** tab, click the **Create** button (see Figure 4.9, callout 4) to open the **Create Data Provider** dialog box. Next to the **Query** field, click the **Query Selection** button (see Figure 4.9, callout 5) and select the Input-Enabled Query **ZSLSPLN_INPUT**.

4. Click **OK** (see Figure 4.9, callout 6) to save changes.

5. In the **Behavior** area, define the settings for the **Analysis Grid** item as shown in Figure 4.9, callout 7, and confirm the settings by clicking **OK** (see Figure 4.9, callout 8).

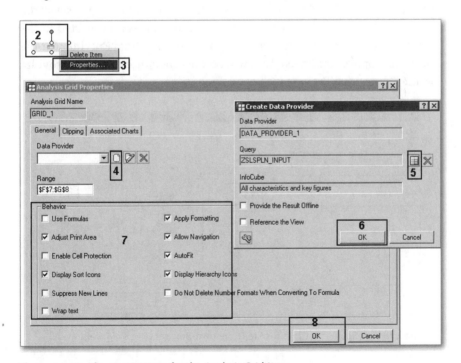

Figure 4.9 Configuring Settings for the Analysis Grid Item

Configuring the Properties for the Dropdown Box Item

The planning application should enable users to restrict the data displayed for planning based on the **Material group** Characteristic. Therefore, we will add a Dropdown Box that will enable users to select a value for **Material group**. Follow these steps:

1. Select a cell in the workbook and click the **Dropdown Box** item in the **Design** pane. This will add the Dropdown Box to the workbook.

2. The next step will be to set the properties for the Dropdown Box item. Right-click the item and select **Properties.** On the **General** tab (see Figure 4.10, callout 9), set the Data Provider to be used for the Dropdown Box item by using the same steps outlined for making the assignment for the Analysis Grid item in the previous task.

3. Click the **Dimensions** tab (see Figure 4.10, callout 10) to select the Characteristic to be used in the Dropdown Box. Choose the **Material group** Characteristic from the dropdown list (see Figure 4.10, callout 11). Select the **Text Type**, **Read Mode,** and **Display** settings as shown in Figure 4.10, callouts 12, 13, 14.

4. Click **OK** (see Figure 4.10, callout 15).

5. Select the **TargetDataProvider** tab (see Figure 4.10, callout 16) to select the target Data Provider that will be affected when values are selected in the Dropdown Box. Because we have assigned only one Data Provider for the planning application, the system will automatically use this Data Provider as the Target Data Provider.

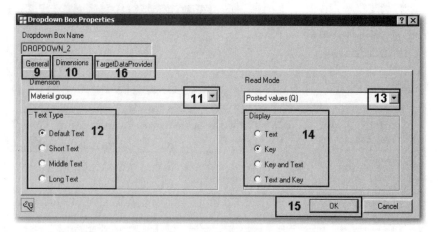

Figure 4.10 Configuring Settings for the Dropdown-Box Item

Configuring the Properties for the Button Item

The planning application should make it possible to use commands for performing tasks such as filtering and drilldown. The **Button** item enables the use of these commands. All of the navigation and command options used in a workbook can be automated via commands. There are also commands that can be used for executing Planning Functions. The necessary command can be enabled by including a **Button** item in a workbook and assigning a command to the **Button**. For our case study, we will include buttons for executing the Copy Planning Function, the Revalue Planning Function, and the Save Area command.

1. Click a workbook cell and add a **Button** item for each of the command that needs to be executed.

2. Right-click the item and select **Properties.** The **Button Properties** window displays. Under **Button Text**, enter the text to display on the button (see Figure 4.11, callout 17).

3. In the **Static Parameters** area of the **Button Properties** window, specify the commands to be executed for each button. The names of the commands and the associated parameters for executing a Planning Function are shown in Table 4.1.

Command Name	Parameter
CMD	EXECUTE_PLANNING_FUNCTION
DATA_PROVIDER_FILTER	<NAME OF THE DATA PROVIDER> The Data Provider that is used as the Filter for the Query is specified here.
PLANNING FUNCTION_NAME	<NAME OF THE PLANNING FUNCTION> The name of the planning function that should be executed is specified here.

Table 4.1 Commands to Execute a Planning Function Inside a Button Item

4. Select the commands under the **Name** column as shown in Figure 4.11, callout 18.

5. In the **Value** column, select the corresponding parameters for the commands. For the command **PLANNING_FUNCTION_NAME**, select **<PLANNING_FUNCTION>** in the **Value** column (see Figure 4.11, callout 19). This displays the **Open** window where you can choose a Planning Function. Select **Copy 2006 sales data as 2007 plan** (see Figure 4.11, callout 20).

6. Click **Open** (see Figure 4.11, callout 21).
7. Click **OK** (see Figure 4.11, callout 22).

Figure 4.11 Selecting the Commands in a Button Item to Execute a Copy Planning Function

8. You can include as many buttons as required into the workbook. Define another button to execute the **Revalue sales amount** Planning Function by following the steps outlined for the Copy Planning Function.

9. Add another button to save the changes made to the plan data. The command you need to use for this button is the **SAVE_AREA** command (see Figure 4.12).

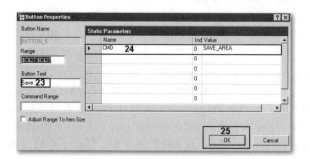

Figure 4.12 Selecting the SAVE_AREA Command

10. Add a **Workbook Setting** item into the workbook and set the properties of the workbook as shown in Figure 4.13.

Figure 4.13 Settings for a Workbook

11. Optionally, you can add a **Message** (see Figure 4.7, callout 12) item into the workbook to display any system and warning messages that relate to the display of data or the execution of commands in the workbook.

12. This completes designing the workbook to contain the necessary design items for our planning application. Save the workbook using the **Save** option (see Figure 4.6, callout 2) in the **Analysis** toolbar and specify a description. The workbook can now be executed by switching from Design mode to Analysis mode.

The planning application now displays inside a Microsoft Excel workbook, as shown in Figure 4.14. Notice the Dropdown Box to select data based on the Material group Characteristic and the Buttons to perform the Copy, Revalue, and Save functions. Key Figures that have been enabled for changes can be modified in the planning application.

After users have entered plan data using this interface, the information can be transferred to the Planning Buffer, which is a temporary area in the SAP NetWeaver BI system to store plan data. To do so, right-click anywhere in the workbook and choose **Transfer Values** (see Figure 4.14, callout 22). This option reads the new and changed values in the workbook, transfers them to the BI server to check consistency against the planning model based on Characteristic Relationships and Data Slices, and transfers the data to the planning buffer.

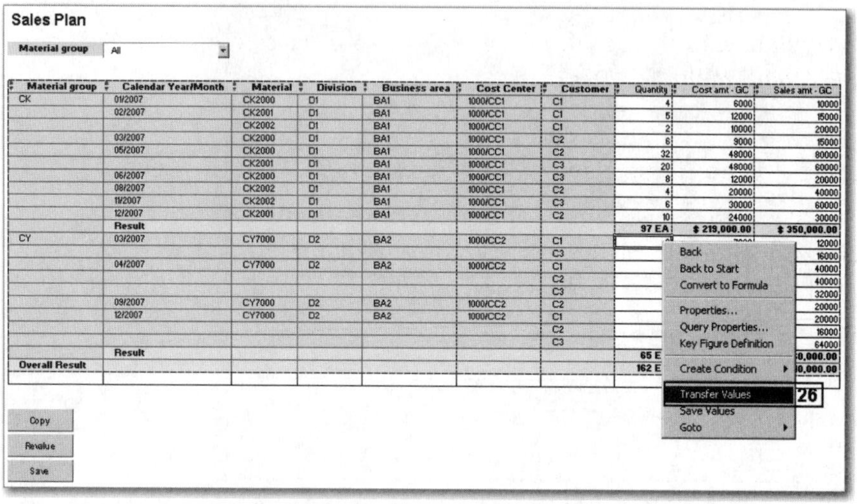

Figure 4.14 A Complete Planning Application in a Microsoft Excel User Interface

Note

Users can create a new plan record by entering the information at the bottom of the Analysis grid.

You have now seen how to create a complete planning application user interface that meets the requirements of our sample company, Rich Bloom, Inc., using the BEx Analyzer tool. In the next section, we will detail the development of the same planning application user interface using the BEx Web Application Designer.

4.4 Creating a Planning Application User Interface Using the BEx Web Application Designer

The BEx Web Application Designer can be used for designing a planning application user interface that is to be used on the Web. It lets you create Web templates that form the basis of building the application. A variety of Web items can be included in a Web template. The Web items to be included in a Web template will depend on the reporting requirements.

The version of the BEx Web Application Designer in SAP NetWeaver 7.0 has several new Web items and enhancements to existing Web items. One of the significant features in the new version is the ability to include commands in a Web application. The command interface allows developers to provide enhanced features when developing a complete Web application for users.

We will now explore some of the Web items that are frequently used in the BEx Web Application Designer.

4.4.1 Web Items Used in BEx Web Application Designer

The BEx Web Application Designer provides several items that enable you to create a complete planning application user interface. The Design model used with this tool is intuitive and enables rapid development of the interface.

Analysis Web Item

The Analysis Web item is a frequently used design element in a Web template. It is used for displaying the results of a query. A Data Provider is specified as the source of data for the Analysis item, and to associate a query, query view, or an InfoProvider to the Web item. The following properties can be set on an Analysis Web item:

▶ **Visibility**
Specifies whether the Web item is visible in the Web application.

▶ **Data Column From**
Specifies the column position from which data is to be displayed. The default value for this parameter is 1.

▶ **Data Column To**
Specifies the column position to which data is to be displayed. The default value for this parameter is 0. When the parameter is set to 0, all of the columns are displayed.

▶ **Data Row From**
Specifies the data row from which the data is to be displayed in the result set.

▶ **Data Row To**
Specifies the data row to which the data is to be displayed in the result set.

▶ **Allow Navigation**
Specifies whether navigation is possible within the Web item. If this property is de-selected, no navigation is possible on this item.

▶ **Data Provider**
Lets you assign a Data Provider to the Web item. The Data Provider that is associated with an InfoProvider, Query, or a Query View should be created before this assignment can be made for the Web item.

Dropdown Box

The Dropdown Box Web item is used for restricting the data displayed in a Web application. A Data Provider is associated with this Web item. A Characteristic used in the Data Provider can be used for filtering data. The values that are displayed in a Dropdown Box can be one of the following:

▶ **Characteristic Values for Filtering**
Enables selecting data based on Characteristic values.

▶ **Query View Selection**
Can be used to select from a list of query views as provider of data for the item.

▶ **Fixed List of Options**
Enables users to select from a fixed list of values.

▶ **Fixed List of Options (Manual Update)**
Enables users to select from a fixed list of values and also maintain the list.

▶ **Variable Selection**
Lets you use a variable that determines the set of values.

Radio Button Group

The Radio Button Group Web item is used for the same purpose as the Dropdown Box Web item. It provides a radio button for each of the entries associated with the Characteristic. Users can choose one value from the set of entries.

Check Box Group

The Check Box Group Web item also is used for the same purpose as the Dropdown Box Web item. It provides a checkbox for each of the entries associated with the Characteristic. Users can choose multiple values from the list of entries.

Navigation Pane

The Navigation Pane is associated with a Data Provider. It provides for further navigational abilities when using the Data Provider.

Report

The Report Web item provides the option to include reports designed in the BEx Report Designer into a Web template.

Charts

SAP NetWeaver 7.0 lets users include charts in a Web template; that is, the data returned by a query can be displayed as a chart in a Web template. Different types of charts can be used for displaying data, including line chart, bar chart, pie chart, scatter chart, and Gantt chart.

Button Group

The Button Group Web item can be used to create a group of buttons. Each button included in the group can be used to execute a set of commands. For example, a button can be included to execute a Web template. We will discuss the different types of commands that can be used in a Web application later in this section.

Filter Pane

The Filter Pane Web item works similar to that of a Dropdown Box Web item. A Characteristic along with the Data Provider is specified for displaying the data. More than one value can be selected when using the Filter Pane Web item.

List Box

The List Box Web item lets you filter data based on a Characteristic by displaying the data as a list. The advantage of using this Web item over the Dropdown Box Web item is that it lets you select multiple values.

Commands

Beginning with SAP NetWeaver 7.0, command wizards can be used in Web templates. Commands are used to automate the steps that are manually performed by using the navigation options in a Web template. The Commands that can be created in a Web application can be grouped as follows:

► **Commands for Data Providers**
These commands affect Data Providers. For example, a query associated with a Data Provider can be changed dynamically using a command.

► **Commands for Planning Applications**
These commands are relevant only in the context of planning applications; for example, the command to save changes made to plan data.

► **Commands for Web Items**
These commands affect the status of Web items; for example, the command to change parameters for a Web item.

► **Commands for Web Templates**
These commands affect the Web template that is being displayed in the Web application; for example, the command to save bookmarks.

Now that we have analyzed the Web items that are frequently used in a planning application, we will examine the details of developing a planning application using the BEx Web Application Designer tool.

4.4.2 Developing a Planning Application Using the BEx Web Application Designer

We already have discussed the steps for developing a planning application using the BEx Analyzer tool. In this section, we will develop the same application using the BEx Web Application Designer. Perform the following steps to develop the planning application using this tool, as illustrated in Figures 4.15 through 4.24:

1. Launch the BEx Web Application Designer from your PC using the menu path **Start • Programs • Business Explorer • Web Application Designer.**

2. Start creating a new Web template by clicking **Create.**

3. Start identifying the Data Provider to be used for the Web template by double-clicking **New Data Provider** (see Figure 4.15, callout 1).

4. In the **Define Data Provider Type** area, select the Data Provider from the appropriate dropdown list. A **Query View**, **Query** or **InfoProvider** can be used as a Data Provider. For our case study, assign the Input Enable Query **ZSLSPLN_INPUT** as the **Data Provider Type** (see Figure 4.16, callout 2). Note that more than one Data Provider can be created and used in a Web template. Confirm the selection by clicking **OK** (see Figure 4.16, callout 3).

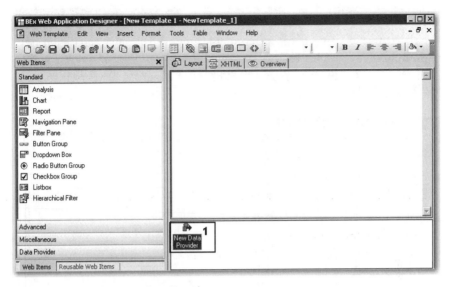

Figure 4.15 Creating a New Data Provider

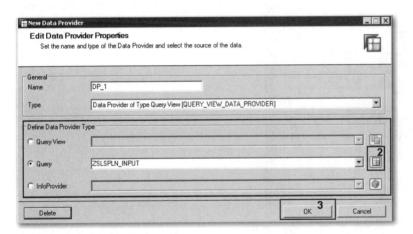

Figure 4.16 Settings for a Data Provider

5. Under **Standard Group** of Web items, in the upper left pane of the Web template, select the **Anaysis** item and drag it into the Web template. The system assigns the name **ANALYSIS_ITEM_1** to the item (see Figure 4.17, callout 4).

6. The properties of an Analysis Item are set by selecting the item in the **Properties** pane and specifying the properties on the **Web Item Parameters** tab. Set the properties of **ANALYSIS_ITEM_1,** as shown in Figure 4.17, callout 5.

> **Note**
>
> To allow users to enter a new plan record using the Web planning application user interface, set the **Number of New Lines** under the **Internal Display** property of the Analysis item to be greater than 0. This displays as many new rows as users need to enter plan data.

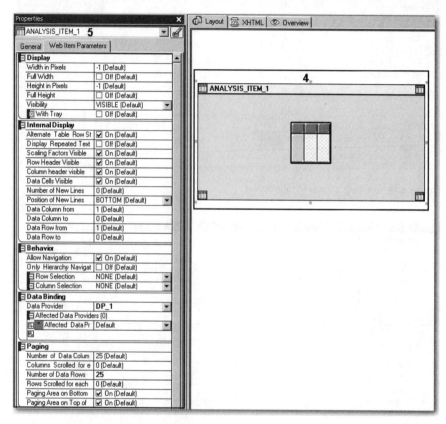

Figure 4.17 Settings for the Analysis Item

7. Under **Standard Group** of Web items, in the upper left pane of the Web template, select **Dropdown Box** and drag it to the Web template. The system assigns the name **DROPDOWN_ITEM_1** to the item (see Figure 4.18, callout 6).

8. The properties of a Dropdown item are set by selecting the item in the **Properties** pane and specifying the properties on the **Web Item Parameters** tab. Set the properties of **DROPDOWN_ITEM_1,** as shown in Figure 4.18, callout 7. For our case study, in the **Data Binding** section of the **Properties** pane, select the **Material group** Characteristic Dropdown Box.

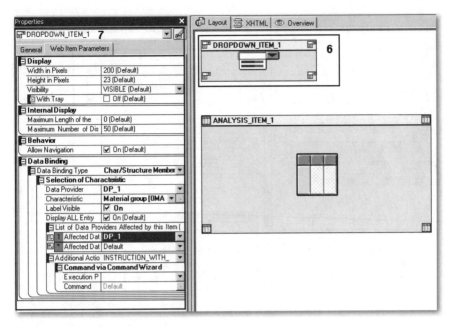

Figure 4.18 Settings for the Dropdown Box Item

9. Under **Standard Group** of Web items, in the upper left pane of the Web template, select the **Button Group** and drag it to the Web template. The system assigns the name **BUTTONGROUP_ITEM_1** to the item (see Figure 4.19, callout 8).

10. The properties of a Button Group Item are set by selecting the item in the **Properties** pane and specifying the properties on the **Web Item Parameters** tab. Set the properties of **BUTTONGROUP_ITEM_1**, as shown in Figure 4.19, callout 9.

11. Select the dropdown list as shown in Figure 4.19, callout 10 to define the settings for the individual button inside the group.

12. Enter the name of the **Caption** for the button; for our case study, this name is "Copy" (see Figure 4.20, callout 11). This will be shown as the description of the button when executing the Web template.

13. Next, you need to specify the command that will be used when executing the button. Click the dropdown list next to **Command** (see Figure 4.20, callout 12) to display the **Edit Command** window shown in Figure 4.21.

14. Select the **All Commands** tab (see Figure 4.21, callout 13).

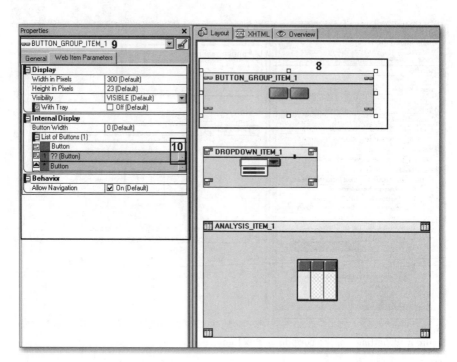

Figure 4.19 Settings for the Button Item

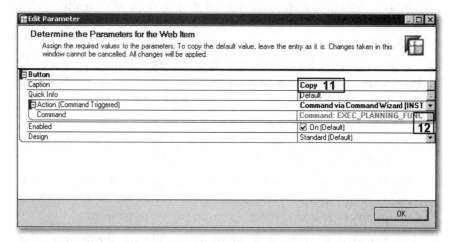

Figure 4.20 Settings for a Command in the Button Item — Copy

15. Under the **Commands for Planning Applications** group, select the checkbox for **Execute a Planning Function (Simple) [EXEC_PLANNING_FUNCTION_SIMPLE]** (see Figure 21, callout 14).

16. Click **Next** (see Figure 21, callout 15).

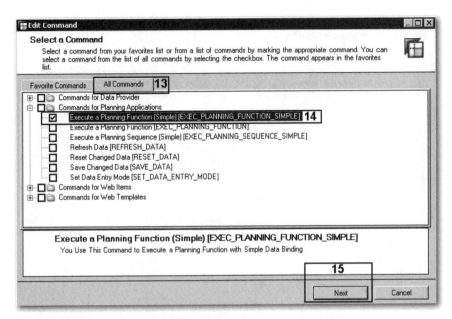

Figure 4.21 Settings for a Command in a Button Item — Choose Command

17. In the next **Edit Command** window, shown in Figure 4.22, you'll need to select the parameters to be used for the command you selected in the previous step. Under **Data Binding**, select the Data Provider **DP_1** to be used as a Filter when executing the Planning Function (see Figure 4.22, callout 16).

18. Under **Command Specific Parameters**, using the Dropdown Box for **Planning Function,** select the Planning Function. For our case study, this is **ZSL_P_COP** (see Figure 4.22, callout 17).

19. Click **OK** to confirm the selections (see Figure 4.22, callout 18).

20. A Button Group can include a list of Buttons. To include another Button in the Button Group, create a new entry as shown in Figure 4.19, callout 10. Repeat the steps you used to add the Copy Planning Function to define another Button that will execute the Revalue Planning Function.

21. The option to save the changes to the plan data should be included in the planning application. Therefore, include a Button called **Save** in the Button Group item. Select the **Saved Changed Data** option in the list of commands displayed under **Commands for Planning Applications** when creating the Button (see Figure 4.23, callout 19).

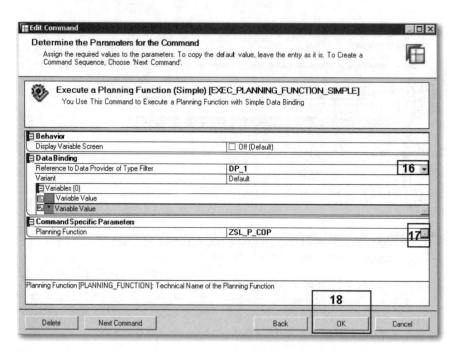

Figure 4.22 Settings for the Button Item — Choose Planning Function

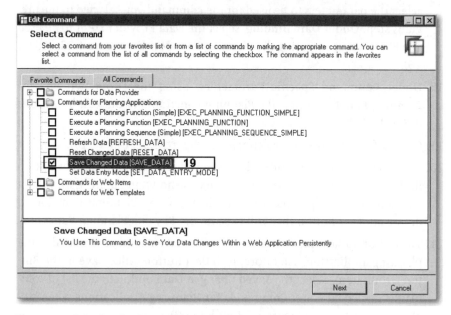

Figure 4.23 Selecting the Command to Save Changes to Plan Data

22. Under **Miscellaneous Group** of Web items, in the upper left pane of the Web template, select the **Text** item and drag it to the Web template. This can serve to describe the purpose of the Web template when users execute it.

23. Save the Web template.

Testing the Web Template

You can now test the Web template by clicking the **Web template Execute** button. The URL that is associated with the Web template can be captured as follows:

1. Click **Web Template** in the menu bar. The menu options are displayed.

2. Click **Publish**.

3. Choose **Copy URL into Clipboard** (see Figure 4.24, callout 20). This saves the URL to the clipboard. You can now copy the URL to the Address bar of your browser and execute the Web template. You can also add this URL to the favorites in your browser.

> **Note**
>
> The URL can also be integrated into the SAP Enterprise Portal and executed from there.

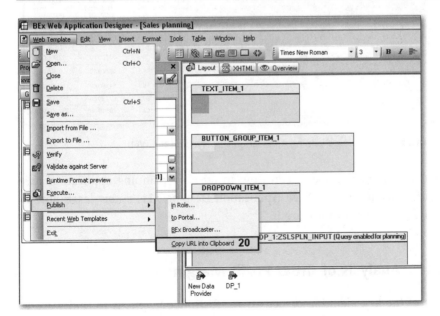

Figure 4.24 Copying the URL of the Web Template to the Clipboard

237

After the Web template is executed, its output displays as shown in Figure 4.25. The planning functions can be executed by clicking the respective buttons created in the planning application (**Copy** and **Revalue** in our example). You can use the **Save** button to make and save necessary changes to the data.

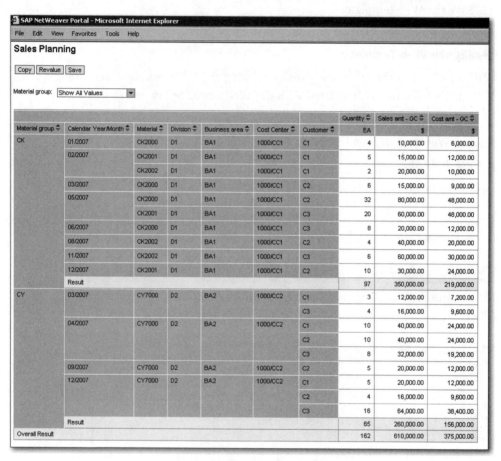

Figure 4.25 A Complete Planning Application Displayed on the Web

In this section, you have seen how to create a planning application user interface using the BEx Web Application Designer. Let's now learn how to analyze the gross profit margin.

4.5 Analysis of Gross Profit Margin

One of the key planning objectives for Rich Bloom, Inc. is to find ways to improve its gross profit margin. Rich Bloom, Inc. hopes to increase the gross profit margin by reducing cost. The company wants to use the planning process to understand where the costs are incurred so that it can find ways to cut unnecessary costs. It is also working to improve its operations in order to reduce labor and inventory costs and increase gross profit margin.

To achieve this goal, we will create a query to help management understand the gross-profit- margin percentage that the company plans to achieve for the different products, both as an actual amount and as a percentage of sales. The results of the query will aid in understanding the different aspects of cost in an effort to reduce costs and increase the gross profit margin percentage. The company also intends to use the results to compare its performance with that of other companies with comparably sized operations in the same business. The goal here is to compare its level of efficiency with that of its competitors.

The following steps are needed to create a query to analyze the gross profit margin, as illustrated in Figures 4.26, 4.27, and 4.28:

1. Launch the BEx Query Designer tool from your PC using the menu path **Start • Programs • Business Explorer • Query Designer.** The BEx Query Designer toolbar displays.

2. Use the **Create** button on the toolbar to start creating a new query.

3. Select the InfoProvider that contains the plan data for creating the query.

4. Add the Characteristics that are required for making the analysis in the **Rows** area of the query (see Figure 4.26, callout 1). For our case study, we will select **Material group** and **Material.**

5. Add the Key Figures to be used for the analysis in the **Columns** area of the query (see Figure 4.26, callout 2). For our case study, select **Quantity, Sales amt — GC,** and **Cost amt — GC.**

6. Create a formula to determine the planned gross profit margin amount. To do so, in the Columns area, right-click **Key Figure** and choose **Create New Formula** (see Figure 4.26, callout 3).

7. The **Properties** window displays. Under **Description**, enter "Gross Profit Margin (Amount)" (see Figure 4.26, callout 4) and click **Enter.** This takes you back to the **Query Definition** screen.

8. Right-click **Gross Profit Margin (Amount),** and choose **Edit** to specify the definition of the formula. The planned gross profit margin amount is calculated by subtracting Planned Cost from Planned Sales (Figure 4.26, callout 5).

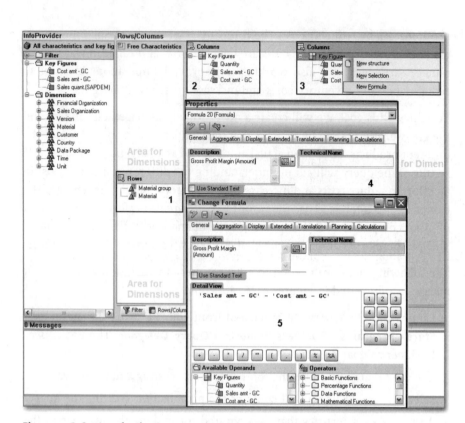

Figure 4.26 Settings for the Gross Margin Analysis Query

9. Using the steps to create the formula **Gross Profit Margin (Amount)**, create another formula, **Gross Profit Margin (%)** to determine the planned gross profit margin as a percentage of planned sales. This formula will be calculated by subtracting the planned cost from planned sales and dividing it by the planned sales. This will be multiplied by 100 to express the result as a percentage (see Figure 4.27, callout 6).

10. Save the query by specifying a **Technical name** and **Description**. The query can be executed by choosing the **Query Execute** button from the toolbar. The output of the query is shown in Figure 4.28.

We have now created a query that can be used for analysis of the planned gross profit margin. The query displays the planned gross profit margin at a Material group level. This helps Rich Bloom, Inc. identify products that yield higher margins, so that the sales team can focus on these products in the future. It also reveals the planned costs of the different products, so that the company can look for opportunities to reduce costs.

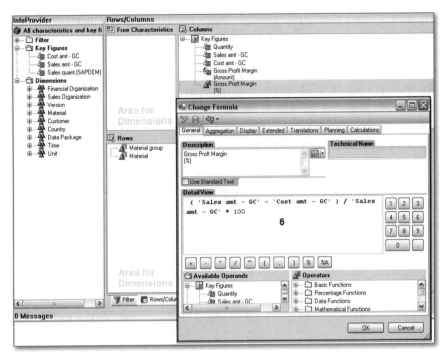

Figure 4.27 Settings for the Gross Margin Analysis Query — Create Gross Profit Margin (%)

Figure 4.28 Output from the Query Created for Gross Margin Analysis

4.6 Summary

In this chapter, we first discussed the different options available for reporting in the SAP NetWeaver BI system. We identified the BEx suite of tools available for reporting and analysisand also discussed how Visual Composer can be used in the context of reporting data from multiple systems.

We then detailed the steps to create an Input-Enabled Query used to manually create and modify plan data. Next, we created a planning application using the BEx Analyzer tool. We then reviewed the steps to develop the same planning application using the BEx Web Application Designer tool. The planning objects created in Chapter 3 were used as the basis for creating the planning application with both tools. Finally, we created a query to fulfill one of Rich Bloom, Inc.'s planning requirements: Establish a process to analyze plan data for gross profit margin reporting.

This chapter illustrated how easy it is to develop a planning application user interface once the planning objects have been created and made available to users. It also emphasized the advantage of using a single tool for entering and analyzing data. The tool allows standardization of planning and reporting requirements using a single solution, which in turn helps to lower TCO.

In Chapter 5, we will discuss several important topics relevant to designing a planning application. These include:

▶ Locking issues when multiple users run a planning application simultaneously.

▶ The Status and Tracking System (STS) used to automate the planning process.

▶ The process of transporting planning objects from the development system to the quality assurance and production systems.

▶ Performance considerations to take into account when designing and developing a planning application.

▶ The process to retract plan data back from the SAP NetWeaver BI system into the SAP R/3 system.

PART III
Developing Planning Applications

Chapter 5 discusses topics that are important to understand when developing and deploying a planning application. The chapter explains the concepts of data-locking in a planning application, the benefits of using the Status and Tracking System (STS) application for planning, authorization concepts in SAP NetWeaver BI, the steps for transporting planning objects, and the meaning of data retraction and how it is used in planning. We'll also offer tips for monitoring and improving the performance of a planning application.

5 Essential Tools for Developing SAP NetWeaver BI Planning Applications

We begin the chapter by explaining the meaning of locking in the context of a planning application. We also explain locking and the settings available for configuring locks.

The next part of the chapter illustrates a typical scenario for using the Status and Tracking System (STS) application. The STS application is an out-of-the-box application provided by SAP that can be customized for enabling workflow in planning and to complete the plan data for a planning scenario.

Subsequently, we provide an overview of the new concept of authorization in the SAP NetWeaver BI system. The different features of authorization and their use are explained.

Later in the chapter, we explain how plan data can be retracted from the SAP NetWeaver BI system to the SAP R/3 system. We also discuss the planning application for which the regression functionality is available. We then demonstrate the process used for transporting planning objects created in the development system to the quality and production systems.

Finally, we analyze the importance of performance when developing a planning application and the areas to consider when evaluating performance.

5.1 Locking

Let's start by understanding the concept and practice of locking so that we can minimize data locking when multiple users simultaneously access a planning application.

5.1.1 What is Locking?

As we mentioned previously, a planning application created using the BI Integrated Planning tool can be used to change the plan data using an Input-Enabled Query and Planning Functions. When a user executes an Input-Enabled Query, the data selected by the query is locked by that user (and only by that user), and the selection information is stored in a selection table in the system. This table is read when a second user subsequently requests data from the InfoProvider while working in a planning application. The second user will be able to continue the request only if the selections for the data do not overlap with the selections recorded in the selection table.

A user who requests the same data or a subset of data that has already been requested by another user will get a message indicating that the data is locked by another user. This prevents two users from changing the data in an InfoProvider for the same selections at the same time. Locks are released when the user leaves the planning application.

Note
The InfoProvider does not have to contain data for a user to make selections.

An Example of Locking

As an example of how locking works, let's assume that three Characteristics and two Key Figures are included in an Aggregation Level used for planning. The Characteristics in the Aggregation Level are Company Code, Division, and Sales Organization. The Key Figures are Quantity and Amount.

User Randy executes an Input-Enabled Query containing all three Characteristics listed above and only the Quantity Key Figure. Randy uses a filter to restrict the data in the Input-Enabled Query using the following values:

▶ C1 for Company Code
▶ D1 for Division

No restrictions are defined for the Sales Organization Characteristic. As a result, the data for all of the Sales Organizations in the InfoProvider will be displayed in the query.

When the Input-Enabled Query is executed, the selections are recorded in a selection table. Because no value is selected for the Characteristic Sales Organization, the value * is used internally in the selection to represent all Sales Organizations. The Characteristics that are not included in the Aggregation Level but that exist in the InfoProvider will also have the * automatically included in the selection table.

Subsequently, user Marsha executes the same Query and Filter that Randy did. The system will first read the selection table to see if the data required by Marsha overlaps with the data already requested by another user. Because Marsha and Randy are requesting the same selections, the system will display an error message indicating that the data requested is already locked by Randy. This situation is a typical example of locking.

Avoiding locks

To avoid locking and ensure simultaneous access of data by multiple users, the following guidelines should be taken into account:

▶ To avoid locking, avoid any overlap in the data selections when two users access data. When selecting data for planning, the users should select different values for at least one Characteristic, in order to facilitate simultaneous access to the data. In the example above, if Randy had required data for company code C1 and if Marsha had required data for company code C2 locking could have been avoided.

▶ If two users make the same selections based on Characteristics, locking can be avoided if the selections involve different Key Figures. In the example above, if Randy had only the Quantity Key Figure in his query and Marsha had only the Amount Key Figure in her query, the system would have allowed Marsha to continue with her request even though the selections are the same.

Locking errors can be avoided by assigning appropriate filters to users in Input-Enabled Queries and Planning Functions to prevent overlapping selections.

We will now discuss the configuration for locking.

5.1.2   Locking Configuration

Transaction **RSPLAN** is used to maintain and analyze lock settings (see Figure 5.1). The transaction can also be accessed from the SAP Implementation Guide (IMG). Click the **Manage Lock Server** button to configure and analyze lock settings.

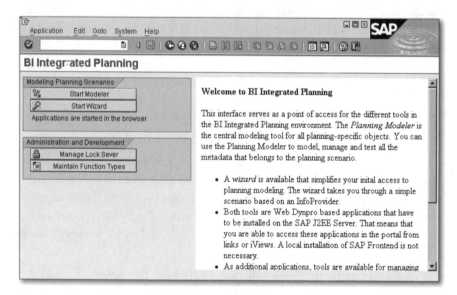

Figure 5.1 Menu to Access Lock Configuration Settings

The following tabs are available to configure lock settings (see Figure 5.2):

► Lock Table
► Locking Characteristics
► Lock
► Locking Conflict

Each tab provides additional information for the settings pertaining to a different area.

Lock Table

The **Lock Table** tab specifies the location of the selection table where the lock table is stored. When a user requests data for a planning application, the system reads the selection table to see if there is a collision before the request is processed. There are three options for setting the lock table:

▸ When the **Lock Server** option is selected (see Figure 5.2, callout 1), the lock table is compressed and stored on the standard lock server. The check for a collision when a user executes a planning application is not carried out on the lock server, however. The selection tables are copied from the lock server to the application server where the user is logged on, and the check is carried out there. A fixed application server can be specified to perform this check and can be set here when using this option for locking.

▸ When the **Shared Object Memory of Server** option is selected (see Figure 5.2, callout 2), the lock tables are stored in the shared object memory area that is connected to an application server used by the system. This is the same server where the collision check is carried out. The application server used to manage locks, also called the enqueue server, is the default location for storing the lock tables when using this option. Using this option for locking ensures that the collision check is performed in the same location where the lock tables are stored.

▸ When the **liveCache** option is selected (see Figure 5.2, callout 3), the lock tables are stored in the application server configured for SAP liveCache. This option can be used only if the SAP liveCache is installed on a separate application server. The collision check is also performed on this server.

Lock Characteristics

The **Lock Characteristics** tab is used to reduce the size of the locking table. When a user requests planning data, the selection for the data that is requested is recorded in the lock table. As users continue to request data, the lock tables get bigger. Before planning data is processed based on requests from users, the lock tables are read and checked to ensure that there are no overlapping selections. This check may result in additional performance overhead when the lock table is big. You can use the **Lock Characteristics** tab to exclude Characteristics from the collision check for an InfoProvider to reduce the size of the selection table and thereby improve the performance of a planning application.

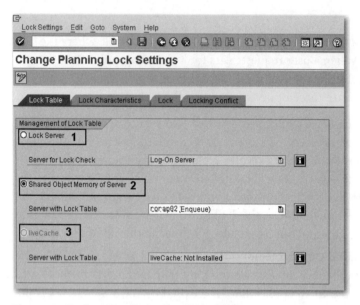

Figure 5.2 Configuration for Locking Table Settings

If the same Characteristics values are used by all of the users for selection in a planning application, then these Characteristics are good candidates for exclusion from the lock check. For example, if the plan year 2007 is used as a selection by all of the users as a Filter in the planning application, then this Characteristic might be excluded from recording in the lock table.

Use these steps to exclude Characteristics:

1. Select the **Lock Characteristics** tab and switch to Change Mode (see Figure 5.3, callout 1).

2. Select the Real Time InfoCube that is used for planning from the drop-down list (see Figure 5.3, callout 2).

3. The Characteristics associated with the InfoProvider are displayed in the **Lock Characteristics** area (see Figure 5.3, callout 3).

4. Highlight the Characteristic in the Lock Characteristics area and use the left arrow button to select the Characteristics that are not required to be recorded in the lock table (see Figure 5.3, callout 4).

5. The Characteristics excluded are displayed in the **Selection of Characteristics** area (see Figure 5.3, callout 5). The values for the Characteristics specified here are not recorded in the lock table and not used when performing the lock check.

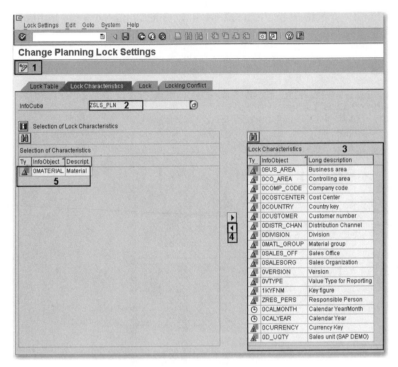

Figure 5.3 Settings to Exclude Characteristics from Locking

Lock

The **Lock** tab displays the active locks in the system, as follows:

▶ The screen provides an area to specify the parameters to display the active locks in the system. An **InfoProvider** can be specified here. For example, an Aggregation Level can be selected as an InfoProvider (see Figure 5.4, callout 1). A **User** can also be optionally specified (see Figure 5.4, callout 2). The system displays the lock entries for the InfoProvider and the user.

▶ The **Locks: Header Entries** table displays the header data for the locked selections. The table displays the InfoProvider, user name, lock mode, locked records and lock handle (see Figure 5.4, callout 3).

▶ The **Lock mode** is set to **E** (Exclusive) if the data that is selected when executing a planning application is requested in change mode by a user. The lock mode is set to **S** (Shared) if the data requested is reference data. The data requested as reference data can be used by multiple users for display only. However, the reference data cannot be changed.

▶ The **Lock Records** table displays the details of the locked selection for each entry in the Header table (see Figure 5.4, callout 4). These details include the lock handle specified in the header entry table, along with the individual Characteristics and the selection values that are locked.

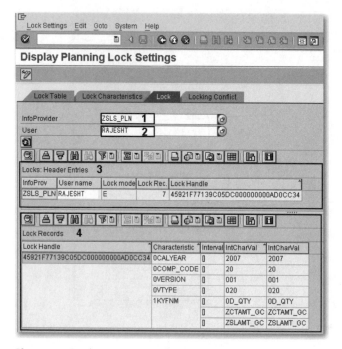

Figure 5.4 Display Active Locks for an InfoProvider

You can use Transaction **SM12** to monitor and delete locks in the system. The name of the table is one of the parameters you can specify when using this transaction and depends on the **Lock Table** option that has been used to configure locking. Table 5.1 lists the Lock Table names for the different Lock Table options.

Lock Table Option	Lock Table Name
Lock Server	RSPLS_S_LOCK
Share Object Memory	RSPLS_S_LOCK_SYNC
Live Cache.	LCA_GUID_STR

Table 5.1 Lock Tables Used for Various Lock Options

Locking Conflict

The **Locking Conflict** tab displays the last time a locking collision occurred in the system. The locks are displayed for an InfoProvider (see Figure 5.5, callout 1), a user who requested the lock (see Figure 5.5, callout 2), and the user who is holding the lock (see Figure 5.5, callout 3).

The selections of the user who requested the lock display in the **Selection in Lock Request** area (see Figure 5.5, callout 4). The selections of the user holding the lock at that time display in the **Locked Selection** area (see Figure 5.5, callout 5). Analyzing which data selections the two users share will help with understanding the source of the lock conflict.

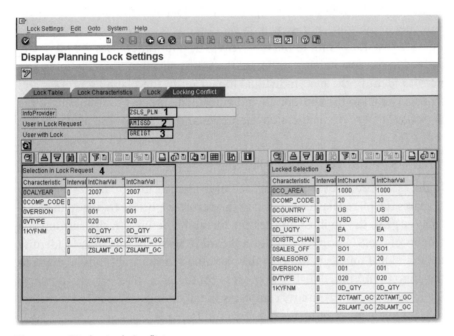

Figure 5.5 Display Lock Conflicts

This concludes our discussion of locking in a planning application. In the next section, we will explore the benefits of using the Status and Tracking System (STS) application in planning.

5.2   Status and Tracking System (STS) Application

SAP provides the Status and Tracking System (STS) as a predefined application that can be used to automate the workflow and monitor the status for a planning scenario. The application can be customized to meet the requirements of an individual planning application.

As we mentioned in Chapter 4, there are two types of planning: bottom-up planning and top-down planning. Bottom-up planning begins at the lowest level of the hierarchy and moves up to the higher levels through an approval process. Top-down planning starts at the top level and filters down to lower levels.

5.2.1 STS and Bottom-Up Planning

In the case of bottom-up planning, the individual at the bottom of the planning hierarchy prepares the plan data and sends the request for approval to a person just above him in the hierarchy. The application uses the hierarchy defined in the customizing section of the STS application (for a Planning Session) to identify the next individual higher up in the planning process and sends an email to the appropriate individual. The process continues until the person at the top of the hierarchy approves and completes the plan data.

5.2.2 STS and Top-Down Planning

In the case of top-down planning, the individual at the top of the hierarchy prepares the plan data and sends it to the person reporting to him in the hierarchy. Again, the application uses the hierarchy defined in the customizing section of the STS application (for a Planning Session), this time to identify the individual one level lower in the planning process and sends an email to the appropriate individual. The process continues until everyone, down to the bottom of the hierarchy, completes the planning process. The direction of planning begins at the top and moves to lower levels.

> **Note**
>
> Planners are provided links to a Web-based planning application via email for preparing, monitoring, and setting the status of plan data. Authorizations are granted to the planners depending on their role in the planning process. This determines the access a planner will have when executing the STS application.

5.2.3 STS Key Points

Be sure to remember the following points about the STS application:

► The entire planning process can be effectively monitored using the STS application. The application can be used to display an overview or provide a detailed view of the status of the planning process. It serves as a visual aid to track the status of the planning process and identify bottlenecks so they can be addressed immediately.

▸ STS supports both bottom-up planning and top-down planning.

▸ In the course of the planning process, data prepared by a user and approved by his supervisor can be protected from further changes. This functionality can be used as an authorization tool to prevent users from changing data.

We can better explain the use of the STS application by presenting a planning scenario, which we will do next.

5.2.4 Planning Scenario for Using the STS Application

Let's say that our sample company, Rich Bloom, Inc., wants to prepare a sales plan. The company has three sales offices representing different regions, and each office has a fully staffed sales team. A sales director is responsible for the company's overall planning.

Historical sales data is to be used as the basis for planning future sales. The plan data is generated based on historical sales data but must be adjusted to reflect the true demand for the company's products in the plan period.

The salesperson is responsible for reviewing the plan data generated by the system and making changes based on the realistic demand for the products in the plan period. The salesperson then sends a request via email to the regional manager to approve the plan data.

The regional manager reviews the plan data sent by the salesperson and either approves or rejects the request. If the regional manager rejects the request, it goes back to the salesperson. The salesperson then will make the necessary corrections and resubmit the request to the regional manager. When the regional manager approves the sales data prepared by the salesperson, it may be further modified by the regional manager and is finally sent to the company's sales director.

The sales director then goes through the process of approving or rejecting the requests sent by the regional manager. Similar to the process described in the previous paragraph, if the request is rejected by the sales director, then the regional manager will make the necessary changes and resubmit the request for approval.

Once the sales director approves the plan data prepared by all of the regional mangers, the planning process is complete.

255

As we can see from this planning scenario, a hierarchy is involved in the planning process. The salesperson reports to his regional manager, and the regional manager in turn reports to the sales director of the company. We will now see how to use STS to automate the process of planning for this planning scenario.

5.2.5 STS Application Concepts

Before configuring STS, you need to understand some of the terms used in this context:

▶ **Planning Area**
Defined to specify the InfoProvider that is to be used in an STS application. The Planning Area is defined using the Business Planning and Simulation (BW BPS) tool for planning.

▶ **Subplan**
Represents a specific area of planning: financial planning, sales planning, investment planning, head-count planning, etc.

▶ **Planning Session**
Associated with a subplan. A subplan represents a specific area of planning: financial planning, sales planning, investment planning, head-count planning, etc. There may be different variations when executing a subplan. For example, a planning process for sales planning may generate different versions of data (1, 2, and 3). The planning process associated with each Planning Session can be specified for each of these variations. The Planning Sessions might be titled Plan1, Plan2 or Plan3. Each Planning Session may correspond to a version in the planning process.

▶ **Hierarchy**
Represents the relationship of individuals involved in the planning process. It is essential to maintain a hierarchy to identify this relationship. Hierarchies can be created and maintained for an InfoObject.

5.2.6 Preparing for the STS Configuration

Before you start configuring the STS application, you need to perform two other tasks, as outlined in the following list:

▶ **BSP application availability**
You need to make available the **Tunguska** and **Tunguska_Detail** Business Server Pages (BSP) applications in the system by activating the service

associated with the BSP using Transaction **SICF**. These applications serve as the front-end interface for STS. The two applications that need to be activated are:

▶ **Enabling hierarchy data**

The STS application also requires a hierarchy to determine the workflow for the planning process. This hierarchy contains the organizational structure for individuals involved in planning. The Real Time InfoCube that is identified for the planning application should contain this Characteristic. The Characteristic should be enabled to contain hierarchy data.

In our Plan InfoCube, we included a Characteristic ZRES_PERS (Responsible Person) and set the Characteristic to contain hierarchy data, as shown in Figure 5.6, callout 1. The hierarchy data can be maintained by clicking the **Maintain Hierarchies** button (see Figure 5.6, callout 2).

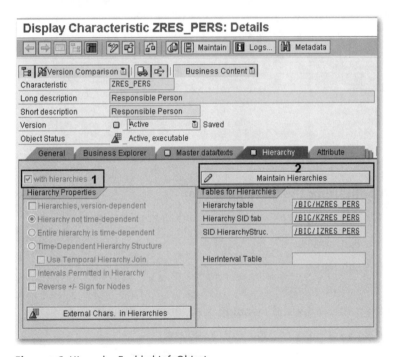

Figure 5.6 Hierarchy-Enabled InfoObject

This displays the screen **Initial Screen Hierarchy Maintenance**, as shown for the ZRESP_PERS Characteristic in Figure 5.7. The actual hierarchy for the ZRESP_PERS Info Object is shown in Figure 5.8.

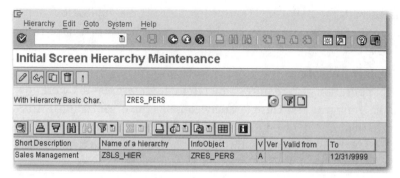

Figure 5.7 Defining a Hierarchy

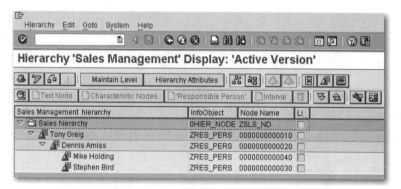

Figure 5.8 Hierarchy Definition for the Responsible Person InfoObject

5.2.7 Configuring the STS Application

Perform the following steps to configure an STS application:

1. Create a Planning Area

2. Create a subplan

3. Create a Planning Session

4. Identify a Hierarchy and Planning Area for the subplan

5. Associate a Planning Session with a subplan

6. Determine the Attributes for the Planning Session

7. Initialize/reset the Planning Session

8. Define Header Characteristics for the Planning Session

9. Determine the Data, Person Responsible, and Layouts

10. Test the STS application

Let's look at each of these steps in detail.

Create a Planning Area

You begin the process of configuring an STS application by creating a Planning Area (see Figure 5.9). A Planning Area identifies the InfoProvider for the STS application. You create it using the BPS tool for planning. Execute Transaction **BPS0** to access the planning workbench in BPS. Then follow these steps to create a Planning Area, as illustrated in Figure 5.9.

1. Create a new Planning Area by selecting the option **Planning • Planning Area • Create** from the menu (see Figure 5.9, callout 1). The **Create Planning Area** dialog box displays. Enter a **Technical name** ("ZASLSPLN") and **Description** ("Sales Plan") for the Planning Area (see Figure 5.9, callout 2).

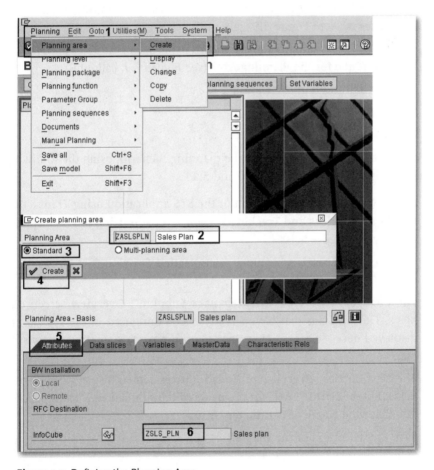

Figure 5.9 Defining the Planning Area

2. Set the type of **Planning Area** to **Standard** (see Figure 5.9, callout 3).

| Note |

A standard Planning Area is created when a single InfoCube is to be used for planning. A Multi-Planning Area is created when more than one InfoCube is required for planning, for example, when a Real-Time InfoCube is used for planning and an additional InfoCube is required to be used as reference data in the planning application.

3. Click **Create** to confirm the settings (see Figure 5.9, callout 4). The settings for the Planning Area can be configured in the window displayed in the right pane.

4. Now five tabs are displayed: **Attributes**, **Data Slices**, **Variables**, **MasterData** and **Characteristic Rels**. For the STS application, we will define the Planning Area that points to the Real Time InfoCube. Click the **Attributes** tab (see Figure 5.9, callout 5).

5. On the Attributes tab, use the dropdown list to select the **Sales plan (ZSLS_PLN) InfoCube** for the Planning Area (see Figure 5.9, callout 6).

6. Save the definition of the Planning Area.

Create a Subplan

We will now create a subplan for the planning scenario, using the following steps, as illustrated in Figures 5.10 and 5.11:

1. Access the Customizing function of the STS application using Transaction **BPS_TC**. The **Status and Tracking System — Customizing** screen displays, as shown in Figure 5.10.

2. In the **General Settings** section, select **Define Subplan** (see Figure 5.10, callout 1) and click **Execute**.

3. The **Change View "View Maintenenace Subplan": Overview** screen displays. The subplans that have already been configured in the system are displayed here. Select the **New Entries** option to start creating a new subplan.

4. The **New Entries: Overview of Added Entries** screen displays (see Figure 5.11). Enter "ZUSSLPLAN" for the name of the subplan and "Sales plan for 2007" for the **Name of Parameter Group**.

5. Save the definition of the subplan.

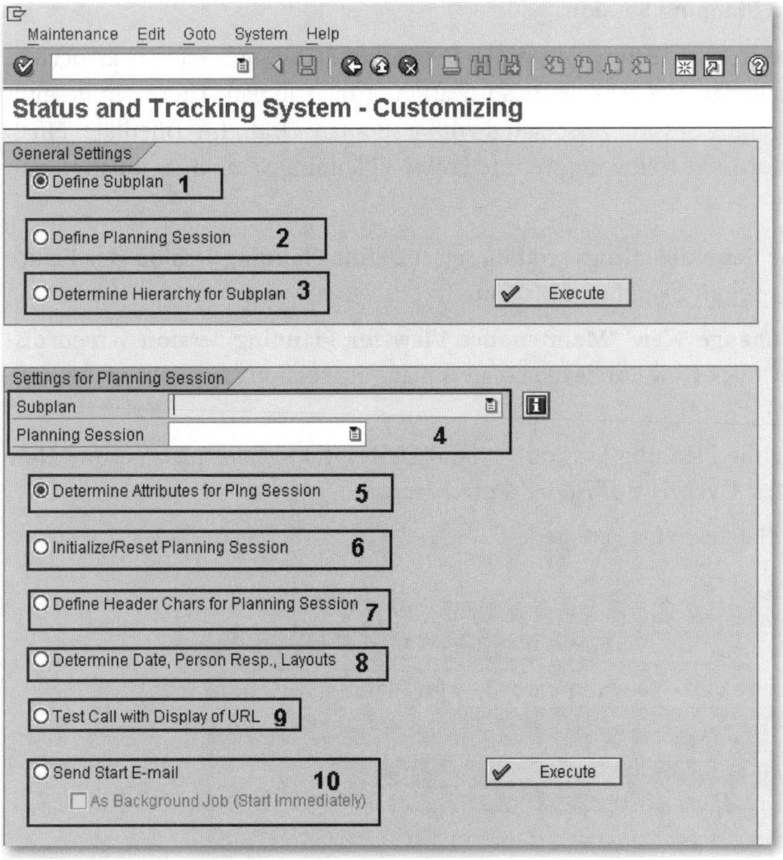

Figure 5.10 The Customizing Screen of the STS Application

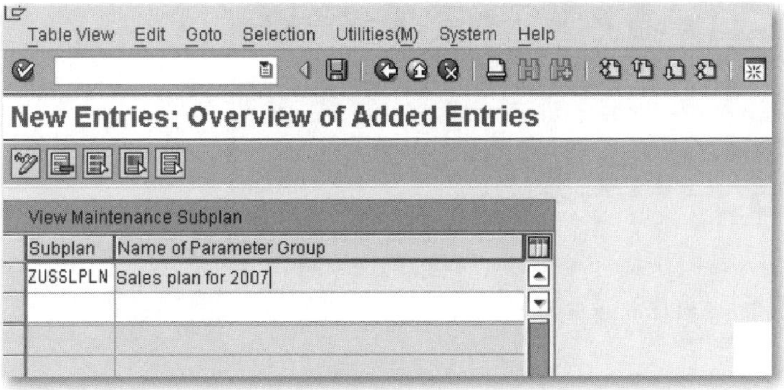

Figure 5.11 Defining a Subplan for Planning

Create a Planning Session

The next step is creating a Planning Session. A Planning Session is associated with a subplan and represents a variation of the subplan. There can be multiple Planning Sessions associated with a subplan: Draft, Intermediate, Final, etc. Perform the following steps to create a Planning Session, as illustrated in Figure 5.12:

1. In the **General Settings** section, select **Define Planning Session** (see Figure 5.10, callout 2) and click **Execute**.

2. The **Change View "Maintenance View for Planning Session** screen displays. Click **New Entries** to create a planning session (see Figure 5.12, callout 1).

3. Enter the Planning Session "1" and Description "Sales plan" in the **New Entries: Overview of Added Entries** screen.

4. Save the new entry created.

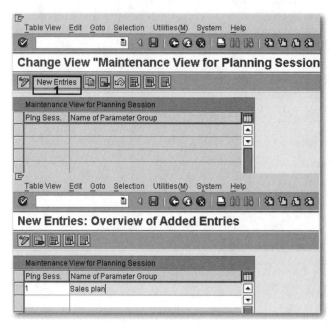

Figure 5.12 Defining a Planning Session

Identify the Hierarchy and Planning Area for a Subplan

In this step, we import and assign a hierarchy to the subplan and specify the Planning Area to be used for the subplan. The following steps are needed to configure this setting, as illustrated in Figures 5.10 and 5.13:

1. In the **General Settings** section, select **Determine Hierarchy for Subplan** (see Figure 5.10, callout 3), and click **Execute**.

2. The **Import BW Hierarchy and Assign to Subplan** screen displays (see Figure 5.13). In the **Specify Hierarchy** section, configure the following settings:

   ▶ Select the **Planning Area (ZASLSPLN)** that includes the Characteristic containing the hierarchy (see Figure 5.13, callout 1).

   ▶ Select the **Hierarchy Basic Characteristic (ZRES_PERS)** in the Planning Area that will be used for the hierarchy (see Figure 5.13, callout 2).

   ▶ Select the **Hierarchy Name (ZSLS_HIER)** for the Characteristic (see Figure 5.13, callout 3).

   ▶ Specify a **To Selection Date (12/31/9999)** for the hierarchy (see Figure 5.13, callout 4).

3. In the **Assignment** section, select the hierarchy **ZUSSLPLN** to assign to a subplan (see Figure 5.13, callout 5).

4. Click **Execute** (see Figure 5.13, callout 6). A message in the status bar indicates that the hierarchy has been successfully imported.

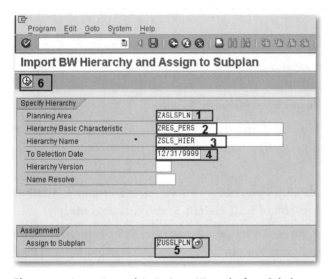

Figure 5.13 Importing and Assigning a Hierarchy for a Subplan

Associate a Planning Session to a Subplan

1. In this step, you associate a Planning Session with a subplan. In the **Status and Tracking System — Customizing** screen, select the subplan and Planning Session that will be used for the STS application (see Figure 5.14).

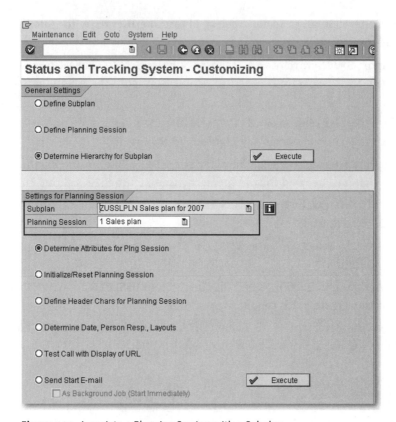

Figure 5.14 Associate a Planning Session with a Subplan

Determine the Attributes for a Planning Session

You now have to specify the Attributes for the Planning Session. The following steps are needed to configure this setting, as illustrated in Figures 5.10 and 5.15:

1. In the **Settings for Planning Session** section, select **Determine Attributes for Plng Session** (see Figure 5.10, callout 5) and click **Execute**.

2. Set the planning direction required for the STS application, either **Bottom-Up** or **Top-Down**. For our scenario, select **Bottom-Up** (see Figure 5.15, callout 1).

3. A Planning Session will pass through different statuses in the course of planning. If a Planning Sequence is to be executed when the status switches, you need to specify the method to be used for executing the Planning Sequence. Check this option only if you want to execute Planning Sequences during status changes. Selecting **Synchr.** runs the Planning Sequence in the foreground. Selecting **As Background Job** runs the Plan-

ning Sequence in the background (see Figure 5.15, callout 2). If **Plng Sequence on Status Switch** is checked, then the system selects the **Synchr.** option by default.

4. To enable the email process for a Planning Session, select **Automatic E-Mail Dispatch Active** (see Figure 5.15, callout 3).

5. Click **Confirm** to save the changes (see Figure 5.15, callout 4).

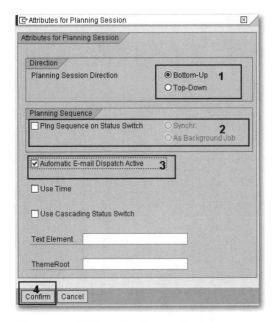

Figure 5.15 Attributes for Planning Session

Initialize/Reset the Planning Session

Initializing/resetting the Planning Session deletes the entire history of statuses and comments associated with an existing Planning Session. You normally do this when a new Planning Session is started. Follow these steps:

1. Select **Initialize/Reset Planning Session** (see Figure 5.10, callout 6).

2. Click **Execute**.

Define Header Characteristics for the Planning Session

The **Define Header Chars for Planning Session** option is used by the system to prevent changes to the plan data after it has been approved. This approach can be used as an additional way of locking data against changes. Perform the following steps to configure this option, as illustrated in Figures 5.10 and 5.16:

1. In the **Settings for Planning Session** section, select **Define Header Chars for Planning Session** (see Figure 5.10, callout 7), and click **Execute**.

2. Define the Header Characteristics as shown in Figure 5.16.

Figure 5.16 Defining Header Characteristics for a Planning Session

Determine Data, Person Responsible, and Layouts

The purpose of the **Determine Data, Person Resp., Layouts** configuration option is to establish the personal information of the people involved in the planning process, completion data for planning, the URL of the Web application used for planning, and the Planning Sequence to be executed when a planner submits or approves a plan. The following steps are needed to configure this setting, as illustrated in Figures 5.10 and 5.17:

1. Select **Determine Data, Person Resp., Layouts** (see Figure 5.10, callout 8) and click **Execute**.

2. Select and double-click an entry from the hierarchy of individuals involved in planning (displayed in the left portion of the screen as shown in Figure 5.17, callout 1).

3. Under the **Personal Information** section you now need to specify the following information: **Selected Unit**, **Person Responsible**, **Name,** and **E-mail** (see Figure 5.17, callout 2). The value entered for the user in **Person Responsible** should match their user ID on the system.

4. The URL of the Planning application the user will execute is specified under the section titled **URL of Planning Application.** This planning application should enable the user to change plan data (see Figure 5.17, callout 3).

5. When additional reports are required for the analysis of plan data, a report including the URL for control reporting can be specified under the section titled **URL of Control Report** (see Figure 5.17, callout 4).

6. When Planning Sequences are to be executed when an individual planner submits or approves plan data, the Planning Sequences that should be executed can be specified in the section titled **Execute Planning Sequence with Status Switch** (see Figure 5.17, callout 5).

7. Save the changes (see Figure 5.17, callout 6).

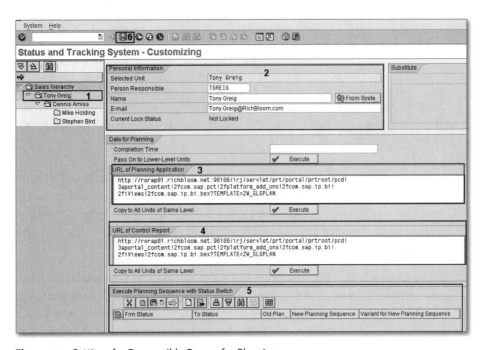

Figure 5.17 Settings for Responsible Person for Planning

Test the STS Application

To test the standard STS application, you use the **Test Call with Display of URL** option as follows:

> **Note**
>
> Make sure the Web-based BSP applications Tunguska and Tunguska_Detail are active before testing the STS application.

1. Select **Test Call with Display of URL** (see Figure 5.10, callout 9) under the **Settings for Planning** section.

2. Click **Execute**.

Alternatively, use Transaction **BPS_STS_START** and specify the subplan and the Planning Session to launch the STS application. You can access this transaction using the following menu path in the SAP GUI from the SAP menu:

Business Planning and Simulation • Status and Tracking System • Execute

5.2.8   Send Start Email to Start an STS Planning Session

The following steps start the email process for a Planning Session:

1. Select **Send Start E-mail** (see Figure 5.10, callout 10) under the **Settings for Planning Session** section.

2. Click **Execute**.

> **Note**
>
> Email notification should have been enabled when setting the Attributes for the Planning Session.

If you have chosen the bottom-up type of planning and email notification is enabled, everyone listed in the hierarchy will get a message saying that a new Planning Session has been started. Those at the bottom level of the hierarchy will start the planning process and send it for approval to their immediate supervisors.

If you have selected the top-down type of planning and email notification is enabled, the person at the highest level in the hierarchy will get a message notification that a new Planning Session has started. That person will create the plan data and send it to his or her immediate subordinates for planning.

For our case study, we have selected the Bottom-up type of planning. The individual planners will receive an email asking them to start planning for their respective areas. You can see an example in Figure 5.18.

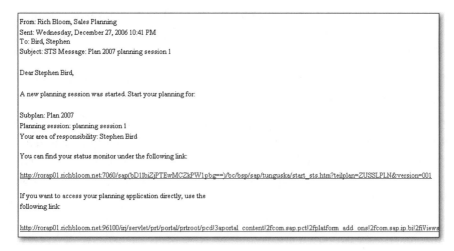

```
From: Rich Bloom, Sales Planning
Sent: Wednesday, December 27, 2006 10:41 PM
To: Bird, Stephen
Subject: STS Message: Plan 2007 planning session 1


Dear Stephen Bird,

A new planning session was started. Start your planning for:

Subplan: Plan 2007
Planning session: planning session 1
Your area of responsibility: Stephen Bird

You can find your status monitor under the following link:

http://rorap01.richbloom.net:7060/sap(bD1lbiZjPTEwMCZkPW1pbg==)/bc/bsp/sap/tunguska/start_sts.htm?teilplan=ZUSSLPLN&version=001

If you want to access your planning application directly, use the
following link:

http://rorap01.richbloom.net:96100/irj/servlet/prt/portal/prtroot/pcd!3aportal_content!2fcom.sap.pct!2fplatform_add_ons!2fcom.sap.ip.bi!2fiViews
```

Figure 5.18 Status and Tracking System Application — Request to Enter Plan Data

Executing a Planning Scenario with STS

If email is enabled and the bottom-up type of planning was selected, the individual planner will get an email message asking him to enter plan data.

A link to the STS application is also sent in the email and can be used to launch the application. When the link is clicked, the user is authenticated for access to the system and the STS application indicating the planning status displays, as shown in Figure 5.19. The information and options displayed here depend on the authorization granted to the user. Click **Details** (see Figure 5.19, callout 1) to access the planning application.

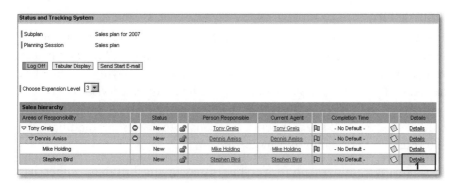

Figure 5.19 Status and Tracking System Application — Initial View

The planning details display (see Figure 5.20) users can use the **Set for Processing** button (see Figure 5.20, callout 1) to set the planning status from

New to **Processing**. They then can click the **Open Planning** button (see Figure 5.20, callout 2) to launch the planning application. They can also enter comments by clicking the **Comments Maintain** button (see Figure 5.20, callout 3).

To access the control report, users can click the **Open Report** button (see Figure 5.20, callout 4). The control report is used mainly for analysis.

Once a user completes entering the plan data for his area, he can use the **Send for Approval** button (see Figure 5.20, callout 5) to send the plan data for approval. The STS application determines the responsible supervisor and sends a request to that individual to approve the plan data prepared by the team member.

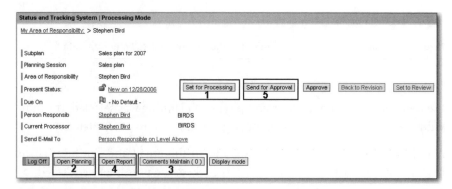

Figure 5.20 Status and Tracking System Application — Processing Mode

In the example shown in Figure 5.21, the planner's supervisor received a message indicating that a person reporting to him has submitted plan data for his approval.

The supervisor can now access the STS application link and either approve or reject the data. If the supervisor approves it (see Figure 5.22), the planner who originally sent the data for approval gets a message saying that the data he had sent to his supervisor has been approved. If the supervisor rejects the plan, the person who submitted the plan data gets a message saying that the request was rejected. The planner can then make the necessary modifications and resubmit the data for approval.

This process continues until everyone listed in the hierarchy either has entered or approved the plan data. When all of the persons listed in the hierarchy have completed planning for their area and it is approved by the most senior person in the hierarchy, the planning process is considered complete (see Figure 5.23). This also signifies that the plan data has been approved by management.

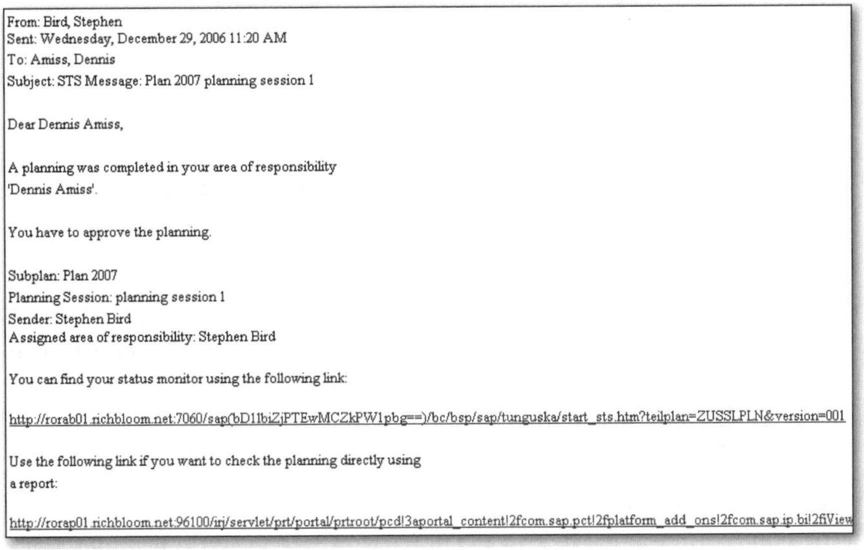

From: Bird, Stephen
Sent: Wednesday, December 29, 2006 11:20 AM
To: Amiss, Dennis
Subject: STS Message: Plan 2007 planning session 1

Dear Dennis Amiss,

A planning was completed in your area of responsibility
'Dennis Amiss'.

You have to approve the planning.

Subplan: Plan 2007
Planning Session: planning session 1
Sender: Stephen Bird
Assigned area of responsibility: Stephen Bird

You can find your status monitor using the following link:

http://rorab01.richbloom.net:7060/sap(bD1IbiZjPTEwMCZkPW1pbg==)/bc/bsp/sap/tunguska/start_sts.htm?teilplan=ZUSSLPLN&version=001

Use the following link if you want to check the planning directly using
a report:

http://rorap01.richbloom.net:96100/irj/servlet/prt/portal/prtroot/pcd!3aportal_content!2fcom.sap.pct!2fplatform_add_ons!2fcom.sap.ip.bi!2fiView

Figure 5.21 Status and Tracking System Application — Request to Approve Plan Data

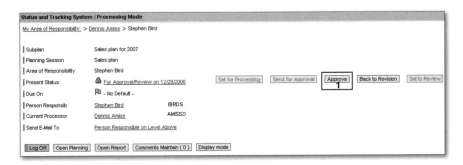

Figure 5.22 Status and Tracking System Application — Approving Plan Data

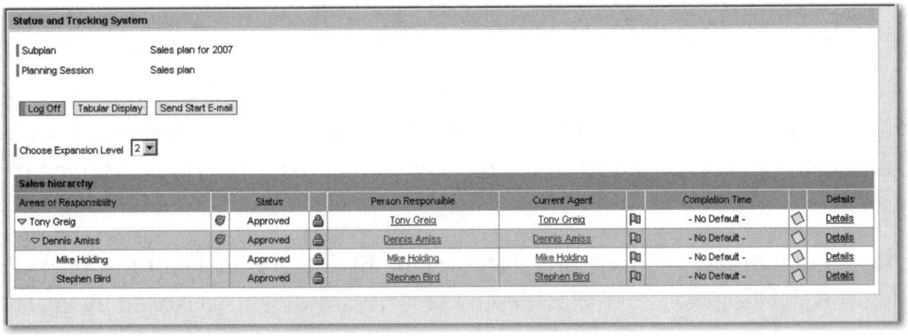

Figure 5.23 Status and Tracking System Application — Completion of Planning

271

Authorizations in STS

The following authorization objects are available for various users of the STS application, as outlined in the following list:

▶ **R_STS_CUST (Plan Administrator)**
This object is assigned to the administrator of the STS application. The technical administrator is responsible for setting the subplan and Planning Session, importing the hierarchy, and assigning the tasks for the planner.

▶ **R_STS_SUP (Plan Coordinator)**
This object is assigned to users responsible for monitoring the entire planning process. A user assigned to this authorization object is given complete access to monitor all of the tasks in the planning process. This user can modify the status of any planning task in the hierarchy.

▶ **R_STS_PT (Planner)**
This object is assigned to give a planner acccess to perform planning tasks and to approve plans submitted by another planner in the planning hierarchy.

In this section, we have explored the steps to configure the STS application and seen the benefits it offers in planning. In the next section, we will detail the process of granting authorization to users in the SAP NetWeaver BI system.

5.3   Authorization

Authorization determines the level of access for a user in a system. Authorizations are granted based on users' roles in the system. A finance user has access to the finance-related applications and data; a sales user has access to the sales-related applications and data, and so on.

The basic element used to administer authorization is called an authorization object. Authorization objects are assigned to a security role held by a user. Transaction **PFCG** is used to create roles and administer the roles assigned to users.

The implementation of an SAP NetWeaver BI Integrated Planning project requires developing a matrix to deploy security for objects accessed by users. A security document will need to be created identifying the different security roles that will be used to administer authorization.

5.3.1 Types of Security Roles

You can specify the following types of security roles:

▶ **Type of User Role**
This determines the role of the user in the planning process; for example, Developer, Planner, Info-Consumer, Power User, and Administrator.

▶ **Data Level Access Role**
This determines the access to specific data within an InfoProvider; for example, access to planning for or reporting on specific business units. This is also referred to as Analysis Authorization.

▶ **Menu Role**
This determines the reporting folders to which users have access. These folders contain the links to transactions, queries, workbooks, and Web applications.

Type of User Role

SAP provides a number of authorization objects that are used to administer security based on the type of user. The authorization objects can be classified for the following:

▶ Using the SAP NetWeaver BI Data Warehousing Workbench

▶ Using the SAP NetWeaver BI Integrated Planning tool

▶ Using the Business Explorer (BEx)

▶ Administering Analysis Authorization

▶ Using Data Mining objects

Table 5.2 lists and describes the authorization objects used in the Data Warehousing Workbench.

Authorization Object	Description
S_RS_ADMWB	Authorizations for working with individual objects of the Data Warehousing Workbench
S_RS_IOBJ	Authorizations for working with individual InfoObjects and their sub-objects
S_RS_DS	Authorizations for working with the DataSource

Table 5.2 Authorization Objects for Using the Data Warehousing Workbench (Source: SAP AG)

273

Authorization Object	Description
S_RS_DTP	Authorizations for working with the data transfer process and its sub-objects
S_RS_ISNEW	Authorizations for working with InfoSources
S_RS_ISOUR	Authorizations for working with InfoSources with flexible updating and their sub-objects
S_RS_ISRCM	Authorizations for working with InfoSources with direct updating and their sub-objects
S_RS_TR	Authorizations for working with transformation rules and their sub-objects
S_RS_ICUBE	Authorizations for working with InfoCubes and their sub-objects
S_RS_MPRO	Authorizations for working with MultiProviders and their sub-objects
S_RS_ODSO	Authorizations for working with DataStore objects and their sub-objects
S_RS_ISET	Authorizations for working with InfoSets
S_RS_HIER	Authorizations for working with hierarchies
S_RS_IOMAD	Authorizations for processing master data in the Data Warehousing Workbench
S_RS_PC	Authorizations for working with process chains
S_RS_OHDST	Authorizations for working with open hub destinations
S_RS_CTT	Authorizations for working with currency translation types
S_RS_UOM	Authorizations for working with quantity conversion types
S_RS_THJT	Authorizations for working with key date derivation types
S_RS_RST	Authorization object for the RS trace tool
RSANPR	Authorizations for working with analysis processes

Table 5.2 Authorization Objects for Using the Data Warehousing Workbench (Source: SAP AG) (cont.)

Table 5.3 lists the authorization objects used in the SAP NetWeaver BI Integrated Planning tool.

Authorization Object	Description
S_RS_ALVL	Authorizations for working with Aggregation Levels
S_RS_PLSE	Authorizations for working with Planning Functions
S_RS_PLSQ	Authorizations for working with Planning Sequences
S_RS_PLST	Authorizations for working with Planning Function types
S_RS_PLENQ	Authorizations for maintaining or displaying lock settings

Table 5.3 Authorization Objects for Using the SAP NetWeaver BI Integrated Planning Tool (Source: SAP AG)

Table 5.4 lists the authorization objects used in the Business Explorer (BEx) for reporting.

Authorization Object	Description
S_RS_COMP	Authorizations for using different components for the query definition
S_RS_COMP1	Authorization for queries from specific owners
S_RS_FOLD	Display authorization for folders
S_RS_TOOLS	Authorizations for individual Business Explorer tools
S_RS_ERPT	Authorizations for BEx Enterprise Reports
S_RS_EREL	Authorizations for reusable elements of a BEx Enterprise Report
S_RS_DAS	Authorizations for working with data access services
S_RS_BTMP	Authorizations for working with BEx Web templates
S_RS_BITM	Authorizations for working with BEx Web items
S_RS_BCS	Authorization for registering broadcast settings for execution.
S_RS_BEXTX	Authorizations for the maintenance of BEx texts

Table 5.4 Authorization Objects for Using the Business Explorer (BEx) Tool (Source: SAP AG)

Table 5.5 lists the authorization objects used for administering Analysis Authorization.

Authorization Object	Description
S_RSEC	Authorization for assigning and administration of analysis authorizations
S_RS_AUTH	Authorization object to include analysis authorizations in roles

Table 5.5 Authorization Objects for Administering Analysis Authorization (Source: SAP AG)

Table 5.6 lists the authorization objects used for the Data Mining object.

Authorization Object	Description
RSDMEMBW	Authorization for uploading Data Mining results into the BI system
RSDMEMODEL	Authorization for working with analytical models
RSANPR	Authorizations for working with analysis processes

Table 5.6 Authorization Objects for Using Data Mining Objects (Source: SAP AG)

Based on the type of user, a user is granted access to InfoProviders and planning objects in the SAP NetWeaver BI system. The InfoProvider, Query, Aggregation Level, Planning Sequences, and Planning Functions are some of the objects to which authorizations can be assigned.

A user must be granted the required authorization to access the InfoProviders and the planning objects included in a planning application. This is addressed as part of any new SAP NetWeaver BI implementation. During this process, the roles of users are identified and the corresponding authorizations are determined.

If an InfoProvider is created exclusively for planning, the required authorizations should be set for any users who will need access to the InfoCube for planning. We will now discuss the authorization needed to access and modify the data in the system.

Data Level Access Role

Starting with SAP NetWeaver 7.0, SAP has renamed the authorization tool available for granting authorization on the data in the SAP NetWeaver BI system from Reporting Authorization to Analysis Authorization. The change in name was prompted by the emergence of planning as an integral part of the SAP NetWeaver BI system and one that includes authorization for both display and maintenance of plan data. SAP has introduced many new features and enhancements to address limitations in the old concept.

The essence of analysis authorization is to grant users access to the data in an InfoProvider based on their role in the organization. For example, a company might have operations in the U.S. and Brazil. Let's say that two company codes exist, one for the U.S. and one for Brazil. A sales analyst working in the U.S. should be given only the access needed to display the sales data that pertains to the U.S. and a sales analyst working in Brazil should be given only the access needed to display the sales data that pertains to Brazil.

In SAP BW 3.5 and earlier releases, Transaction **RSSM** was used to administer authorization. In SAP NetWeaver 7.0, a new Transaction **RSECADMIN** is available to maintain Analysis Authorizations. SAP recommends that customers move their existing authorization setup for data to the new method when they upgrade their SAP BW system to SAP NetWeaver 7.0. While the authorizations specified using Transaction **RSSM** will continue to work, SAP recommends customers use the Analysis Authorization concept from now on.

Note
SAP provides a migration tool, RSEC_MIGRATION, to help with moving existing authorizations based on Reporting Authorization to the new Analysis Authorization. This simplifies migration of authorization administered using Transaction RSSM to the new process.

Use Transaction **RSECADMIN** to access the interface for managing authorizations in the SAP NetWeaver BI system, as shown in Figure 5.24. Three tabs are displayed: **Authorizations**, **User**, and **Analysis**. Let's look at each in more detail.

Authorizations

The **Authorizations** tab is used for maintaining, generating, and transporting authorizations. Three buttons are displayed when the authorization tab is clicked: **Maintenance**, **Generation**, and **Transport**. We'll look at how to use each of these in detail.

▶ **Maintenance**

The **Maintenance** button is used for displaying and maintaining authorization objects. Authorization objects form the basis for defining the Analysis Authorization.

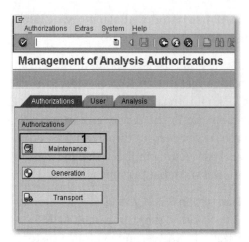

Figure 5.24 Transaction RSECADMIN for Maintaining Analysis Authorizations

Perform the following steps to maintain an authorization object, as illustrated in Figures 5.24 through 5.28:

1. Click the **Maintenance** Button (see Figure 5.24, callout 1).

2. The **Maintain Authorizations: Initial Screen** displays. Enter a name for the authorization object ("ZACC") and click **Create** to create a new authorization object (see Figure 5.25, callouts 2 and 3).

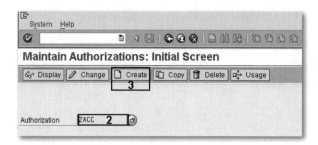

Figure 5.25 Creating an Analysis Authorization Object — Part 1

3. The **Maintain Authorizations: ZACC Create** screen displays (see Figure 5.26). Enter the **Description** "Company Code" **Medium Text** "Auth object for Company Code" and **Long Text** "Auth object for Company Code" for the authorization object (see Figure 5.26, callout 4, 5 and 6).

4. Select the InfoObject to use for administering Analysis Authorization. Click **Create** to define the authorization structure. Select the InfoObject by entering it manually or by using the dropdown box (see Figure 5.26, callout 7 and 8).

5. Certain InfoObjects play a special role in authorization. They are called Special InfoObjects. Click **Special InfoObjects** (see Figure 5.26, callout 9a) to include the InfoObjects in the list that follows (see Figure 5.26, callout 9b):

   ▸ **0TCTAACTVT**

   This InfoObject can be used to provide read and write access for objects. The possible values are 02 (Change data) and 03 (Display data). The default value is 03.

   ▸ **0TCTAIPROV**

   This InfoObject lets you specify the InfoProviders for which the authorization object is applicable.

   ▸ **0TCTAVALID**

   This InfoObject can be used to specify the validity of an authorization object. Before the release of SAP NetWeaver BI 7.0, authorizations could be enforced only at the role level. By using this option, validity can be enforced at the authorization object level. The InfoObject also provides options for excluding time periods and using relational operators such as LE, GT, GE, and LT to define the validity of the authorization. For example, authorization can be set to be valid only on specified dates in a month or a year.

   ▸ **0TCAKYFNM**

   When a Key Figure has been marked as authorization relevant, authorization will be enforced on all InfoProviders that contain the Key Figure. For a user to access the Key Figure, this InfoObject must be included as an authorization object and assigned to the user. Possible values are: single value, range, and pattern. The default is * (All Key Figures).

6. Double-click the InfoObject selected to set the permitted values for the authorization object (see Figure 5.26, callout 10).

7. The **Maintain Authorizations: ZACC Create** screen displays again. The **Value Auths.** and **Hierarchy Authorizations** tabs are available on this screen. The **Value Auths.** tab is used for specifying the values of the Info-Object to be used in the authorization. The **Hierarchy Authorizations** tab is used for specifying the values to be used in the hierarchy authorization. You use this if the InfoObject contains hierarchy data and you need to define authorizations based on the hierarchy. Intervals can also be specified (see Figure 5.27, callout 11).

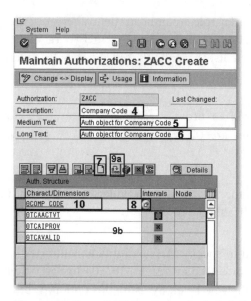

Figure 5.26 Figure 7. 26 Creating an Analysis Authorization Object — Part 2

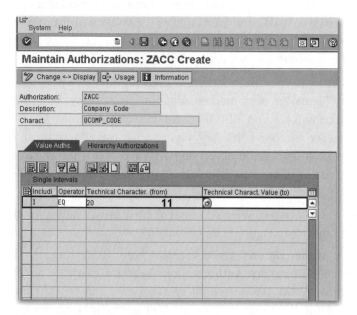

Figure 5.27 Creating an Analysis Authorization Object — Part 3

8. Repeat the previous two steps for the other InfoObjects included in the authorization structure.

9. Figure 5.28, callout 12, displays the values set for the **0TAACTVT** Info-Object. This is a Special InfoObject. The values set here dictate whether

a person can only display or can display and change data for the Info-Object included in the authorization object.

10. Save the authorization object.

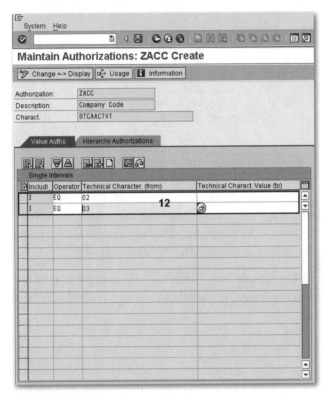

Figure 5.28 Creating an Analysis Authorization Object — Part 4

▶ **Generation**

SAP NetWeaver BI supports the generation of analysis authorizations from other source systems such as the SAP R/3 system and the flat-file system. For example, if a user has access to a specific Human Resource (HR) Organizational Level in the SAP R/3 system, the same access can be made available in the SAP NetWeaver BI system by generating the authorization based on information in SAP R/3. The data coming from these systems are loaded into specific Data Store objects. SAP provides Business Content objects to facilitate the loading of these Data Store objects from the R/3 system. The Data Store objects are then used as the source of data for generating authorizations in the SAP NetWeaver BI system. Figure 5.29 displays the screen used for generating authorizations in SAP NetWeaver BI based on data in the Data Store objects.

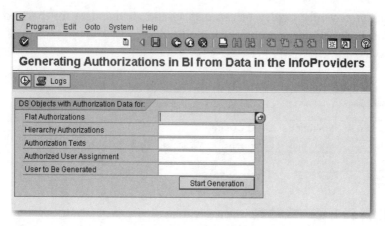

Figure 5.29 Generating Authorization from Data in an InfoProvider

▶ **Transport**

The Transport button is used for transporting authorization objects created in the SAP NetWeaver BI development system to the other systems in the landscape — namely, the Quality and Production systems.

We are now done looking at the configuration options that are available on the **Authorizations** tab. Next, we will detail the settings available on the **User** tab.

User

The **User** tab is used for assigning the necessary authorizations for users. The following options are available when assigning authorization to a user:

▶ **Individual Authorization**

In this case, a user is selected and a corresponding authorization object is assigned to the user.

▶ **Group Authorization**

In this case, the authorization objects are grouped into a hierarchy, and a user is granted access to one or several authorization groups.

▶ **Role-Based Authorization**

In this case, an authorization object is assigned to the role and the role is assigned to a user. This option has been available since earlier releases. When using the Analysis Authorization, you can assign the authorization to authorization object S_RS_AUTH. This lets you assign authorizations created using the Analysis Authorization method to traditional security roles.

The following are the steps to assign an authorization object to users, as illustrated in Figures 5.30 and 5.31:

1. In the **Analysis Authorizations** area, click the **Assignment** button (see Figure 5.30, callout 1).

2. The **BI Reporting: Init Screen Assignment of User Authorizations** screen displays. Click the **Change** button to switch into change mode (see Figure 5.30, callout 2).

3. Enter the user for whom the authorization is to be set (see Figure 5.30, callout 3) and click **Enter**.

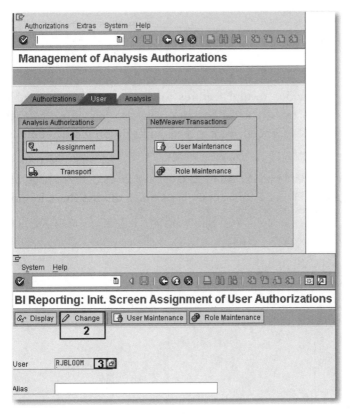

Figure 5.30 Assigning User Authorization — Part 1

4. Select the authorization object to be assigned to the user from the dropdown list and click the **Insert** button (see Figure 5.31, callouts 4 and 5). The authorization object selected is assigned to the user.

5. Click the **Save** icon (see Figure 5.31, callout 6).

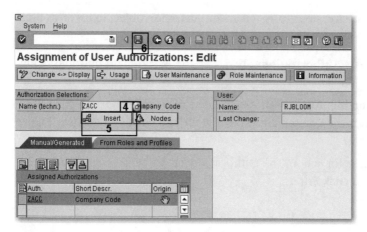

Figure 5.31 Assigning User Authorization — Part 2

Analysis

The analysis tool provides several features that are useful when trouble-shooting users' issues related to authorization. It also lets you effectively monitor the security setup needed for a legal audit by providing complete logs of users' activities.

Three buttons are available on the Analysis tab: **Execute as...**, **Error Logs,** and **Generation Logs** (see Figure 5.32, callout 1). We will discuss these in more detail.

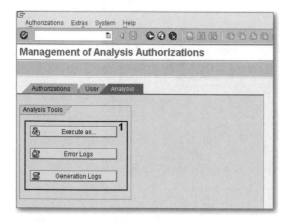

Figure 5.32 Management of Analysis Authorization — Part 1

► **Execute as...**

Using this option, a user can be logged into the system using his user ID and then simulate the identity of another user to perform actions. For example, suppose that a user from the development team wants to view a problem faced by another user who is executing queries. In this case, it will be helpful for the developer to enter the application as that user and see the actual error. The user ID of the specific user can be entered or selected from a dropdown list in the **Execution as User** field, and the desired transaction executed. The transaction that needs to be simulated is selected from the **Possible Transactions** area shown in the screen.

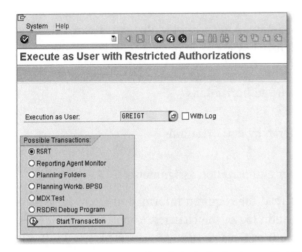

Figure 5.33 Management of Analysis Authorization — Part 2

▶ **Error Logs**
When logging is enabled for a user, details of Analysis Authorization checks carried out by the system can be displayed.

▶ **Generation Logs**
After an authorization generation is complete, you can use this option to view a detailed log for the authorization generation.

The error logs and generation logs provide complete data when the system is subject to a legal audit. The logs can also highlight any security-related short-comings in the system and help to address them. In the next section, you will see how changes to authorizations can be tracked.

Menu Role

The menu role contains links to the following objects:

▶ Transactions

▶ Queries

▶ Workbooks

▶ Web applications

The role provides users with access to these objects. Users who are assigned to menu roles see their roles displayed as menu items when they sign onto the system.

5.3.2 Legal Auditing

As part of SAP Technical Content, SAP provides Virtual InfoProviders to track changes to authorizations. They are as follows:

▶ **0TCA_VAL**
Change documents for value authorizations

▶ **0TCA_HIE**
Change documents for hierarchy authorizations

▶ **0TCA_UA**
Change documents for user authorization assignments

These Virtual InfoProviders read the required information from the associated tables that contain the audit log of the changes. You can create queries for these InfoProviders to monitor the activities.

In this section you have seen how the new Analysis Authorization concept in SAP NetWeaver 7.0 helps define authorization objects that can be used for both planning and reporting and how easily an authorization object can be assigned to users. This section has also highlighted several new features that can be used when troubleshooting authorization-related issues. The ability to display authorization-related errors encountered by users and the ability to generate change logs related to authorization objects both highlight the multifaceted approach to security in SAP NetWeaver 7.0. In the next section, we will discuss the details of transporting objects in the SAP NetWeaver BI system.

5.4 Transporting Planning Objects

Planning objects created in the development system will need to be transported to the quality assurance and production systems for testing and final implementation. To start this process, you create a transport request in the development system that contains the planning objects for the application and transport it to the quality assurance system. A user-acceptance test is then performed in the quality assurance system to ensure that the functionality works as expected. After the objects are tested successfully in the quality assurance system, they are transported to the production system.

The process of transport involves the following steps:

1. Create/Edit Objects in the development system.
2. Create a transport request in the development system for the objects created or modified.
3. Transport the request to the quality assurance system.
4. Perform user acceptance test in the quality assurance system.
5. If the test passes, the transport request is moved to the production system.

5.4.1 Change Control Process

A good change-control process should be in place to ensure that the changes made to planning objects are authorized, documented, and well-tested in the respective systems before moving a transport request to the next system in the landscape. This prevents more problems than following a process that allows unintended transports across the landscape.

5.4.2 Creating a Transport Request

Creating a transport request for planning objects is relatively simple when compared to the complexity of transporting SAP NetWeaver BI-related objects. The planning objects that can be transported in the context of SAP NetWeaver BI Integrated Planning are Aggregation Level, Filter, Planning Function, and Planning Sequence.

The following steps are needed to transport planning objects, as illustrated in Figures 5.34 through 5.37:

1. Use Transaction **RSA1** to access the Data Warehousing Workbench. Select the **Transport Connection** option.
2. Before starting the process of creating a transport request, set the **Grouping** and **Collection Mode** in the Transport Connection tool. We recommend that you set the **Grouping** to **Only Necessary Objects** and the **Collection Mode** to **Collect Automatically** (see Figure 5.34, callouts 1 and 2).

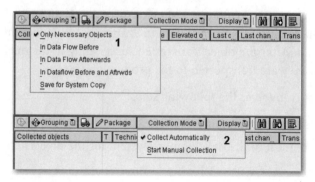

Figure 5.34 Transporting a Planning Object — Set Collection Mode

3. Select the object type for the transport. The type of planning objects that can be transported are shown in Figure 5.35, callout 3.

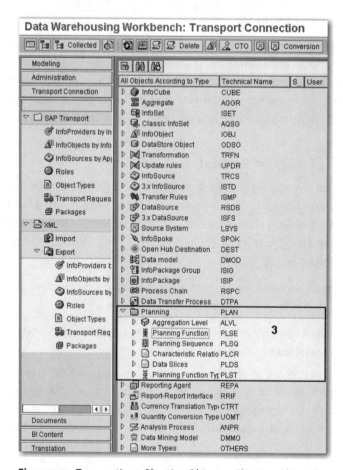

Figure 5.35 Transporting a Planning Object — Planning Object Types

4. Select and then double-click the object type to start the process of selecting the objects for the transport (see Figure 5.36, callout 4). The **Input help for Metadata** dialog box displays the list of objects for the object type. Select the object from the list and click **Transfer Selections** (see Figure 5.36, callouts 5 and 6).

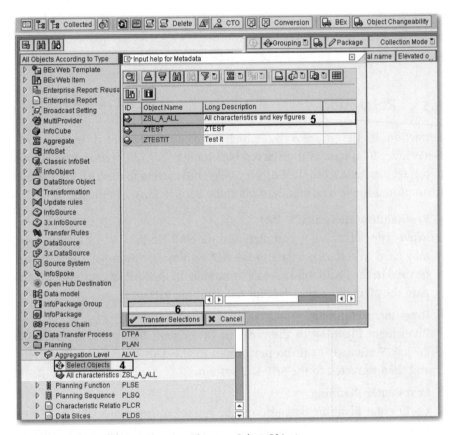

Figure 5.36 Transporting a Planning Object — Select Objects

5. Click the **Transport** button to create a transport requests for the objects selected (see Figure 5.37, callout 7). The system prompts you to assign the objects to a transport request.

In this section, we showed you the steps involved in creating a request to transport objects across the landscape. In the next section, we will examine the process to retract plan data from the SAP NetWeaver BI system to the SAP R/3 system.

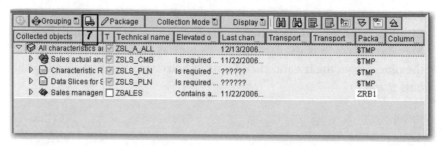

Collected objects	7	T	Technical name	Elevated o	Last chan	Transport	Transport	Packa	Column
▽ 🌍 All characteristics a	☑		ZSL_A_ALL		12/13/2006...			$TMP	
▷ 🗒 Sales actual an	☑		ZSLS_CMB	Is required ...	11/22/2006...			$TMP	
▷ 🗐 Characteristic R	☑		ZSLS_PLN	Is required ...	??????			$TMP	
▷ 🗐 Data Slices for S	☑		ZSLS_PLN	Is required ...	??????			$TMP	
▷ 🔷 Sales managen	☐		ZSALES	Contains a...	11/22/2006...			ZRB1	

Figure 5.37 Transporting a Planning Object — Create Transport Request

5.5   Retraction

Retraction is the process by which plan data completed in the SAP NetWeaver BI system is transferred back to the SAP R/3 system. The ability to retract plan data from the SAP NetWeaver BI system to the SAP R/3 system is supported for several standard planning applications, as follows:

▶ **Profitability Analysis (CO-PA)**
When sales planning is completed in the SAP NetWeaver BI system, you may need to retract the data to the R/3 system. For example, the data can be used in the Profitability Analysis module in the SAP R/3 system to compare the plan and actual data for determining variances.

▶ **Investment Planning**
Investment Planning in the areas of Investment Management (IM) and Project System (PS) can be performed in the SAP NetWeaver BI system and then retracted to the SAP R/3 system.

▶ **Cost Center Planning**
Cost Center Planning data also can be retracted from the SAP NetWeaver BI system to the SAP R/3 system. Users have a great deal of flexibility in doing primary cost planning in the SAP NetWeaver BI system. After primary cost planning is completed, the data can be retracted to the SAP R/3 system, which usually handles secondary cost planning. As of this writing, there is no function module available with which to retract secondary plan costs from the SAP NetWeaver BI system to the SAP R/3 system.

Retractors fall into two types:

▶ **Pull Mechanism**
In this case, the data is requested and initiated from the SAP R/3 system. An example of a retractor that belongs to this type is Sales and Profitability Planning (Controlling: Profitability Analysis application).

▶ **Push Mechanism**

In this case, the data is pushed from the SAP NetWeaver BI system to the R/3 system. An example of a retractor that belongs to this type is Cost Center Planning, where primary cost plan data can be retracted from the SAP NetWeaver BI system to the SAP R/3 system.

The following steps are needed to retract the plan data pertaining to the Profitability Analysis module (CO-PA) from the SAP NetWeaver BI system to the SAP R/3 system, as illustrated in Figures 5.38 through 5.42:

1. Create a query by including the necessary Characteristics and Key Figures for the transfer in the SAP NetWeaver BI system. The query should be enabled for access to third-party applications (see Figure 5.38).

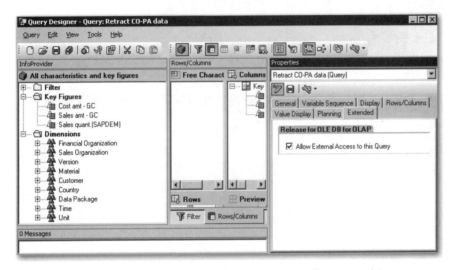

Figure 5.38 Retracting CO-PA Data to the SAP R/3 System — Allow External Access

2. Use Transaction **KELC** in the source system to maintain the settings for the transfer. The system prompts you to enter the operating concern before executing the transaction (see Figure 5.39).

3. Specify the query that will be used in the SAP NetWeaver BI system as the basis for extracting the data (see Figure 5.40).

4. Maintain the mapping of InfoObjects used in the query in the SAP NetWeaver BI system within the fields maintained in the R/3 system (see Figure 5.41).

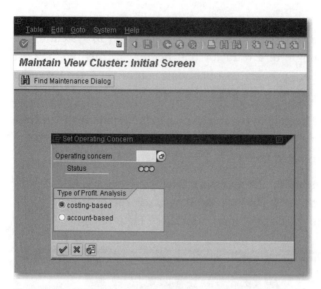

Figure 5.39 Retracting CO-PA data to the SAP R/3 System — Transaction KELC

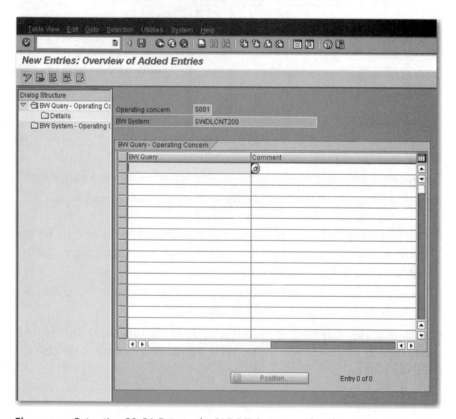

Figure 5.40 Retracting CO-PA Data to the SAP R/3 System — Identify Query for Retraction

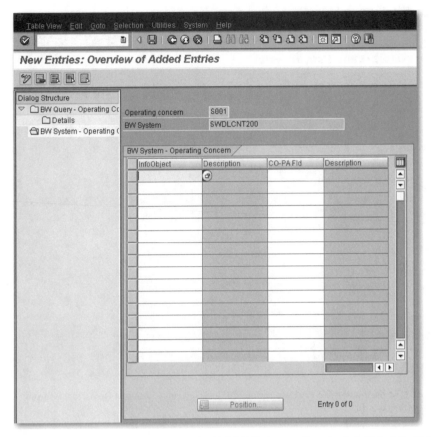

Figure 5.41 Retracting CO-PA Data to the SAP R/3 System — Mapping InfoObjects to Fields

5. Initiate the data transfer from the source system using Transaction **KELR** (see Figure 5.42). Select the SAP NetWeaver BI system and the query to be used for transferring the data. If variables are used in the query, specify a variant for the query that contains the values to be used for the variables. In this transaction, the type of update (actual or plan) can be specified.

   Because the SAP R/3 system is normally the source of the actual transaction data, the type of update should be set to **Plan**. The transaction type and version values to use for extracting the plan data can be specified. The transaction can also be executed in test mode. The option of reversing the data previously extracted is also available.

You have now seen how to retract plan data from the SAP NetWeaver BI system to the SAP R/3 system. In the next section, we will discuss the importance of monitoring performance and the areas to review when analyzing performance issues.

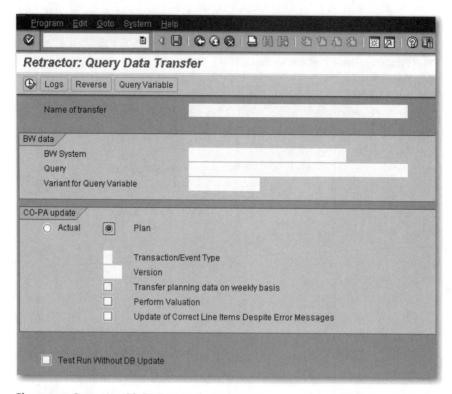

Figure 5.42 Retracting CO-PA Data to the SAP R/3 System — Request Data Transfer from SAP NetWeaver BI

5.6   Performance Monitoring and Analysis

Performance monitoring and analysis is an integral part of the planning application development process, and you should allocate enough time for this purpose.

You should identify and include key business processes in the planning application when analyzing performance. Each key business process must be broken down into individual steps. One of the techniques that SAP recommends is a case-based approach for analyzing performance. A case is a series of no more than 15 steps. An Input-Enabled Query or a Planning Function can be considered as a step in this process.

It is important to record the time taken to complete each step to know whether the process was completed efficiently. The bottlenecks with respect to runtime and memory consumption are identified in the analysis.

During performance analysis, the system should closely resemble the same environment that will exist in the production system. You should pay particular attention to configuration, number of users and volume of data. Performance analysis can be done during the testing phase and also just before the go-live date.

Consider the following points for improving performance of planning applications:

▶ The performance of a planning application starts with the modeling of InfoProviders created for planning and analysis. A robust data model lends itself to improved performance when analyzing data. InfoProviders should be designed for optimal performance because the data for planning is read from the InfoProviders.

▶ The sizing of the SAP NetWeaver BI system plays an important role in the performance of systems. It should take into account the volume of data, the number of users simultaneously accessing and using the system at different times, the complexity of the application, and data growth. It is important to focus on sizing during the initial phase of the project. Incorrect sizing can contribute to a host of problems; performance might be affected and users might lose confidence in the system.

▶ Create Aggregates on InfoCubes to improve the performance of queries.

▶ Compress data in an InfoCube on a regular basis so that the number of records in the InfoCube is reduced. This will help improve the performance of queries.

▶ On a periodic basis, perform Database Statistics on tables in the SAP NetWeaver BI system.

▶ Deploy Statistics InfoProviders to measure application use and performance. The Business Content InfoProviders for recording the statistics of the BI system can be activated and analyzed regularly to understand the performance of the planning applications.

▶ The Planning Functions provide functionality for automatically generating and modifying plan data. Consider the following when designing Planning Functions.

  ▶ Use the generic planning functions (copy, delete, repost, etc.) provided by SAP as much as possible.

  ▶ Use formula (FOX) and user exit-based functions only when necessary. Use them when it is efficient to combine multiple functions into one formula function or exit function. They provide flexibility and help when there are complex requirements.

▶ Do not use nested FOREACH statements in formulas in a Planning Function. They increase overhead and might produce erroneous results.

5.7   Summary

This chapter covered topics you must understand to be able to work with planning applications. We discussed the concept of locking and the different options that are available to configure locks in the system, including the settings that help prevent locking conflicts.

We also explained in detail the benefits of working with the STS application, using a typical planning scenario as an example and we showed you the steps involved in customizing the STS application for the planning scenario.

Further, we discussed the new concept of Analysis Authorization for administering authorizations. We explained the many advantages this offers and showed you the steps for setting up an authorization object. We also specified the authorization objects that are used in SAP NetWeaver BI Integrated Planning.

Later in the chapter, we examined the process of transporting planning objects from the development system to other systems in the landscape. We also highlighted the importance of change management when administering the transport process.

Next, we listed the planning applications that can be used for retracting data from the SAP NetWeaver BI system back to the SAP R/3 system, and we illustrated the steps to retract the Profitability Analysis data (CO-PA) from the SAP NetWeaver BI system to the SAP R/3 system.

Finally, we stressed the importance of good performance for a planning application and explained what to look for when analyzing performance.

In the next and final chapter, we will look at SAP's recommended approach to implementing projects using the Accelerated SAP (ASAP) methodology and best practices to adopt when implementing a SAP NetWeaver BI planning project. The chapter ends with a summary of the key points discussed in the book and how SAP NetWeaver BI Integrated Planning can be used to effectively fulfill the planning requirements of a business.

6 SAP NetWeaver BI Integrated Planning — Implementation and Best Practices

This chapter provides an overview of the implementation steps for an SAP BI Integrated Planning project using the Accelerated SAP (ASAP) methodology and the best practices to be followed for a successful implementation

We start the chapter by discussing the steps in the implementation of a project using ASAP. In the subsequent section, we detail some of the best practices that can be deployed for ensuring success in any software implementation. This also applies to the SAP BI Integrated Planning project.

6.1 SAP ASAP Methodology

The SAP BI Integrated Planning tool provides the framework for realizing the planning, forecasting, and budgeting requirements of an organization. The architecture incorporates the following components:

- Storage platform (Enterprise Data Warehouse layer) for maintaining plan data in multidimensional data storage containers called InfoCubes.
- Data-processing layer that enables users to modify plan data using Business Planning tools.
- Presentation layer that presents the planning application in Microsoft Excel and the Web interface.
- Additional tools such as the BEx Broadcaster that allow dissemination of information and provides the security mechanism that restricts users based on the their profiles, and utilities that allow for efficient execution of the planning process.

Figure 6.1 provides an overview of the architecture used in SAP BI Integrated Planning.

Planning is a key component of any business. The benefits of planning depend on how well a plan is conceived, developed, and executed. The SAP BI Integrated Planning tool addresses the need for a stable and flexible planning solution.

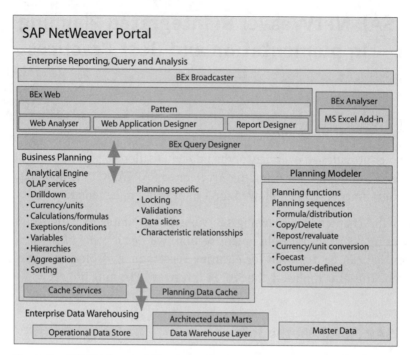

Figure 6.1 SAP BI Integrated Planning Architecture (Source: SAP AG)

SAP recommends a project management methodology known as ASAP. This is a proven, repeatable, and successful approach to implementing an SAP solution. The methodology consists of the following phases:

▶ Project preparation

▶ Business Blueprint

▶ Realization

▶ Final preparation

▶ Go-Live and support

Figure 6.1 depicts the stages in an implementation using the ASAP methodology.

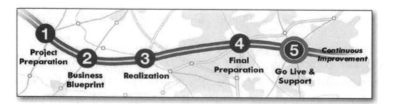

Figure 6.2 Steps in the Implementation Using ASAP Methodology (Source: SAP AG)

The objectives of the project are clearly defined in the project preparation phase. It is during this phase that the timelines for the different milestones are defined, the budget for the project is allocated, and resources are assigned. The remaining phases are described here:

▶ **Business Blueprint phase**
The functional requirements are gathered during workshop sessions. A detailed blueprint document is prepared, which highlights the objectives of the project and the schedule of delivery of functionality to users.

▶ **Realization phase**
The configuration and development of objects are performed based on the objective outlined in the blueprint document. After completion of the configuration and development, an integration test is performed to ensure the quality of the software. End-user documentation is also prepared for users. This serves as a reference to the functionality being deployed.

▶ **Final preparation phase**
The final phase of testing—end-user training—transports objects to the production system; final cutover activities are performed.

▶ **Go-live and support phase**
Users start using the functionality in the production system. The project team is responsible for providing production support, ensuring optimal performance of the system, and monitoring system activities.

The next section discusses some of the best practices you can employ during a project implementation.

6.2   Best Practices for Project Implementation

Best practices are proven methodologies that have produced desired results in the past. These best practices apply to most software implementations. The following points need to be considered to ensure success in the implementation of the SAP BI Integrated Planning project.

▶ Project sponsorship is the key to ensuring the success of a project. The project sponsor is the person who has a clear vision of the business requirements and who drives the project in a manner that realizes an organization's objectives. The project sponsor is also responsible for providing high-level direction.

- The scope of a project is used to define the project's deliverables. The project outcome, along with the timelines in which they will be delivered, needs to be clearly communicated to business users and project team members. This aids in managing user expectations.

- A project's implementation involves teams that combine resources from the business and the IT departments. Business users drive the requirements of the project, while the IT department works with the business to deploy software solutions. It is important for the business and IT team members to work together toward this common goal. The two teams must also communicate well with each other to ensure that everyone involved in the project knows what is happening at all times.

- It is helpful for project team members to be in one location. Team members need to be able to collaborate easily, and putting them all in one location helps to create a sense of working on a team.

- Implementing a software project will have a direct impact on the users who use the tool. It could change the way users perform a particular task, and that can cause some anxiety among the staff. This is typical in most big implementations. To help alleviate this problem from occurring, the change should be managed by communicating the benefits of the tool to the end-users early in the project rather than springing the tool on everyone and expecting them to be productive.

- It always helps to network with other organizations involved in implementing the BI Integrated Planning tool in their organizations. This allows you to exchange ideas and follow the best practices that other teams have found beneficial.

- An implementation's success is measured by the use of the tool. End-users need to be trained on the tool as well. The benefits of using the tool need to be communicated during training.

- Documentation is often left for last, but it is a key part of any software implementation. The functional and technical areas of your implementation should be well-documented, and the earlier you start the documentation, the better. The documentation will help developers who may need to modify the configuration at a later time, and a reference guide that explains how to use the tool should also be made available to business users.

This wraps up our coverage of SAP BI Integrated Planning for Finance. We hope that we were able to help you accomplish a smooth project implementation in your own or your client's organization. In the next section, we will summarize the important topics that we have discussed in this book.

6.3   Summary

SAP NetWeaver 7.0 provides the key capabilities for integrating people, information, and processes as well as the actual application platform. Business Intelligence falls under the information integration capability and provides the tools needed to integrate, analyze, and distribute information. This helps organizations make decisions in a timely manner and stay ahead of the competition.

The BI Integrated Planning tool is a solution you can use to address the financial planning, forecasting, and budgeting needs of an organization. The contents of this book were covered in three major sections.

▶ The first section included the Introduction and Overview and Chapter 1. It provided an introduction to financial planning and discussed the evolution of the planning software provided by SAP. SAP NetWeaver BI Integrated Planning is the latest tool offered by SAP in the area of planning, and is available with SAP NetWeaver 7.0.

▶ The second part included Chapters 2, 3, and 4. These chapters discussed the concepts and terminology used in the SAP Business Intelligence system and analyzed the framework that is available for planning. You saw a case study for a model company, Rich Bloom, which is a clothing retailer that caters to the teenage market. The company's operations are located in the United States, the United Kingdom, and Germany, and the requirement of the case study was to project the gross profit margin of its operation. You saw how to configure the planning application using the SAP BI Integrated Planning tool. You also developed a complete planning application, using the BEx Analyzer and the Web Application Designer tools, to meet the planning requirements of the case study.

▶ The third part included Chapters 5 and 6. These chapters presented topics that would help with the smooth functioning of the BI Integrated Planning tool. In Chapter 5, the steps used to implement the SAP solution using the ASAP methodology were discussed. In this chapter (Chapter 6), you learned about some of the best practices you can deploy for a successful implementation.

In this book, you have also seen how BI Integrated Planning helps reduce TCO. Here are some of the important reasons:

▶ The front-end toolsets, such as the BEx Analyzer and the Web Application Designer used to analyze data in the SAP Business Intelligence system, can also be used in the context of planning. This is a major change when compared to the SAP BPS software and directly contributes to better usability. It also reduces TCO.

▶ You can leverage the power of the OLAP functionality in the SAP BI system to develop a sophisticated financial planning application. This not only provides better performance, but also allows certain functionalities, such as drill-down capabilities, unit of measure conversion, currency translation, and so on.

▶ The BI Integrated Planning tool enables objects to be reused, thus reducing the time needed to develop planning applications. Further, the data that already exists in the data warehouse can be used as reference data for the purpose of planning. This provides access to information and aids in planning.

The SAP BI Integrated Planning tool provides the framework to plan and analyze data with the goal of enhanced user productivity and reduced total cost of ownership. The planning software in SAP has evolved to meet the vital requirements of business users. Making the right choice of planning tool ultimately can determine the success of your organization.

Appendix

A   Author Biography

Sridhar Srinivasan

Sridhar Srinivasan is a Senior Business Intelligence Architect for Zebra Consulting, Inc, in Phoenix, AZ. He holds a bachelor's degree in Engineering from the College of Engineering in Guindy, Chennai, India.

Sri has two decades of information-technology experience and has been working with SAP products since 1995. He has been directly involved since 1998 with implementations of the SAP NetWeaver Business Intelligence (BI) product, originally called SAP Business Warehouse (BW). He is certified in all of the versions of the product, including SAP NetWeaver BI 2004s. Sri has helped several clients in the U.S. manage and implement solutions in business intelligence, covering application areas that include Finance, Controlling, Sales and Distribution, Customer Relationship Management (CRM), Service Management, Inventory Management, Plant Maintenance, and Human Resources. He has also been working as lead consultant in managing the entire lifecycle of BI project implementations, from the blueprint phase through post-go-live support.

Sri has been living with his family in the U.S. for the last 17 years and now lives in Houston, Texas. He can be reached at *zebraus@yahoo.com*.

Kumar Srinivasan

Kumar Srinivasan is a Senior Business Intelligence Consultant working for Zebra Consulting Inc. in Phoenix, AZ. He holds a master's degree in Finance from Loyola College in Chennai, India. He is also a certified cost accountant.

Kumar has almost two decades of experience in information technology and has been working with SAP products since 1999. He has been involved since 2000 with implementations of the SAP NetWeaver Business Intelligence (BI) product, originally called

SAP Business Warehouse (BW). He provides solutions to clients in various areas of business intelligence, dealing both with back-end configuration and front-end user-interface development. Kumar has expertise providing solutions in the area of SAP Business Planning and Simulation (BPS) and using the SAP NetWeaver BI Integrated Planning tool. His articles on SAP BW have been published in *BW Expert* magazine.

Before working with Zebra Consulting, Inc., Kumar worked as an information officer with The World Bank. During this time, he worked with relational database management systems using Ingress, Informix, and Oracle software. He also has extensive experience in the development of applications using messaging tools such as Lotus Notes.

Kumar has been living with his family in the United States for the last 15 years and now resides in San Diego, California. He can be reached at *kshrini77@yahoo.com*.

B   Sources and Further Reading

B.1   Sources

▶ SAP Help Portal: **http://help.sap.com**

▶ SAP Developer Network : **http:/www.sdn.sap.com**

▶ SAP Service Marketplace: **http://www.service.sap.com**

▶ SAP ASAP Methodology: The information about the SAP recommended project management methodolgy can be accessed on the SAP Help Portal (**http://help.sap.com**)

B.2   Further Reading

Additional SAP PRESS titles related to the subject matter the authors recommend include:

▶ Business Planning with SAP SEM by Roland Fischer

▶ SAP Business Intelligence by Norbert Egger, Jean-Marie Fiechter, Sebastian Kramer, Ralf-Patrick Sawicki, and Stephan Weber

C   Glossary

Administrator Workbench The Administrator Workbench for SAP BW 3.x (Transaction RSA1) is the main tool for performing back-end configuration. It provides data-modeling functions as well as functions to control, monitor, and maintain processes associated with data procurement, data retention, and data processing.

Aggregate An Aggregate stores the dataset of an InfoCube redundantly in summarized form. It is an InfoCube that is defined to contain a subset of the Characteristics and Key Figures for improved performance in reporting.

Aggregation Level Aggregation Levels are used in planning as InfoProviders. An Aggregation Level contains a set of Characteristics and Key Figures from a Real-Time InfoCube. It forms the base on which other planning objects like Filters, Planning functions, and Planning Sequences are created when using the BI Integrated Planning tool. It provides the foundation for manual planning of data or changing of data using Planning Functions.

Attributes Attributes are InfoObjects that are logically assigned or subordinated to other InfoObjects of the Characteristic type.

Attribute Change Run If hierarchies and attributes for Characteristics have changed, then it is necessary to make structural changes to the aggregates in order to adjust the data accordingly. The attribute change run activates master and hierarchy data and adjusts data in aggregates.

Authorization Objects These objects provide access to system, transactions, menus, tasks, queries, and data.

Basic Cube The Basic Cube is a type of InfoCube that contains data.

Business Explorer (BEx) Analyzer This is an add-on tool used in the SAP NetWeaver BI system that makes it possible to create queries, query views, and workbooks using Microsoft Excel.

Business Explorer (BEx) Query Designer This is an add-on tool for creating queries for reporting data in the SAP NetWeaver BI system. The query created here can be used by the BEx Analyzer, BEx Report Designer, and BEx Web Application Designer.

Business Explorer (BEx) Report Designer This add-on tool is used to design formatted reports.

Business Explorer (BEx) Web Application Designer This add-on tool is used to develop templates for reporting on the Web.

Business Content Business Content is a predefined set of objects provided by SAP to expedite development of business-intelligence projects. The list of objects includes InfoObjects, Info-

Providers, Roles, Queries, InfoSources, and Web Applications.

Business Planning and Simulation (BPS) This tool is available in the SAP SEM-BPS and SAP NetWeaver BI systems to plan, forecast, and budget for various application areas.

Calculated Key Figure A Calculated Key Figure is one that represents a formula. An example is the sum of two different values.

Characteristic This is a type of Info-Object in the SAP NetWeaver BI system. Characteristics represent character values of data. Examples of Characteristic are Customer, Material, and Employee.

Characteristic Relationships These are the relationships between data used in the derivation and validation of planning data.

Communication Structure In the SAP BW 3.x system, this represents the structure of an InfoSource and is independent of data coming from a source system.

Crystal Report This third-party tool is used to develop formatted reports.

Data Provider A Data Provider is used in the BEx Web Application Designer tool for reporting. It is an object that contains the data used as the source for a Web item in a Web template. It can be an InfoProvider, Query, or Query View.

Data Slices Data Slices are used to explicitly lock certain subsets of plan data so they cannot be changed.

DataSource A DataSource is an object that defines the source of data from a source system.

Data Store A Data Store is an object that contains detailed data in a relational-database format. The data is stored as a transparent table.

Data Target A Data Target is an object in SAP that contains data. An InfoCube, an InfoObject, and a DataStore are examples of Data Targets.

Data Transfer Process (DTP) A Data Transfer Process is an object that determines how data is transferred between two persistent objects in the SAP NetWeaver BI system.

Data Warehouse Data warehousing with SAP NetWeaver BI supports an extensive business-intelligence solution for converting data into valuable information.

Data Warehouse Workbench The Data Warehouse Workbench for SAP NetWeaver BI 2004s (transaction RSA1 is the main tool for performing back-end configuration in the SAP NetWeaver BI system. It provides data- modeling functions as well as functions to control, monitor, and maintain processes in SAP NetWeaver BI that are associated with data procurement, data retention, and data processing.

Delta Load The Delta load to the SAP NetWeaver BI system contains changes to the data coming from a source system since the last load.

Dimension A dimension is a grouping of Characteristics that relate to each other. When an InfoCube is defined, Characteristics are summarized in dimensions in order to store them in a table of the star schema (dimension table).

Dimension Table A dimension table stores the dimension IDs and surrogate

IDs of the Characteristics that make up a dimension.

Extract Structure The extract structure is the structure of data that is extracted from the source system before being loaded to the SAP NetWeaver BI system.

Extractor An extractor is a set of ABAP programs, database tables, and other objects that SAP NetWeaver BI system uses to extract data from SAP systems.

Fact Table The fact table is the table in an InfoCube that contains the dimension IDs and the Key Figures. This table forms the central unit of the star schema.

Filter Filters are used in reporting and planning to restrict data based on Characteristic values.

Flat File A flat file is a data file with a format similar to that of a text or comma-separated file.

Full Load A full load is a load to the SAP NetWeaver BI system that represents a full extract of data from a source system. The full load can also be based on specific selections.

Hierarchy A hierarchy represents the parent-child relationship of data. Examples of hierarchy are cost center hierarchy, customer hierarchy, and material hierarchy.

InfoCube An InfoCube is a Reporting Object in a data warehouse that has a structure of a star schema.

InfoObject This is the basic building block of objects in a SAP data warehouse. It includes Characteristics and Key Figures.

InfoPackage An InfoPackage defines an object that is used to schedule a load of data from a source system to the SAP NetWeaver BI system.

InfoProvider These are objects in the SAP NetWeaver BI system that contain data and can be used for reporting.

InfoSet An InfoSet is an InfoProvider that joins data in objects such as the InfoCube, Data Store, and InfoObjects.

InfoSource An InfoSource is an object that represents the data coming from a source system into the SAP NetWeaver BI system.

Input-Enabled Query An Input-Enabled Query is one that is defined for purpose of planning in SAP NetWeaver BI. This query allows users to enter plan data.

Key Figure This type of InfoObject in the SAP NetWeaver BI represents quantitative values of data. Examples of Key Figures are Sales Amount, Sales Quantity, and Count of Items.

Locking Locking is the process by which the system manages conflicts when different users try to access the same data at the same time.

Manual Planning This term is used for manual entry of plan data using a planning application in the SAP NetWeaver BI system.

Operational Data Store (ODS) ODS objects contain detailed data in a relational database format. This term has been replaced by the term Data Store in NetWeaver BI 7.0.

Planning Area These planning objects in SAP BW-BPS define the InfoCubes that are used as the basis for creating a planning application.

Planning Function A Planning Function is an object used to automate the generation and modification of plan data. For example, a Planning Function can be used to copy actual sales data to a version of the plan data.

Planning Level This planning object in SAP BW-BPS defines the set of Characteristics and Key Figures that are used as the basis for creating a planning application.

Planning Modeler This tool, available in the SAP NetWeaver BI Integrated Planning application, is used to create planning objects.

Planning Package This planning object in BW-BPS further restricts Characteristics whose values have not already been restricted in the planning level. The Planning Package is used for manual planning or when executing a planning function.

Planning Sequence This object in SAP NetWeaver BI Integrated Planning is used to combine and sequence multiple planning functions and execute them one after the other.

Planning Workbench This tool is available in the SAP BW-BPS application to create planning objects.

Process Chains These objects are used to schedule and sequence the loading and administration of data in the SAP NetWeaver BI system.

Query A query is the definition of the layout of a report. It consists of rows, columns, free characteristic, and filter.

Query View A Query View is the customized view of the results of a query.

Real-Time Cube A Real-Time InfoCube is one that is optimized for write mode and used planning. In the BW 3.x system, this type of InfoCube was referred to as a Transactional InfoCube.

Remote Cube A Remote InfoCube is an InfoCube that provides a logical view of data that physically exists in a remote system.

Requests These are requests for data to be transported from a source system to the SAP NetWeaver BI system.

Restricted Key Figure A Restricted Key Figure is one that is limited based on Characteristic values. An example is the sales amount for the month of May 2007.

Retraction Retraction is the process of moving data from the SAP NetWeaver BI system back to the SAP R/3 system.

SAP NetWeaver BI Integrated Planning This tool is available as a part of the Business Intelligence 2004s system for planning, forecasting, and budgeting in various business application areas.

Status and Tracking System (STS) This system provides a workflow that enables the monitoring and approval of a planning process.

Surrogate ID (SID) A Surrogate ID is a unique identifier for Characteristic data.

SID Table This table contains the SIDs and the corresponding Characteristic values.

Transfer Rules These govern the transformation of data from the transfer structure to the communication structure in the SAP BW 3.x system.

Transfer Structure The Transfer Structure replicates the extract structure used in the SAP BW 3.x system.

Transformation This business rule is used to connect two persistent objects in the SAP NetWeaver BI system (used in BI 7.0).

Transport Transport is the process of migrating objects from the development system to the Quality Assurance and Production systems.

Update Rules These rules govern the transformation of data from an InfoSource to a data target and are used in the SAP BW 3.x system.

Variables Variables are objects used to allow selection of data in queries and planning applications.

Virtual Cube This is a new term introduced in BI 7.0 to refer to a Remote InfoCube.

Web Application A Web application is one that is deployed on the Web and that contains business information for users.

Web Item A Web item is a component used to design a Web template in the SAP NetWeaver BI system. Examples of Web items are Analysis Web items and Chart Web items.

Workbook A workbook contains the results of one or more queries, displayed in a Microsoft Excel spreadsheet.

XML XML (eXtensible Markup Language) is a W3C-recommended markup language that supports several applications and is a standard for describing data.

Index

Uncover the real-world applications of the Balanced Scorecard and SAP CPM

Gain practical information about the Management Cockpit, creating scorecards, crucial tips, tricks, and more

Up to date for SEM 6.0

387 pp., 2006, 69,95 Euro / US $69.95
ISBN 978-1-59229-085-7

CPM and Balanced Scorecard with SAP

www.sap-press.com

Marco Sisfontes-Monge, Marco Sisfontes-Monge

CPM and Balanced Scorecard with SAP

Organizations planning to initiate the implementation of SAP CPM, using the Balanced Scorecard approach, need this practical guide. Get a clear understanding of the Balanced Scorecard and its relationship with SAP CPM, while gaining a thorough knowledge of the central concepts of both. With a foreword by Dr. David Norton, this book includes practical information about the management cockpit and teaches you how to create SAP CPM scorecards.

**Efficient Reporting with BEx
Query Designer, BEx Web, and
SAP BW Information
Broadcasting**

**Step-by-step instruction to
optimize your daily work**

Up-to-date for SAP BW 3.5

578 pp., 2006, 69,95 Euro / US$ 69,95
ISBN 978-1-59229-045-1

SAP BW Reporting and Analysis

www.sap-press.com

N. Egger, J.-M.R. Fiechter, J. Rohlf, J. Rose, O.
Schrüffer

SAP BW Reporting and Analysis

Mastering reporting with BEx Query Designer, BEx
Web, and SAP BW Information Broadcasting

In this book you'll find everything you need to
configure and execute Web reporting and Web
applications, as well as detailed instruction to take
advantage of the resulting possibilities for analysis
and reporting in SAP BW.
First, you'll be introduced to the basic topics of BEx
Query Designer, BEx Web Application Designer, BEx
Web Applications, BEx Analyzer, and SAP Business
Content. Then, expert guidance shows you, step-by-
step, how to master the process of creating custom
reports and analysis. That's just for starters. You'll
also learn best practices for creating your own SAP
BW Web Cockpit and much more.

SAP BW Data Retrieval

N. Egger, J.-M.R. Fiechter, R. Salzmann, R.P. Sawicki,
T. Thielen

SAP BW Data Retrieval

Mastering the ETL process

This much anticipated reference makes an excellent
addition to your SAP BW Library. Read this book and
you'll discover a comprehensive guide to configuring,
executing, and optimizing data retrieval in SAP BW.

The authors take you, step-by-step, through all of the
essential data collection activities and help you hit the
ground running with master data, transaction data, and
SAP Business Content. Expert insights and practical
guidance help you to optimize these three factors and
build a successful, efficient ETL (extraction, transformation,
loading) process. This all-new edition is based on the
current SAP BW Release 3.5, but remains a highly valuable
resource for those still using previous versions.

How to succeed with InfoObjects, InfoProviders, and SAP Business Content

Step-by-step instruction to optimize your daily work

Up-to-date for SAP BW 3.5

437 pp., 2005, 69,95 Euro / US$ 69,95
ISBN 978-1-59229-043-7

SAP BW Data Modeling

www.sap-press.com

N. Egger, J.-M.R. Fiechter, J. Rohlf

SAP BW Data Modeling

This book delivers all the essential information needed for successful data modeling using SAP BW. In a practice-oriented approach, you'll learn how to prepare, store, and manage your data efficiently. Essential topics such as data warehousing concepts and the architecture of SAP BW are examined in detail. You'll learn, step-by-step, all there is to know about InfoObjects, InfoProviders, and SAP Business Content, all based on the newly released SAP BW 3.5.

Complete and targeted overview of all new BI features and functionalities

Comprehensive information on SAP NetWeaver Visual Composer and BI Accelerator

Up-to-date for SAP NetWeaver 2004s BI

656 pp., 2007, 69,95 Euro / US$ 69,95
ISBN 978-1-59229-082-6

SAP Business Intelligence

www.sap-press.com

N. Egger, J.-M.R. Fiechter, S. Kramer, R.P. Sawicki, P. Straub, S. Weber

SAP Business Intelligence

Up-to-date for SAP NetWeaver 2004s BI

This book provides information on all the important new BI features of the SAP NetWeaver 2004s Release. Essential subjects like data modeling, ETL, web reporting, and planning are covered along with all of the newest functions making this book an unparalleled companion for your daily work. Real-life examples and numerous illustrations help you hit the ground running with the new release. Plus, useful step-by-step instructions enable the instant use of new features like Visual Composer, and many more.

**A practical guide
to implementing and using
SAP xApp Analytics**

**Easily deploy, configure, and
combine analytic applications
to customize SAP xApp
Analytics for your needs**

408 pp., 2006, 69,95 Euro / US$ 69.95
ISBN 978-1-59229-102-1

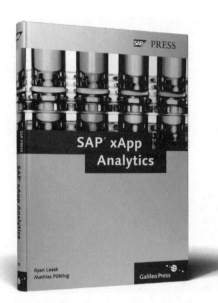

SAP xApp Analytics

www.sap-press.com

Ryan Leask, Mathias Pöhling, Ryan Leask,
Mathias Pöhling

SAP xApp Analytics

A practical guide to implementing and using
SAP xApp Analytics

This book fulfills two goals. First, it gives readers a
look at the technology behind building Analytic
Applications within SAP. Second, it gives a business
perspective as to why xApp Analytics are beneficial.
It addresses how SAP meets industry-specific
challenges with various pre-packaged Analytic
applications. Practical examples and the authors'
experiences while working with Analytics are
valuable resources for readers. Readers will also
obtain insight into the future of xApp Analytics.
Other topics include installation, administration,
transporting, and coverage of the Visual Composer.

Obtain the knowledge and tools for a smooth-running SAP BW implementation

Understand common practices and resource constraints for SAP BW projects

407 pp., 2007, 69,95 Euro / US$ 69,95
ISBN 978-1-59229-105-2

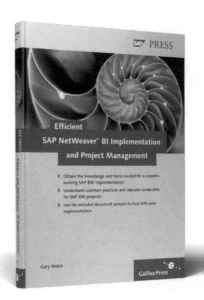

SAP NetWeaver BI

www.sap-press.com

Gary Nolan

Efficient SAP NetWeaver BI Implementation and Project Management

Gain a clear understanding of the SAP NetWeaver BI/BW project-management process and its attendant problems. This book helps you prepare for a largely problem-free BW project by alerting you early on to possible issues. These issues can be cultural, political, fiscal, or technical, and this book helps you deal with all of them and other problems. Understand how to properly resource a project, how to scope it, and above all how to create a successful implementation strategy. Gain from the author's experience by following the lessons-learned approach in the book. An added bonus is the appendix, which contains important sample documents including project plans, project charters, and cutover plans.

>> www.sap-press.de/1317

Complete details on customization and application of the New General Ledger

Techniques for flexible reporting and faster execution of period-end closing

Comprehensive information on integration and migration

approx. 300 pp., 69,95 Euro
ISBN 978-1-59229-107-6, Aug 2007

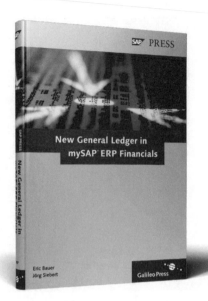

New General Ledger in mySAP ERP Financials

www.sap-press.com

E. Bauer, J. Siebert

New General Ledger in mySAP ERP Financials

Faster, more efficient, and more transparent: This book enables you to implement and use the new General Ledger in mySAP ERP Financials. Readers get an insightful overview of all the most important new functionalities and advantages that the new GL has to offer. You'll quickly learn about the definition of ledgers and document breakdown, with the help of practical examples.

Gain in-depth knowledge
about the core functions of
SAP Funds Management (FM)

Learn about important
SAP FM issues such as budget
execution, budget availability
control, year-end closing, key
integration points, and more

approx. 405 pp., 69,95 Euro / US$ 69,95
ISBN 978-1-59229-151-9, Sept 2007

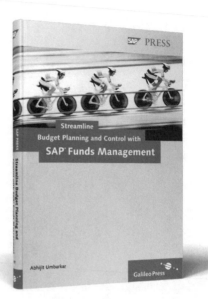

Streamline Budget Planning
and Control with SAP Funds Management

www.sap-press.com

Abhijit Umbarkar

Streamline Budget Planning and
Control with SAP Funds Management

If you are a project manager, consultant, or customer
in the process of adopting SAP Funds Mangement
(FM), this book will help you meet your organizational requirements.
In addition, financial controllers, budget directors,
and finance managers will gain a clear understanding
of how SAP FM can help streamline their budget
planning and control processes.

Interested in reading more?

Please visit our Web site for all
new book releases from SAP PRESS.

www.sap-press.com